The Saints Of God

The
Saints
Of
God

Getting back to
the grass roots of
Christianity

Michael Biagioni

Michael Biagioni Ministries, Inc.
Kissimmee, Florida 34744

Unless otherwise noted, Scripture quotations are taken from the King James Version of the Bible sixteen hundred translation.

Scripture quotation marked NIV are taken from the Holy Bible, New International Version. Copyright © 1973, 1978, 1984, International Bible Society. Used by permission of Zondervan. All rights reserved.

Scripture quotation marked AMP are taken from the Amplified Bible. Holy Bible, New International Version. Copyright © 1954, 1958, 1962, 1964, 1965, 1987 by The Lockman Foundation used by permission.

Printed in the United States of America
First Edition March 2015
Second Edition January 2023

10987654321

Michael Biagioni Books, is a division of Michael Biagioni Ministries, Inc, Kissimmee FL,

The Saints of God name and logo is a trademark of Michael Biagioni Ministries, Inc.

Biagioni, Michael:
The Saints of God: Returning back to the grass roots of Christianity / Michael Biagioni / Linda Biagioni. --- 1st ed. 300 p. 23 cm.

Summary: "In this work, renowned speaker Michael Biagioni shares a wealth of knowledge for people who are desperate to exercise ministry. Within the pages of this manuscript, there is something for everyone including the history of God's generals, church revivals, and the coming days of glory. But the topic perhaps closest to his heart is the preparation of prophetic teams from a first century perspective that will empower believers to demonstrate God's character during tribulation. "

– Provided by Publisher

ISBN-10   06152921655
ISBN-13   978-0-615-92165-5

"Fools enter in where angels dare not tread"

A special appreciation for Pastor Prophet David Paul for the many years that he invested in training and influencing my life for the journey that lays before me.

CONTENTS

CONTENTS

*The Coming Forth of God's
Christian Saints*

*Empowered to take back
the kingdom by force*

*Debunking some
religious myths*

*Experiencing the tangible
Shekinah glory of God*

ACKNOWLEDGEMENTS

First and foremost, I want to give God all the glory and all the praise for preserving my life to write this book which is above and beyond anything that I could have ever imagined.

To my amazing wife, Neida, who has stood beside me during the good times and the bad while continuing to be an undying support in the face of adversity. I am indebted for her care of my son during the difficult years of my life. I thank God for allowing me to connect myself with such an amazing woman.

To Michael, my son, who without complaining always sought after my time though often unfulfilled. Who even after the early years of struggle, remained faithfully by my side with laughter, undying strength, and who really believed in my ministry.

To Mom, whom I love dearly, and who stood relentlessly by my side in the good and bad times. Who, even to this day, forgets not to mention me in her prayers. Mom truly knew what it meant to be alone; she was indeed one of the strongest women I know. God put my name Michael into her ears. Her vision was to have a godly family. She loved being close to family but at the same time, trusted God during her times of loneliness. All of us could always count on Mom to listen to all of our growing pains. She is an amazing woman as well as a wise counselor. Each time one of her children called, she always provided sound advice to carry us through.

To Dad, who I learned to love and appreciate later in life as a true counselor, provider, and father. Dad and his wonderful wife Linda paid my tuition for both Electrical Engineering and ORU. I never knew how much my father loved to travel until much later. He took our family on amazing vacations to Providence Rhode Island and the Cape. Never did we ever go hungry nor did we lack any clothing on our back. He became a true father and a friend when I was older. Dad loved family reunions, he loved to socialize and

ACKNOWLEDGEMENTS

in fact my father never lost an argument. My father has an amazing memory and a high IQ.

FOREWORD

INTRODUCTION

> " You get out there and fight."
> --Mom

I wrote this book with the intention of justifying why God is preparing his Saints for tribulation. I base this on the fact that God had a specific purpose for completing the rebuilding of the Fivefold ministry. The term Fivefold ministry referenced by Ephesians 4:11,12 refers to the offices held by the Apostle, Prophet, Evangelist, Pastor and Teacher. This term was probably coined during the twentieth century. For some time, I was puzzled as to why God completed the rebuilding of the Fivefold ministry in the twentieth century? I asked myself, what would be the purpose of restoring Fivefold leaders if most ministries belief that the world could come to an end tomorrow? The answer is a no-brainer. God completed the reconstruction of Fivefold ministry so that these leaders might bring unity, perfect the Saints, and equip them to fight during the great tribulation of the book of Revelation.

For nearly 200 years, prior to the dawning of Islam, Christians were persecuted under Roman occupation. Later, by decree of King Constantine, Christianity made a paradigm 180 degree shift becoming the state religion of the entire Roman Empire. Unbeknownst to many believers, from the early 600's to 1521AD, the early church slipped into apostasy while only the Roman Catholic Church remained viable.

In 1521AD, Martin Luther decried the Catholic doctrine of indulgence and declares "for by grace ye are saved through faith, and that not of yourselves" (Rom 2:8, 9) and the "just shall live by faith and not works" (Gal 3:11). Since then, God has progressively restored the church from the desolation of the middle ages.

xvii.

INTRODUCTION

Each century after the reformation, God has continued to restore his church with first century biblical norms i.e. gift of life, water baptism, holiness and sanctification.

Fast forwarding 492 years, apart from any cultural differences, how closely do we as a church resemble the early church? Are we too lax and complacent to be effective witnesses before this generation? Have we switched our focus from winning souls for the kingdom to great building projects?

Based on every discipleship training course on evangelism, it is abundantly clear that we should manifest the love of Christ which is an expression of the fruits of the Spirit. However, God wants leaders to go one step farther and that would be to train and equip the Saints to be demonstrators of His character. By "equipping" I mean balancing the church in such a way so that not only do we express our love by charitable works, but also, we have the power to loose the tongue, open blind eyes, cleanse the lepers, and once again, look death in the face and command life.

Hence, not only is the church growing, but God is preparing her for peak performance, without spot and wrinkle, equipped to deal with the rise of Islamic fascism, and enable men to walk with the spirit of power of Elias at the last day.

In this book, I blow the lid off the false doctrine "rapture" concocted by Jesuit Priest Emmanuel Lacunza in 1811. In addition, we shall explore some of today's contemporary interpretations of the more controversial scriptures written by Paul the apostle.

This is a new generation of prophetic evangelism that will play a pivotal role in accelerating the restitution of all things, so that atheists and agnostics will witness God's power through a great awakening of biblical proportion.

INTRODUCTION

"Repent ye therefore, and be converted, that your sins
may be blotted out, when the times of refreshing shall
come from the presence of the Lord. And He shall send
Jesus Christ, which before was preached unto you:
Whom the heaven must receive until the times of
restitution of all things, which God hath spoken by the
mouth of all His holy prophets since the world began."
--Acts 3:19-21)

For this work, I used the C.I. Scofield Bible King James 1611
translation unless otherwise noted for I have found that it is the
best translation from Greek, Hebrew and Aramaic. On the other
hand, translations such as the Amplified Version tend to be more
semantic in style with the intent of simplification whereby
changing the meaning of the interpretation of the original text.

A relevant example would be the ongoing debate over
whether a good God would allow sickness, create disease, or
infirmity. In these cases, the Amplified version tends to add a
more humanistic view of the text suggesting that since God is
good he is only capable of "calamity" not evil. On the other hand,
I believe that the KJV translation better represents the sovereignty
of God. Below I provided a relevant example for your evaluation.

[7] I form the light and create darkness, I make peace
[national well-being] and I create [physical] evil
(calamity); I am the Lord, Who does all these things.
--Isa 45:7 (AMP))

[7] I form the light, and create darkness: I make peace, and
create evil: I the LORD do all these things.
--Isa 45:7 (KJV)

Chapter 1

THE PROPHETIC VISION

Time waits for no man – A Proverb

Two horns shall rise in the USA, Islam and the homo-sexual society. I see several missile launches in the days to come. Russia will push forward like a ram until Putin dies. American will step into position #2 on the world stage. Knowledge will increase with companion AI robots that will speak and walk. A successful moon landing and a new frontier to mars. I see a new form of currency similar to a cashless society. Some will take leisure trips to the moon. I see a moon space station. A plethora of hybrids and electric cars integrated with an intelligent traffic control system. Trump will run for a second term. Slowly but surely, theologians will admit that the church is in tribulation. The day of the mega church has come to an end. As the powers of darkness increase, so shall there be outbreaks of revival with less name-brand preachers and more Saints operating in a word of knowledge, wisdom and prophecy. As a witness, more people will be healed outside of the four walls of the church. Just a snapshot, more to come.

--Prophet Michael Biagioni

THE SAINTS OF GOD

Purpose for Writing this Book

During my impressionable years in the Catholic Church, I continued to ask the question, "where is the power of God"? As a spiritual mentor, I would ask my mother, "Where are the signs, wonders and miracles that I heard about while growing up? Do you believe in miracles? Can God perform a miracle and restore my divorced grandparents?" I posed all of these questions but unfortunately, no one had any answers.

I was just a teenager when I asked these questions in my mind over and over again. Some 15 years later, I had a divine encounter in a particular revival service. I'll never forget the impact it had on me when God revealed my name to a prophet during that meeting. As he approached me he stated, "you have seen yourself being used like Apostle Peter in the bible." After this event, my life would change forever.

As I read the Bible, I continued to ask God what happened to the tangible expression of God. Where did the glory cloud go? When ministers are denied access to a country on a particular assignment, why are they not translated in the Spirit? When Christians pray today, what happened to the sign of the ground shaking like it did in the book of Acts? The Bible records numerous episodes where the earth shook marking God's approval of a notable event. These types of unanswered questions provoked me to begin seeking for an awakening within my own self and would be the catalyst that prepared me to stir up awareness amongst Christian Saints. As a result, this book was written with the Saints of God in mind.

Later, at the Polish National Home in Hartford, CT, in the 1980's, a prophet distributed a prophetic letter to each Saint in the service. My letter, which was decorated with a trim around the border, quoted the verse Jeremiah 1:5, 6. At that time, I truly did not understand the significance of this prophetic letter, but later, I realized I was called from my mother's womb as a prophet unto the nations. As I began to mature in the anointing, I became aware of the fact that most sincere Christians had very little knowledge of church history. I'll explain. As I began to research church history, a pattern of restoration of biblical principles became apparent. For the last 492 years since Martin Luther, God has been restoring many of the principles lost during the dark ages. As I read the Bible backdropped by church history, I received some revelation as to the direction that God is taking the church in the days to come.

Today, there are literally hundreds of cults being practiced in the world. As people from every walk of life go about their business, many are not even aware of the other religions that are contending for the souls of men. Many of these cults have been active for hundreds of years, probably more today than ever before. For that reason, God has raised up some great men and women of the twentieth century that not only can talk the talk but walk with power and demonstration of the kingdom.

I envision a great awakening that will transport the church back to a first century standard. In the days to come, church culture will be more closely aligned to the first century model. God is revealing the importance of developing apostolic teams like Jesus, who appointed a select group of men to train before His ascension. Albeit things have been changing slowly but surely, still today few pulpits in America recognize the office of the apostle and prophet in their local setting. Moreover, where the first century apostle bore witness of the resurrection of the dead with signs and wonders, I see many spirit-filled Saints embracing the same type of anointing. Although God wants to impart those mantels pronto, many Christian Saints are simply satisfied with the status quo or modus operandi of "qué será, será, whatever will be will" mentality.

As time goes on, believer's eyes shall be illuminated to see that the rapture doctrine of "fly in the sky in the sweet by and by" over the last 203 years has duped many generations of Christians into believe that the church is not in tribulation. As I have stated succinctly with ad nauseam, that now more than ever before, the Saints need to demonstrate the character of God.

There are two expressions of Christ, the divine nature of God and the character of God. For the last 492 years, the Saints have learned to express the nature of God through love, joy, peace, and long suffering, which represent the fruits of the Spirit found in Galatians 5:22.

However, I see a new generation that shall emulate the biblical character of God tantamount to "strong and mighty", " a man of war, that shouts from heaven", " raising the dead", and speaking to storms "peace, be still". Sadly though, nearly two thousand years later, unlike Jesus, the church expresses works of love without infallible proof of powerful signs and wonders.

In my view, I believe that folks need to get ready for tribulation. In fact, though some of my scholarly proponents refute this conjecture, I believe that Christian Saints will come out of great tribulation before the second advent of Christ occurs in Revelation chapter 19:11. Later, in another chapter, I will prove to you that God will protect the "remnant" with his seal during the day of wrath.

I see 2023 as a new season to step into assignments where uncommon manifestations shall occur like in the first century. Moreover, ministry shall move to a new level when believers discover that seeking the "glory of Him that sent Him" was the main focus of Jesus Christ. Although we don't overtly state it, many justify their impotent Christian walk by simply stating that "I am not Jesus Christ". That said we still have a small problem, what about John 14:12? Jesus said "the works I do ye shall do and greater works shall he do." Later on, Jesus declared to his disciples "ye shall not only do this which is done to the fig tree" (Jn 21:21). This is why I see God raising up a new generation that will demonstrate the character of God.

In a later chapter, we shall walk down memory lane and discover how the Church was in decline during the dark ages from the fifth to the fifteenth century. Ironically, during the same period of proliferation of Islam, Christians forgot how to express the character of God. Even today, many don't realize that redemption; the cross, salvation, and altar calls are incomplete vis-à-vis the lack of the first century model.

During recent years, I have been impassioned to enlighten readers regarding the spiritual state of the church. For example, I transport readers into a thought provoking realm with unusual illustrations like:

> "Remember the last time you went to Israel on a sabbatical? You found yourself hungry in the Negev, but you and your team forget to bring adequate supplies, only 5 pita breads, 2 avocados, and $100. At lunch time when your group gets hungry, what do you suppose the typical solution would be for a leader in this situation? Does he put a demand on the anointing by multiplying the food or does he send someone back to Be'er Sheva to buy 500 loaves of Bread? Unfortunately, more emphasis is placed on the latter, rather than putting a demand on the anointing."

I hear some people saying "amen" Michael. There must be a balance between the fruits of the Spirit and the power of God that is lacking in this generation. Listen, Jesus was the epitome of love and compassion. Christians today have learned to express agape love, you know "Simon, son of Jonas, loveth thou me?"

Our lack illustrates the fact that our expression of love is limited to the natural cosmos. On the other hand, Jesus expressed his love with power to produce mighty works. During the life of Jesus, when people were hungry, the Lord expressed his love and compassion by dividing loaves and fishes. When the Romans demanded that they pay taxes, again, his compassion was expressed by sending Peter fishing with the intent of finding a gold coin in a fish's mouth.

During the account when the apostles were in the boat fearful for their lives, the love of Jesus was expressed by commanding the wind and sea "peace, be still" (Mark 4:39). Today, our love is filled with passivity; we have become a nation of sissies and "wussies" in the Holy Ghost, bad grammar but a good gospel. Yeah, we're bold behind the pulpit, but when we find ourselves in the theatre of battle, are we suddenly weak in bodily presence? Sadly, we have lost the fortitude that the men of the first century possessed. In short, this generation has compromised the truth of God.

As the church enters tribulation, God revealed to me the need for Fivefold ministry and why God reconstructed the Fivefold ministry in the 20th century. We teach ad nauseam in our institutions that God is raising up a "Joshua generation" but I see the spirit and power falling upon an "Elias generation". We've already passed over to the other side, now it's time to train and fight. But in part, here is the problem, many churches only endorse the pastoral mantel at the exclusion of the other four, namely the Apostle, Prophet, Evangelist and Teacher. Without these other four offices, how will God implement his divine plan for the "perfecting of the Saints, work of the ministry, and edifying of the body of Christ"? (Eph 4:11). In the days to come, the spirit and power of Elias will rest upon the Saints to give witness to a substantive anointing.

In light of church history, many are unaware of the fact that over the last 100 years, the offices of the prophet and apostle were the last to be restored. As a result, apostolic and prophetic leaders are the most rejected offices today amongst rank and file Christians.

For that reason, I elucidate the need for ministries to have prophetic schools to train, equip, and bring awareness to the Saints in preparation for end-time revival. Look, we need Fivefold leaders to bring unity to the body of Christ when the seals are being opened. Team leaders with the wisdom to implement strategic planning with the intent of developing the army of God before the seven trumpets start sounding. Anointed presbyters who can recognize, activate, and impart anointing, raise up prophets with eyes that can see terrorism, invasions, tornados, earthquakes, and weapons of mass destruction before these events occur. We must understand that Fivefold leaders represent the hand that God will use to minister to both Jewish and Gentile Saints.

Unlike the first century primitive church, most Saints enjoy a cushy lifestyle, commuting back and forth to church, occupying their favorite spot, never intimidating the realm of darkness, and have made a peace treaty with the devil. Believer, you must forsake all in order to hear God's voice. We need a word now more than ever before. God will anoint you to demonstrate the power of God especially during tribulation and great tribulation. What happened to the Peter's, Paul's, Stephen's, John's, and James', "men that hazarded their lives for the name of Jesus Christ" (Acts 15:26)?

Now, more than ever before, leaders must activate the Saints for public ministry implementing a prophetic team approach. Currently in Kissimmee, Florida, my wife and I are training prophetic-apostolic ministry teams. In fact, the twelve disciples of Jesus ultimately were trained as an apostolic ministerial team to express the character of God. They emulated Jesus by ministering with the anointing and gifts that descended after he ascended. I want to unveil the secret as to why an apostolic prophetic team approach is much more powerful than just a group of missionaries. I believe that every Christian should have the existential experience of joining an apostolic, prophetic team. Later, I'll illustrate how all Saints can work together in a team setting. As one gives a word of knowledge, another may intercede, while a third person sees a particular detail that will convince the unbeliever that God is real.

Sadly today, scholars set a standard for evangelism by presenting a form of godliness and denying the power thereof. And as a result, the acceptable way to reach the lost is with tracks, not operating in the gifts.

Truly, I believe that we need to literally reenact the book of Acts so that our eyes can be open to the revelation of the Spirit. I believe God is about to reveal to you that the Bible is prophetic in its entirety, and that we are returning to the garden to eat of the tree of life at the appointed time. Walking the book of Acts will reposition us to experience the great grace of God including resurrections of the dead, translations in the Spirit, visions of glory clouds, open heavens, angelic visitation, earthquakes during praise and worship, and much more.

Look, we need to reevaluate the doctrines that we've been taught over the last 492 years. My desire is to help you see the difference between tribulation and the day of vengeance of our God. We have been indoctrinated to believe that God will not subject the church to tribulation but somehow snatch his people bald-headed to join the Lord in the air during an arguably controversial "secret coming." Look, I do believe in a tangible return of Christ in the future, but in 90% of scripture, tribulation applies to the Saints, not ungodly men. The coming of the great and dreadful day of the Lord is reserved for God haters, atheists, and wicked men. Even the apostle John assured future generations that he would "be with us in tribulation".

As the remnant of God, we are living in the finest hour to witness the restoration of the Saints of God. Theology arguably diminishes the role of Christian Saints after Revelation chapter 3. However, I will show you in the chapters that follow, why the word Saint in the book of Revelation must be applied to both Gentile and Jewish believers alike.

Unfortunately, many believers assume that if some renown theologian writes a reference book on eschatology it must be revelation from heaven regarding the catching away (rapture) of the church. One big problem, it's not for us to know the times and the seasons.

One of the reasons for publishing this book was to debunk many of the myths regarding the rapture. Doctrines and traditions are number one factors that limit the restoration of the Christian church. In fact, the rapture doctrine based on "fly and eat your pie in the sky, in the sweet by and by" coined by Joe Hill has done a disservice to many and may be one of the leading causes of apostasy in the days to come.

In this book, "The Saints of God", I wrote an extensive chapter on Islam. From the experience that I gleaned from trips to Pakistan and India, I've experienced firsthand Islam and its radical fundamentalist movement across the globe. Unfortunately, the liberal left has turned a blind eye to the Islamic extremism that is right at our back door. In fact, many Christians are bowing down to these radical groups for fear of retaliation and beheading. Today's prophets have been warning the Saints about the radical Islamo-fascist agenda that has pervaded our society. Sadly, many of my Christian colleges have bought into the Koran's doctrine, implying that it is a book of peace when in fact it was written by a military leader who embraced a war-like mentality. Quite frankly I find it appalling that many Christians have no knowledge of Islam and think that they are isolated from its imperialist mentality. I prophetically declare the dangers of radical Islam in this book. For this reason, we need to be anointed and gifted to deal with the invasion of Islam that is coming to America.

But perhaps the hottest topic of revelation today is the coming tangible glory of God. I want to inform my reader that we as a Christian nation have lost the knowledge of the Glory of God. As such, many of us are living in compromise not understanding the dimension of God's glory. In a following chapter, we return back in time when Christ introduced his inner circle of believers to the glory. We need the knowledge of the glory of the Lord more that ever before. How will we gain this knowledge? I believe that the knowledge will come forth from God's prophets in the twenty-first century. I see God unveiling the secrets that Daniel dictated from the angel Gabriel and then was told to seal them until the end. Those secrets regarding the tribulation will empower his saints with knowledge of his glory. God will not be made manifest just by preaching, but by demonstration of his character, which is his glory. By demonstration I mean, operating in the gifts of God to edify his people.

Get ready for the most exciting journey of your life as. I immerse you in a new realm of glory. By the time you finish learning about who you are, you'll be putting a demand on God for a greater glory in your ministry.

So, without further ado, let's move on to chapter two.

Chapter 2

A GLANCE AT
THE PAST

The writing of this book was in no way intended to be a course on religious history. Neither am I claiming to be a biblical scholar. However, I believe that it is important to illustrate that God continues to revive the lost secrets and prophecy of the Bible. The knowledge of His glory, clearly an important truth, was forgotten during the middle ages between the sixth and sixteenth century AD. From the age of enlightenment until the present, God has been reviving the works of the Holy Spirit in preparation for a kingdom that will inevitably suffer violence in tribulation. Much knowledge of scripture was lost as the church slipped into decline just before Muhammad the prophet died in 632 CE. Later in this chapter, I have supplied a list of the most important movements during church history over the last 492 years. In order to grasp the revelation of where God is taking the church, we must first understand church history.

For the moment, perhaps church history is not extremely fascinating to the average reader, but when you become aware of the chronology of restoration of Christendom, you are more apt to grasp why certain doctrines or church culture exists today. First and foremost, when you understand the progression of history, it reveals a divine pattern from heaven. As I have mentioned elsewhere in this book, since I had been enlightened about the events of Azusa Street, Los Angeles California on April 5, 1906, I always dreamed about having my own personal experience in this area. Finally, I was blessed to be part of the Lakeland Revival also dubbed "the Lakeland Outpouring" in 2008.

There, I witnessed reenactments of the book of acts. The Saints descended from every corner of the globe to attend service each night. We witnessed the Dunamis (dynamite) power of God on display. God was training and equipping the Saints both at the coliseum in Lakeland, and under the clear span tent. Many said it was "the third wave or third great awakening."

Fivefold ministry was represented in those glorious services and the services were even broadcast on www.god.tv for months. In essence it was certified by men such as Prophet Bill Hamon, and Apostle Peter Wagner.

PRAY FOR THE SAINTS EXPERIENCE

Today, more than ever before, people want more than just theory, they want someone that not only can teach about angels, but has had a tangible experience with angels. Not someone who can only hypothesize about the glory, but Saints who have had a tangible, experience in the glory. As believers, more than ever before, the eyes of our understanding need to be enlightened to see the hope of His calling in this century.

As I have repeated ad nauseam, many are complacent in the pews today and have more emphasis on principles of the doctrines of Jesus than on moving on to perfection. If all you preach each week is the blood of Jesus, then unbelievers will get saved but you will never witness the power and demonstration of God. If the emphasis is on deliverance, then you may never witness the prophetic. If the church's prime focus is on missionary work, it's quite possible leadership never acknowledges the restoration of apostles, prophets, and evangelists. Look, the pastor, teacher, and missionary do not possess all the attributes required in Fivefold ministry to fully execute the perfecting of the Saints, the work of the ministry, and the edifying of the body of Christ (Eph 4:12).

As you pour over the details of the greatest movements of our time, open your eyes to see that for some 492 years, God has been preparing His Saints for tribulation. Meanwhile, God is restoring the body of Christ with the objective of preparing a bride without spot or wrinkle, a church in peak performance for the wedding supper of the Lamb, equipped for warfare, and anointed to take the kingdom by force.

MOVES OF GOD

1521 Protestant Reformation
Martin Luther, German Augustinian friar, pioneer of the protestant movement against the Catholic Church, declared that "salvation is by grace through faith and not by works "(Eph 2:8, 9)

1581 Puritanism
Puritan separatists or Pilgrims, immigrated to America seeking reform from the Church of England, began a grass roots movement at Plymouth Rock, notably seeking separation of church and state; emphasis on Calvinistic water baptism, movement pioneered by Jonathan Edwards, publish the King James Bible, Book of Common Prayer suppressed.

1824 Holiness Movement
The church set apart from the world by means of conversion, justification, salvation, and sanctification.

1846 Faith healing
Charismatic figures such as Ethan Allen, John Alexander Dowie, pioneered this divine movement characterized by healing of the physical body through atonement.

1906 Pentecostal Azusa Street (April 14, 1906)
Holy Spirit baptism with speaking in tongues, gifts of the Spirit pioneered by William Seymour and Charles Parham.

1950 Deliverance Evangelism
God completed the rebuilding of the ministry of the evangelist and mass evangelism was in full gear.

1950's Latter Rain Movement
Office of the prophetic presbytery recognized, renewed revelation of the need for praise and worship.

1960 Charismatic Movement
Albeit, this Movement has a character of its own, essentially, it is the composite of the former movements since the Pentecostal Movement of the turn of the century. Some charismatic figures include Kenneth Copeland, Oral Roberts, Kenneth Hagin and Benny Hinn. The 1960 Charismatic reformation was most notable for tongues, gifts of the Spirit, elitism, and desperation for His presence compared to past movements in churches history. During this period, God completes the rebuilding of the pastoral ministry. Pastors are recognized as sovereign heads of local churches.

1970's Word of Faith Group
Visionary Kenneth E. Hagin's is notable for the "Word of Faith Movement" that encapsulated declaring, establishing confessions, prosperity and victorious living. Ministry of the teacher is embraced as a major Fivefold minister. During this period, long-lasting terms were coined such as declaring health, calling wealth, "name-it claim-it", "blab-it grab-it", and "confess-it possess-it".

1980 – 1990's   Restoration of the Prophetic and Apostle Offices
Office of prophet restored, activation of gifts, warfare praise, prophets sent to nations, prophets equip saints with the gifts of the Holy Spirit, bring unity during tribulation, showdowns with false prophets, witches and sorcerers, miraculous signs and wonders apostolic ministry, and unity, great harvest of souls, ministry of apostle recognized to bring order and structure.

2000 Prophetic Saints
Office of the apostle and prophet started to become common place amongst the churches. Not one but many prophetic people were

empowered with, mantles, anointing, and grace. At the turn of the millennium, many feared apocalyptic events. When the stock market crashed, God preserved marriages, homes, and employment.

2008 Lakeland Outpouring Power Evangelism
Ingathering of people from all nations by means of the internet, tens of thousands came from around the world to experience the manifest power of God, remarkable, notable, amazing signs and wonders manifested, people were thirsty, hungry, and desperate for His presence.

2015 Glory Days
A time for change to the world as we know it, apostasy, storms, hurricanes, earthquakes, and sorrows will mark the end time. However, what lacks today in Christian circles are demonstrative manifestations of God's glory. If you recall, in the Old Testament, the cloud and pillar of fire had been taken away until Joshua reached Jordan. However, in the New Testament, God revealed His glory cloud (His presence) again on the mount of transfiguration.

Sadly today, our agape love has been tainted with complacency, as the church draws closure to the end of the age. During great tribulation, there will be violence in the Kingdom as we relive the book of the Acts of the Holy Spirit. Ultimately, those who are enlightened by revelation, desperate, will witness the pillar of fire and visions of the cloud again during revival meetings.

As I traveled, I discovered many passive leaders were not interested in our radical views regarding restoration of biblical truth. Ironically, to their disadvantage, what truly offsets the Saints of God from radical Islam is not just love by itself, but the truth that by the anointing we can express love through the demonstration of His character. This is truly illustrated by the acts of the Holy Spirit in the first century. Will there be extremes on the left and right? Church history denotes it, but don't throw out the baby with the bath water. Every work of Jesus was based in love after His passion, why should Christian Saints be any different? Expect unusual events, such as uproars, visions, dreams, outpouring, and new beginnings.

PROS AND CONS

1970's Word of Faith Movement
When you use the word reformation, most Christian Saints cannot relate to the implication of church reformation due to lack of knowledge of church history. It's important to understand the progression of history so that you may know where you are heading. Some notable leaders have described this current time as a "third wave" of restoration or another great awakening sweeping the globe. Although this book was not intended to be a dissertation, I would like to share my experience regarding the Word of Faith Movement.

Throughout history, during times of reformation, some groups broke off into fanaticism that focused on certain aspects of scriptural truth with certain intolerance.

FAITH WITHOUT WALKING IN DENIAL

One day, while raising funds to travel, God directed me to enter a particular church in Kissimmee in 2008. Unbeknownst to me, the church was a deliverance church in reformation. Explosive preaching, "Dare to believe God" rallies were heard from the pulpit from the Pastor. Moreover, this particular leader promoted Fivefold leadership amongst his ranks while helping to defray expenses for outreach in foreign countries.

Later however, during his transition from pastor of a local church to missionary work to win the nations, he appointed a new pastor to take his place. Essentially a "Bapta-costal", this co-pastor undertook the task of heading the church as he stepped down as senior pastor. With the new leader in place, I noticed, by degrees, the essence of The Word of Faith doctrine, permeating his preaching night after night.

Later, it was apparent that this particular pastor had attended Rhema Bible Training Center founded by Kenneth E. Hagin. Not a Sunday would pass without this pastor declaring, confessing, naming and claiming things he deemed necessary. If resources were needed, they would shout "money come", or that everyone in service would be healed on a particular night according to scriptures.

Regarding prosperity, I don't believe that we can achieve wealth by a simple confession alone, but "whatsoever a man soweth, he reapeth" (Gal 6:7). Remember that with every move of God, there will be extremists who pontificate that the rules shall be their way or else the highway. It is alright to confess faith but don't deny reality. I truly believe one component of apostasy occurs because Christian Saints get tired of unfulfilled confessions and declarations and finally quit. Case in point: if you are afflicted with fibromyalgia, naming and claiming your healing is excellent just as long as you don't deny the pain in the joints and muscles.

DECLARATIONS, PROSPERITY, EXPOSITORY FAITH

During the restoration of doctrine lost in the dark ages, certain groups became obsessed with extremes of revelation. One such group was the Word of Faith People. During this movement, extremists developed the attitude that anyone who lived by the gospel should experience health and wealth every day or else you must be out of the will of God. It caused people to have a nervous breakdown in the process of deliverance from generational curses so that they could be blessed like all the other "testa-liars".

Opponents developed the notion that Christians have no control over their lives, that all poverty and sickness were used by God to work perfection, and whatever came their way was the will of God. Many believed that poverty and sickness had to be endured gracefully and peaceably. Former controversies occurring during the divine healing movement of the 1880's was inflamed again among the Word of Faith group. Christians that needed medicine, consulted a physician, or had surgery were isolated by this movement.

AVOID EXTREME ELEMENTS

Moving to the opposite extreme, the Word of Faith people claimed that all trials and test were of Satan, and that God does not test the righteous. Those who were suffering tribulation must not be "standing on the word". Furthermore, miracles and prosperity should be a normal daily occurrence; else, you were not a person of faith. Other extreme views consisted of positive declarations and confessions until it approximated the doctrine of Christine Science. Opponents labeled these doctrines as: name-it claim-it; blab-it grab-it; health-n-wealth, and confess-it possess-it theology.

STRIVE FOR A BALANCED DOCTRINE

I believe that prosperity is the result of first sowing and later declaring to reap by faith. Furthermore, we should confess healing but without denying reality. Our belief in the gospel defines one's thinking thereby defining destiny giving one much control over the future. Not all dysfunction, calamity, trials, dumbness, blindness, paralysis, and lameness are of the devil. In fact, there are moments when we can view sickness as God's perfecting process. When necessary, we should take medicine and submit to surgery. On the other hand there are moments depending on one's proportion of faith that it is God's will to forego medicine, doctors and surgery. Unlike the opposition's philosophy, a born-again Christian cannot be demon possessed, but can be externally oppressed by principalities, powers, and wickedness in high places.

A GLACE AT THE PAST

Wise men say that hindsight is 20/20 in as much as when we look at days-gone-by, we see God preparing us for the next dimension of glory. I am convinced that we are about to witness one of the greatest revivals in church history. Moreover, one of the last things that shall be restored is His glory. In fact, the book of Psalms 97 declares that all people will see His glory.

"The heavens declare His righteousness, and all the people see His glory."   --Psalm 97:6

Adam and Eve saw the glory of God. Jesus walked in the glory of God according to Hebrews 1:4, 5.

"Who being the brightness of His glory, and the express image of His person, and upholding all things by the word of His power, when He had by Himself purged our sins, sat down on the right hand of the Majesty on high: Being made so much better than the angels, as He hath by inheritance obtained a more excellent name than they."

While Jesus walked on the earth, He was the very epitome of the express image of His (God's) person, much better than angels, and the brightness of His glory. Look at the history trail, everything points to a greater glory in the last day. Although theologians tend to dumb-down the expectation that we shall witness his glory again, just read the book of revelation. Revelation hints that many tangible signs shall come down from heaven during the tribulation period.

As we will discuss in a later chapter, some scholars deny that the Saints on earth will witness certain eschatological events thereby justifying a secret advent of Christ. But if the advent of Christ occurred tomorrow, this last generation of Saints would not witness firsthand the glory of God on the earth according to Psalms 97:6. Later, we will discuss how the perpetuation of the doctrine "rapture" has been a disservice to the revelation that God is equipping his bride specifically for tribulation, not to avoid it.

Chapter 3

CULTS OF
THE WORLD

In the Amazon jungles of Peru, children that are considered cursed are buried alive. In India, groups of Hindu people walk down the street in catatonic states, demon possessed, while Islamic extremists strap C4 (C4 is a substance used in the military to create explosives) to their waists, ready to lacerate, destroy and maim in the name of Allah. Arguments constantly arise between adherents to validate their religious practices. Through the years many have posed the question as to why there are so many different religions, and which one is authentic. Arguments constantly arise between constituents to validate their religion. In fact, it's not the first time that the Bible was used to justify heinous crimes against humanity. In fact, slavery was instituted by the Spaniards that founded the San Miguel de Guadalupe colony in 1526. According to the Bible, Black men (Biblical Cushites) were considered cursed by the Spaniards of the day. So naturally all Black men from Africa were assumed to be of the descendants of the ancient Canaanites from Palestine.

For the last 1,000 years, many of middle-eastern religions teach their adherents that the crusaders of 1096-1099AD were Christians. Would you call French and German mercenaries Christians whom after first being coerced to be baptized later repelled the Seljuk Turks from Jerusalem by massacring everyone in their path? Were these men Christ-like?

CHRISTIAN CRUSADES

First Crusade, Pope Urban II had encouraged the Iberian Christians to re-conquer Tarragona, using much of the same symbolism and rhetoric that was later used to promote the crusade to the people of Europe.

Defending your homeland, getting physical with an intruder entering your home is one thing. On the other hand if you pillage, plunder, commit heinous acts, rape, burn, murder, commit genocide, destroy everything in your path because you're hungry and want compensation from Rome is reprehensible. In fact its diametrically opposite to the word of God. Therefore, I refuse to call those men that raided the holy city, "Christian Crusaders."

Initially, the objective of Western Christianity, under the Papacy's directives, was to finance a campaign to win back Jerusalem from the Islamic crusades by the Turks.

Saint, did you know that during the first Crusade, crusaders would shout "the will of God" before they destroyed and plundered Constantinople?

"According to ancient accounts, while attacking, one version of the speech, the enthusiastic crowd responded with cries of "Deus Vult" or "God wills it!".

Was Christianity founded upon bloodshed by Christians?

JIM JONES

"What you need to believe in is what you can see ... If you see me as your friend, I'll be your friend. As you see me as your father, I'll be your father, for those of you that don't have a father ... If you see me as your savior; I'll be your savior. If you see me as your God, I'll be your God"

The former statement is according to former Temple member Hue Fortson, Jr. as quoting Jim Jones in the documentary *Jonestown: The Life and Death of Peoples Temple.*

In one of the largest losses of human life in any single disaster recorded in history next to the 9/11, 2001, terrorist attack on America's financial institutions, 913 inhabitants including 276 children lost their lives at the hands of a demented sociopath. Some would say, "It's hard to imagine that a man obsessed with socialism could exploit the Bible in such a way as to deceive so many people to participate in an unconscionable act".

JONES' HIDDEN AGENDA

Albeit, he was deceptive with an underlying communist agenda, still many of these people probably bought into his ideological views early on. Not only was Jones obsessed with religion at an early age but was an alleged homosexual as well as an opportunist taking advantage of other women in the temple.

In the middle of the 1950's, Jones became the founder of the Peoples Temple Full Gospel Church probably to facilitate his social goals. Apparently, a charismatic figure in many circles, he may have acquired his skills by mimicking such notorious people including Karl Marx, Joseph Stalin, Mahatma Gandhi, and even Adolf Hitler. He also became aware of the close ties between faith healing and charitable contributions inspiring him to open his own church that would provide the resources for his socialist agenda. It's obvious that no valid miracles ever occurred at the hand of this monster.

During the 1940's, it is alleged that Jones often sympathized with minorities in repressed African communities due to his early childhood of being a misfit social outcast. Furthermore, many of his adherents were duped into believing his deceptive convictions after he integrated or adopted children from other races. One clue into the personality type of Jones would be to look at his relationship with his father. Sources alleged that his father was an active member of the Ku Klux Klan. It's not hard to discern that a white supremacist father would have nothing in common with a communist Nazi. In fact, for over a decade, Jones who developed close ties to black African Americans, hated his father and had no conversations with him for years.

FALSE PROPHETS AND TEACHERS IN TRIBULATION

I would like to point out that Jesus warned believers that false prophets and Christ's would come during tribulation in the gospel of Matthew 24:24:

"For there shall arise false Christ's and false prophets, and shall show great signs and wonders; insomuch that, if it were possible, they shall deceive the very elect. "

As I build the argument that Christian Saints endure great tribulation, it is evident in the case of Jones who masqueraded as a faith healer with a hidden agenda was able to deceive the very elect. For that reason, it is imperative for God's people to receive the gift of discerning of spirits (1 Cor 12:10) to expose leaders who outwardly appear righteous but inwardly are committed to a demonic purpose.

I believe that it is quintessential for leaders to empower their believers with gifts of the Holy Ghost during these times of tribulation by ungodly men.

During the McCarthy hearings of the 1950's, Jones began searching for a means to express his socialist views. Witnesses stated that Jones happened upon a Baptist superintendent that helped establish him as a pastor at the Sommerset Southside Methodist Church. It wasn't long before they abrogated him for wanting to integrate blacks into the congregation.

In 1956, Jones launched his public ministry at the Cradle Tabernacle Church in Indianapolis, IN. In fact, he allegedly arranged to share the pulpit during a miracle service with a very prominent leader of his time. All of these schemes helped elevate Jones to a place of preeminence. Unfortunately, no one discerned his true intentions until it was too late.

But I digress; adopting orphan children of other ethnicities during times of war can be honorable as long as the motive is not to portray yourself as a civil rights leader. In fact, sharing wealth with others under coercion is essentially socialism 101, regardless of race, color or creed. Conversely, the biblical example of sharing wealth found in the book of Acts is quite different. In Acts 4:32-37, the primitive church shared such as was needed in as much as there was no lack among them but with one big difference, all gifts laid before the apostles were free-will offerings and not mandated by government or crude dictator!

Cleary Jones tried to begin in the Spirit, but later attempted to perfect himself after the flesh because at the core he was truly a communist. Inasmuch as appearing to have the right heart by integrating men of different races into the ranks, his agenda was truly satanic. Fact is that from the beginning, he had already premeditated the ultimate demise of himself and would-be followers.

On one trip in particular, Jones makes a stop at Guyana on his way to Brazil perhaps to study how the minorities would react to some of his religious tactics. Instead of portraying himself in the light of Karl Marx or Joseph Stalin, he used a more apostolic biblical approach that diverse racial groups might relate to. Essentially, he was a wolf in sheep's clothing. His high-pitched charismatic voice seemed to electrify the atmosphere wherever he preached causing people to be drawn by his theatrics.

FALSE PRETENSE OF DESEGREGATION

During the sixties Jones continued to search for outlets where he could promote communism. Jones proved to be an unusual integrator of mixed ethnicities and was appointed as director of the Human Rights Commission. To his credit, Jones was a forerunner of desegregation in Indianapolis including amusement parks, police station, hospitals, theatres, churches, restaurants, and many more.

JONES MAKES TRANSITION TO SOCIALISM

After returning to Indiana, Jones declared an apocalyptic "end of the world" scenario in order to influence the Temple to move to Redwood Valley, California. By this time, Jones had made a complete reversal in his daily cultic dialogue by imparting \a more socialist type of gospel with his Temple disciples. His concept he called enlightenment appeared innocent but later used stronger language grouping individuals who were capitalist, racists or fascist as sinners and anyone who was a communist as free.

At this point, any person with some knowledge of the Bible should have raised a red flag when their leader suddenly shifted his doctrine from Christianity to communism. Some Christians knew that his views had nothing to do with God but were fearful for their lives. As he tainted the apostolic doctrine with Marxism, maybe other people simply ignored the typical warning signs because of personal issues with anti-government sentiment and racial inequality.

OCUPY WALL STREET MOVEMENT

I would equate Jones' sentiment to the Occupy Wall Street Movement in 2012 that started out as a genuine grievance of Americans regarding the corruption of Wall Street's financial institutions. Occupiers alleged that bankers lined their pockets during a recession while real Americans lost employment, homes, and ultimately filed for bankruptcy. Unfortunately, with many such uprisings, what often began with valid principles later became corrupt. After a period of denial, the liberal media aired vivid images of hypodermic needles removed from the tent sites in Zuccotti Park. Arguably, the original group that had a legitimate argument had been infiltrated by thugs, anarchists, and intimidating nut-cases. Finally, class warfare erupted between the Occupiers who were viewed as liberal while the Tea Party people were viewed as fascists.

Jones' rhetoric heightened with such reprehensible statements such as "If you see me as your savior, I'll be your savior. If you see me as your God, I'll be your God." During cultic worship not only did he declare that he was God but performed false signs and wonders.

Around 1970, Jones decided to build his socialist utopia at Jonestown, a temple commune, stating racial purity as a communist community. As a member, you were not able to leave Jonestown once initiated. Many sympathized with him for setting up a racial community due to the fact that many of the citizens were black. Some people joined because they needed help, others simply were missionary volunteers that enjoyed giving their time.

SOCIALIST UTOPIA BEGINS

About the time that Congressman Leo Ryan visited Jamestown in November of 1978, families were already planning to defect from the Jamestown utopia that Jones had created. Although many wanted to escape, the Jamestown camp was strategically located deep within the jungle. With the arrival of Ryan, Jones called for "white nights" where he woke up everyone in the commune early in the morning and rehearsed a mass suicide. By this time, his drug use was evident causing him to become delusional. He mastered-minded this mass murder with the intent to make a statement to the world. He was undoubtedly influenced by satanic powers to concoct such a plot. Interestingly enough some believe that his beginnings were genuine, but the fact remains he was a habitual liar, psychopath and a fake.

But things turned ugly against Jones when Leo Ryan who was on a fact-finding mission in Jonestown was assassinated by the Red Brigade armed guard while boarding his plane. At that moment, Jones became paranoid and psychotic when stating conspiracy theories of "intelligence organizations allegedly conspiring against the People's Temple and that men would parachute in here on us and shoot some of our innocent babies." He created an atmosphere of paranoia and fear among temple members when lying about a plot of the government to airdrop hostile forces that would supposedly convert members and children to fascism.

This same rhetoric was used by Jones to justify what he dubbed "revolutionary suicide" to crying temple members. According to sources, Jim Jones had rehearsed mock suicide procedures many times in the past just for the final day. Finally, vats were brought out with flavor-aid laced with cyanide poison. Arguments were raised about a plan to take asylum in the Soviet Union, but Jim Jones was determined to make a final stand before the Intel organizations.

When Coroners examined Jones' body, they found evidence of barbiturate pentobarbital at lethal levels, a drug used in physician-assisted suicide. According to documentaries, Jim Jones died of a single gunshot wound to the head. It was evident that he was coward not able to subject himself to the same painful death that he diabolically planned for his followers. Since the forces to be were greater than Jones, his last and final statement to the world would be that "we committed an act of revolutionary suicide".

If anything good can be extracted from this mass murder, Jones' son Stephan survived the ruthless killing and is married today with 3 daughters. Fortunately, Stephan and his brothers were playing with the Peoples Temple basketball team against the Guyanese national team in Georgetown. Marceline Jones, Stephan's mother, also a victim of this ruthless monster, was found poisoned at the pavilion.

RISE OF ISLAM

At its inception, Islam was born out of a militant atmosphere in Saudi Arabia. Eventually dominating all of the Arab nations for the last fourteen hundred years, Islamo-fascism, the term commonly used today, is quickly becoming a formidable force to be reckoned with. One may view Islam as part of the beast or one of the heads of the beast described in the book of Revelation that has seven heads and ten horns ultimately making war with Christians Saints (Rev 13:7). Quran, Muslims' holy book which means "recitation", was authored by Muhammad, and written after his death in 632AD. The adherents of Islam are called Muslims. Islam is the Arabic word for submission to Allah.

Although illiterate, he was a political, religious and military leader in Saudi Arabia. Muhammad supposedly received words from the angel Gabriel while in a trance. According to tradition, Muhammad received the Quranic verses during trances, seizures, comas and convulsions. According to oral tradition, Muhammad married a woman named Khadija. Essentially, it was Khadija's uncle who began writing the Quran from the oral revelation of Muhammad.

Again, the word Quran truly means recite, and was written in ancient Arabic but not by Mohammed who was illiterate and could not write. Today's Quran contains some 114 Surahs or chapters. Many of the Surahs originated from Muhammad's experience while praying in a cave.

According to oral traditions, Mohammed supposedly received the Quran from the angel Gabriel which creates a point of contention with Christian scholars. How could the angel that spoke with Mohammed be Gabriel if the doctrine that he conveyed to Muhammad is false? According to Muhammad's account from the angel Gabriel, our Lord and Savior Jesus Christ is nothing more than a prophet and did not die. The effects of such Surahs have lasting implications suggesting that our salvation as

Christians is invalid if in fact Jesus was not God in the flesh and did not ultimately die for our sins.

FACT FROM FICTION

On the other hand, most Islamic scholars purport that any Bible that records that Jesus is begotten of God is simply corrupt due to issues of translations from Hebrew to Greek and them later to English. Most Muslims that speak Arabic pride themselves because no translation exists, but simply read the original Arabic text until today. When Muslim clerics state that the Bible is flawed, it is because the English version of the Bible was translated from lost ancient texts that were later transcribed from Hebrew into Latin, Greek and Aramaic. Unfortunately, all of the books written in Hebrew that comprise the Septuagint were lost. Isaiah is the only book preserved by the Essenes, a Jewish sect that transcribed the ancient book Isaiah during the time of the occupation of the Roman Empire.

A SECULAR HISTORIAN VALIDATES JEWISH HISTORY

Josephus, one of the most revered ancient historians, records that the Essenes existed in large numbers, and thousands lived throughout Roman occupied Judea. Unfortunately, any scholarly authority like Josephus would be considered by Muslim clerics diluted and not factual. Keep in mind that the Hebrew text was authored by Moses before Muhammad was a twinkling in his mother's eye. Let's face it, for thousands of years the Arabs did not have a gospel. During Muhammad's time the only thing that existed in that part of the world was Latin, Greek and Aramaic texts of the Bible. It's not hard to draw a conclusion that Khadija's uncle who was able to read, and socialize with Christians and Jews, simply borrowed Bible verses from the Torah to write the Quran. It's hard to imagine how an illiterate man like Muhammad could have concocted a book with over 114 Surahs. In fact, the various authors of the Quran even incorporated the deception of the Jews regarding the resurrection of Jesus. When the Jews could not explain what happen to the body of Jesus, they paid the officers money to lie to the then governor Pontius Pilate, that the body of Jesus was stolen.

> " [12]And when they were assembled with the elders, and had taken counsel, they gave large money unto the soldiers, [13] Saying, Say ye, His disciples came by night, and stole Him away while we slept. [14]And if this comes to the governor's ears, we will persuade him, and secure you."   --Mt 28:12

Case in point, any Mullah, Cleric, Sheik, or scholar would simply say that the truth of the following verse was lost in translation. I truly think that for the last 1,400 years, Muslim scholars have stayed awake late at night attempting to concoct a wild explanation why Muhammad and the angel Gabriel authored the Quran but the Bible categorically disagrees with their hypothesis.

According to Muhammad, Jesus neither died nor did Allah beget a son but Christ was simply a messenger. Where Christians embrace Jesus to be God in the flesh, the Quran regards Jesus as a mere prophet.

> "O People of the Scripture do not commit excess in your religion or say about Allah except the truth. The Messiah, Jesus, the son of Mary, was but a messenger of Allah and His word which He directed to Mary and a soul [created at a command] from Him. So believe in Allah and His messengers. And do not say, "Three"; desist - it is better for you. Indeed, Allah is but one God. Exalted is He above having a son. To Him belongs whatever is in the heavens and whatever is on the earth. And sufficient is Allah as Disposer of affairs."

Bible scholars suggest that the Septuagint (LXX) was composed around 200 B.C., the Dead Sea Scrolls around 100 B.C. and the Masoretic text of the Hebrew Bible about 100 A.D. Based on the previous assumptions, how would the Quran composed and published after the death of Muhammad in 632 A.D be considered an authority? In fact, it would be more likely that verses of the Quran originated from the original Hebrew and Greek tongues. The following represents what likely transpired regarding the writings of the Quran.

Khadija's uncle and other writers of the Quran simply modified the story from the initial Hebrew and Greek versions that Jesus never died but was translated to heaven. In actuality, the Quran itself confirms the life cycle of Jesus:

"Peace is on me the day I was born, the day that I die, and the day that I shall be raised up to life (again)!"
--Surah Maryam 19:33

Not only Jesus but the Quran confirms the death of John the Baptist (Yahya):

"So Peace on him [Yahya] the day he was born, the day that he dies, and the day that he will be raised up to life (again)!"   --Surah Maryam 19:15

Why would the transliteration for the word "die" be unique regarding Jesus but signify a literal death for John the Baptist (Yahya)?

THE QURAN IS FILLED WITH THE SPIRIT OF ERROR

It's unconscionable for Christians to believe that Jesus bypassed death before ascending into heaven according to the Quran, but the most blasphemous statement of all is that Allah does not have a Son, making Islam an anti-Christ religion according to 1 John 2:22.

> "²²Who is a liar but he that denieth that Jesus is the Christ? He is antichrist that denieth the Father and the Son."   --1 John 2:12

> "And the Word was made flesh, and dwelt among us, (and we beheld his glory, the glory as of the only begotten of the Father,) full of grace and truth."
>   --John 1:14

Simply stated, Muslims don't deny that Jesus was the Christ, but argue that Jesus was NOT the son of God begotten of the father. Moreover, Islamic scholars will compromise a bit by acknowledging that like Jesus, we are all sons of God, but categorically denounce the evidence that every Bible written literally records that Jesus was The Begotten of the father. The error which I have eloquently disclosed probably originated in the first century when Satan cast aspersions on Jesus in Matthew 4 and the Jewish high priests in Matthew 26:63 attempted to refute His deity during his trial. Since the concept of the Holy Ghost that bears witness of the truth is peculiar to Christians but not evident in Islam, then it would be deduced that the Quran is more of an intellectual creation than a divine inspiration. Yet Muhammad's authors of the Quran in the seventh century were well versed in the controversy between Jews, Christians and Pagans surrounding the virgin birth of Jesus as elaborated by Surah 2:116:

> "And they (Jews, Christians and pagans) say: Allah has begotten a son (children or offspring). Glory be to Him (Exalted be He above all that they associate with Him). Nay, to Him belongs all that is in the heavens and on earth, and all "   --Surah 2:116

A LACIVIOUS DOCTRINE

Albeit it is not written literally in the Quran, most Muslim proponents teach that 72 virgins in heaven await those who are martyred on earth. Now why would a man be excited about virgins in heaven when according to the Judeo-Christian Bible, men shall be like angels in heaven? It's absurd to imagine some type of sexual encounters with a celestial body. No one shall be given or taken in marriage and least of all would they be consummating marriage. Christian and Jews, people of "the book", are called infidels if they do not believe the words of the prophet Muhammad. One of the most outrageous stories is that of Muhammad's wife Khadija who claims that he traveled to Jerusalem on a winged camel. Once there, the angel Gabriel accompanied Muhammad to heaven. What most Westerners do not know is that trips to heaven were common among Arabs during the seventh century.

SAKIR NAIK ON THE NO-FLY LIST TO THE USA

Unlike the belief system of foremost scholars like Sakir Naik, no prophesy in the Bible exists concerning the coming of Muhammad. In fact, Muhammad was a self-acclaimed prophet that does not even meet the biblical standard. A trip down memory lane reveals how supposed Prophet Mohammed began to grow in strength at Medina by convincing two savage tribes, Oas and Khasrej, to wage war against the Arabian tribes in order to subdue them and convert them to Islam. It is not even plausible to conceive how a military leader like Muhammad could possibly author a book of peace.

If historical scholars agree as to the true violent nature of Mohammed and his men, then the question arises, how can the Quran, a "book of peace", be written by a man that resorted to violence?

Similar to the way Islamic scholars deny the existence of Solomon's temple, so they deny the foremost secular historians like Flavius Josephus, Eusebius of Caesarea, and Herodotus that have validated many biblical facts of the Bible. According to Islamic Scholars, they are the only foremost authorities that have factual records of the rise of Islam in the hadith. The translation of the Arabic word "hadith" means both the actions and oral sayings of Muhammad.

As one of the most dangerous cults on the earth today, many scholars believe that Islam personifies one of the heads of the beast in chapter thirteen of the book of Revelation. Meanwhile, the legacy continues with proponents such as Mahmoud Ahmadinejad, president of Iran, who believe that Jerusalem does not have a right to exist, and the temple of Solomon was nothing but a Zionist myth.

THE BEAST OF REVELATION 13

As I previously mentioned, Islam will probably take an active role as one of the seven heads of the beast that will wear out the very elect. Not only is the beast given power to war but at one point overcome the Saints of God. Of course the Saints, whose names are written in the Lambs book of life, will soon experience victory upon the return of Christ. For this reason, I believe that the Saints need to be equipped to fight a spiritual warfare against Islam, like in the days of old.

Contrary to theological scholars, the Saints of God don't just stand around acting dumb while the horn of the beast is making war with them. Over the last 492 years of church restoration, God has been equipping his Saints for the final battle.

> "3And I saw one of his heads as it were wounded to death; and his deadly wound was healed: and all the world wondered after the beast."   --Rev 13:3

The verse above reveals that one of the heads of beast was wounded to death then was healed. No doubt that one of the heads of the same beast is Islam that will fight against Messianic Jews and Gentile Christians Saints during tribulation.

Most western liberal minded Americans of the twenty first century have no idea what they are dealing with. I submit that there is little difference between the Islamic culture of the East and West, what separates the two is democracy; remove democracy from western Islam and it will morph into the same militant religion that it truly is. The ultimate goal of Islam is to legislate sharia law and conquer the entire known world.

Islam impetuously attempts to prove that Prophet Muhammad had power to work miracles. Unfortunately, Muhammad is dead but Jesus is alive. If Christians only witnessed what Jesus did, we are men most miserable. There would be no line of demarcation between Jesus Christ and Muhammad. Aren't you glad that Jesus never stopped working miracles?

SHOWDOWNS BETWEEN TRUE AND FALSE PROPHETS

Even to the present day we witness Jesus performing signs, wonders and miracles. That said, false Christ's and prophets are standing up around the world and only Christian prophets will refute their false claims by the demonstration of power.

"[10]And Moses and Aaron went in unto Pharaoh, and they did so as the Lord had commanded: and Aaron cast down his rod before Pharaoh, and before his servants, and it became a serpent. [11]Then Pharaoh also called the wise men and the sorcerers: now the magicians of Egypt, they also did in like manner with their enchantments. [12]For they cast down every man his rod, and they became serpents: but Aaron's rod swallowed up their rods."
--Exo 7:10-12

God sent Moses to demonstrate signs before Pharaoh's magicians and sorcerers. The above text demonstrates the power of God pitted against the power of darkness. It's evident that the Egyptians practiced magic, witchcraft and sorcery. It probably explains how the ancient Egyptians where able to build pyramids by levitating large blocks weighing 2-15 tons apiece. While the miracles of the rod changing to a serpent represent the glory of God, the feats of the magicians simply attempted to emulate God's glory. If you did not believe before regarding the validity of black magic, perhaps now you will understand that the kingdom of darkness has power to affect objects on the earth. Lucifer, the light bearer, the Devil, Satan is the prince of the power of the air (Ephesians 2:2) and is able to levitate, possess, transform as an angle of light, kill, steal, destroy, lie, accuse, and quote scriptures more accurately than the finest minds. Let me be clear, the days are coming and now are, when God's prophets will oppose the powers of darkness just like Moses. Most likely these encounters will not be televised, but will happen in remote places just like the events that took place in Egypt.

Elijah had a showdown in the valley between him and 450 prophets of Baal. As I have emphatically stated in another place, although there are many cults in this world, our God, the Lord Jehovah, is the only God that answers by fire.

> "24 And call ye on the name of your gods, and I will call on the name of the LORD: and the God that answereth by fire, let him be God. And all the people answered and said, it is well spoken."   --1 Kings 18:24

ISLAM ASSERTS GRIP OVER THE WORLD BY DEGREES

As recent as February of 2012, a first-time-ever event occurred in Grand Junction Colorado, at Grand Junction high school. Allegedly, a student quit attending after school choir when he learned the translation of an Islamic song entitled "Zikr".

When translated from Urdu to English, one verse in particular translated "There is no truth except Allah" and "Allah is the only eternal and immortal". Although students were not required to participate in choir rehearsal, the school embraced the choir director's decision to select the song for its rhythmic tempo. This is the ignorance of the great liberal compromise occurring amongst rank and file educators today. Fear is the major contributor to acquiescence amongst many Americans. It is implicit in the mindset that, "if something doesn't interfere with my self-indulgence, then, I could care less" attitude. Fear of Islam is a major problem in America but no one has the moxie to admit it.

Likewise, many in this country have been duped into believing that Islam is an innocuous religion of peace. It is this same delusional liberal mindset (mental disorder) that impetuously embraces the subtle destruction of our most precious document, the Constitution. The day shall come when the sun arises over Islamic courts practicing Sharia law in this country. It is unconscionable but true.

Incidentally, did you know that the word Allah has no derivative anywhere in the Bible? Again, it appears that Islamic mullahs and scholars stay awake all night looking for a scheme that will prove that the transliteration of the word Allah means God. Unfortunately, Allah is not found in Hebrew, Aramaic, or Greek. However, there are two words in the Hebrew language that sound the same but have different meanings and these are "Alah" and "Elah."

Again, Allah is not the same as Jehovah Yeshua, the Judeo-Christian God of the Bible. For centuries, Islamic scholars never cease to be on the defense while attempting to substantiate the writings of the Prophet Muhammad whom I've stated before was both illiterate and could not write in Arabic.

ENGLAND'S SHARIA LAW, LIBERALISM, AND GRADUAL OVERTHROW OF A SOVEREIGN NATION

Our mother country, even England, has already experienced the devastating effects of Islam. Since 2008, as England parts from its Christian roots into modern secular humanism, it has quietly sanctioned Sharia law where Muslims can now be tried under their own religious law. Sharia law, in essence, blends the concepts both of the Quran and hadith (the words and actions of Prophet Muhammad), and will have lasting effects in the years to come. In fact, as many as 85 Sharia courts in England deal with a variety of topics including politics, economics, crime, as well as personal matters such as hygiene, diet, prayer, fasting and sexual intercourse. These county high courts are enforced with full power by the Supreme Court system. Sadly, women do not have equal rights under Sharia law. It is a well-known fact by scholars that the male-dominated society of the Old Testament tended to rate women as second-class citizens under Judaism similar to the seventh century Sharia law of today.

Case in point, brothers and sisters are treated unequally when dealing with an inheritance under Sharia law. Males are always granted a larger portion of the inheritance than females. Actually, a sister will only receive one half of the amount a brother receives of the inheritance. Sharia flies in the face of western civil liberties as we know it.

According to Etymology, the word Sharia means "pathway to be followed", or "path to the water hole". Sharia is a divine law from the Quran. Breaking a law is sin and ultimately one will answer to Allah in the Day of Judgment.

But sadly, the creation of a cultural stronghold over Muslim communities in the UK is leading to an Islamification of the entire society one court at a time. In communities where the majorities are Bangladeshi Muslim women, Sharia courts are staunchly opposed to equal rights. Sharia law favors men by keeping unloved women trapped in their marriage. While man can be divorced by uttering one word, "talaq", women must elect official channels chaired by men in Sharia court in order to gain a divorce. And if the women's marriage is not registered, then the UK civil court has little recourse to help her when it comes to the division of property.

America, read the handwriting on the wall, the enemy is already within our borders and it is a force to be reckoned with.

JEHOVAH'S WITNESS AT LARGE

I always found it curious how that Islam and the Jehovah's Witness both have one thing in common, neither believe that Jesus is God in the flesh (1 Tim 3:16). Where Islam alleges that Allah has taken no son (Surah 17:111), the Jehovah's Witness acknowledge the son but logically conclude that Jehovah is greater (John 14:29) hence Christ cannot be God. This is plainly a spirit of error and a departure from the truth. In fact the bible is emphatically clear when it states in John 1:2, 14 (KJV) "In the beginning was the Word, and the Word was with God, and the Word was God" and "the Word was made flesh, and dwelt among us, and we beheld his glory, the glory as of the only begotten of the father full of grace and truth".

The fact that Jesus is not only the son but fully God in the flesh is the cornerstone of Christianity.

SOME FACTS ABOUT THE JEHOVAH'S WITNESS

- Founded by Charles T. Russell in 1870 – 1916
- Frederick Franz chief theologian
- Author of New World Translation
- The Three Worlds published that Christ had returned in 1874
- Prophesied Armageddon in 1914, 1925, 1975
- All 21st century prophets are false

- Witnesses believe that Archangel Michael, or "Apollyon" in Revelation 9:11 actually refer to Jesus
- Jesus is not God in the flesh but Michael, the Archangel
- Adherents worship God not Jesus because he was only a prophet
- Un-regenerated man can worship Satan
- After death the soul is non-existent without consciousness, detached from memory of the past
- The last day of God's judgment was 1914
- All other religions are false
- Due to life in the blood, no blood transfusions allowed
- Criticized for refusal to reveal the names and academic credentials of their faithful Translators
- On September 1922, a new emphasis was made on house-to-house preaching
- When a Christian dies, the soul returns to the grave into oblivion, it has no memory of the former life

BUDDHISM

- Buddha began teaching between the 6th and 4th centuries BCE in India
- Buddhism evolved into Hinduism
- Karma (from Sanskrit: "action, work") in Buddhism is the force that drives "samsāra" essentially the cycle of suffering and rebirth for each being.
- Out of Buddhism comes reincarnation, return in another state to prefect oneself, it rejects the concepts of permanent self or an unchanging eternal soul
- Yoga is practiced to become aware
- Buddhism is a philosophy, not a truth
- Belief in many deities and gods
- Constant change of things in flux, things come to be and then cease to be
- Reincarnation or continual change ceases when one has been perfected

HINDUISM

- Based on the notion of karma, Hinduism is practiced largely in India
- Practice Yoga traditions
- Third largest religion after Islam and Christianity
- Hindu divides into Śruti ("revealed") and Smriti ("remembered") texts. These texts discuss theology, philosophy and mythology, and provide information on the practice of dharma (religious living)
- India means "The Land of the Hindus"
- Hindus embrace a diverse system of thought with beliefs spanning monotheism, polytheism, pantheism, monism, atheism, agnosticism, Gnosticism among many
- No declaration of faith or creed, instead an umbrella term comprising plurality of religion
- Hinduism is devoid of the concepts of apostasy, heresy, blasphemy, and righteousness
- Hindus worship and give food and blood sacrifice to deities or gods
- Hindus practice vegetarianism
- Cow in Hindu society is traditionally caretaker and a maternal figure, Hindu society honors the cow as a symbol of unselfish giving. Cow-slaughter is legally banned in almost all states of India
- Adherents march in rituals in the streets manifesting demon possession
- Worship of snakes

WITCHCRAFT, SORCERY

1. Sorcery

The counterpart to a Witch is a Sorcerer who practices black magic though both can interchange powers of darkness. The Bible calls sorcerers children of the devil, similar to the way Jesus spoke with the Pharisees in (John 8:44). In the book of Acts 13:6,

Paul engages with Elymas the sorcerer who sought to pervert the truth and deceive Sergius Paulus. Essentially, sorcery is consistent with the subtle shift and perversion of truth. Case in point, the author of Acts 13:6, informs the reader about a certain Jew by the name of Barjesus who was a sorcerer. Being a Jew, containing the name "Jesus" in a compound name, was quite deceptive in itself. However, this false prophet was no match for the weight of the anointing that rested on the life of Paul the apostle in the first century church. God is restoring this type of anointing to empower the Saints both to discern and deal with false prophets and sorcerers in the days to come.

Black magic is closely tied to Middle Eastern folklore including Aladdin and the Magic Lamp, Sinbad the Sailor, and One Thousand and One Nights that have roots both in China and Saudi Arabia. Many of these classics became animated adventures out of the Disney Renaissance period. But to our shame, the one thing that is lacking today is the authority to demonstrate the power of God like in Paul's time. The bible makes it emphatically clear that Paul the apostle discerns Elymas' true nature, and then commands blindness to fall upon him.

Paul being filled with the Holy Ghost needed to teach the Sorcerer a public lesson. So shall we teach sorcerers and witches a public lesson when we evangelize. For this reason, the world needs to witness the power of true apostles in this last day.

2. Witchcraft

A witch typically is a female that practices voodoo, magic, idol sacrifices, casts spells, makes potions or poison, and conjures the dead. She will influence mind, body and property in a negative way using black magic. There is a very close tie between witchcraft and spiritual things. Deuteronomy 11–12 and Exodus 22:18 therefore produce "Thou shalt not suffer a witch to live" which was seen as providing scriptural justification for Christian witch hunters in the early Modern Age .We see that God has anointed Jehu to deal with whoredoms of King Joram's mother Jezebel who practiced witchcraft (2 Kg 9:22). The word whoredom really implies a relationship between a Christian and a false deity other than God. Jezebel is even viewed as a false prophetess who seduces over 400 prophets of Baal that sit at her table (1 Kg 18:19). Not only does she seduce God's servants through indoctrination but teaches them to commit fornication by eating things sacrificed to idols in the church of Thyatira (Rev 2:20).

The prophetess, like Jezebel, and witches attempt to kill the prophetic word of the prophets (1 Kg 18:13) of the twenty-first century.

I believe that this chapter has enlightened us as to the type of dangerous deceptions that are in the world today. Although many books have been written on this subject, I have by no means covered the depth of the topic in this chapter. I added this chapter so that believers may understand the necessity of having anointed leaders in our places of worship that can both anoint and train us for the coming warfare. To be forewarned is to be forearmed.

My prayer is that God will anoint you to discern those spiritual types previously mentioned in this chapter in order to avoid being seduced like so many others in times past. Protect yourself with the whole armor of God so that in an evil day you can both stand and "wrestle against principalities, against powers, against rulers of the darkness of this world, and against spiritual wickedness in high places" (Eph 6:12).

Chapter 4

THE HOMOSEXUAL AGENDA

> In the beginning God created Adam
> and Eve, not Adam and Steve

I had prophesied that during the Obama Administration, the homosexual agenda would make huge strides toward equal protections. For those who are not familiar with the history of homosexuality, this rising class may seem mesmerizing at first, but in fact, it's not a new class at all but has been around since Noah. Paul admonished the Roman church regarding the unnatural use of the man and the women.

> "[27]And likewise also the men, leaving the natural use of the woman, burned in their lust one toward another; men with men working that which is unseemly, and receiving in themselves that recompense of their error which was meet. "   --Romans 1:27

As the book of Timothy so eloquently stated, there would come a time when men would not endure sound doctrine (2 Timothy 4:3) but seek after teachers that preached secular humanism, liberalism, philosophy, and new age religion. Every time you mention the Bible, they either cry foul, you're a hater, or a discriminator

I would guess that many of our opponents would say that God is one of the biggest discriminators of all time. How did this all begin? All you Bible scholars will remember that the first act of homosexuality occurred between Noah and his grandson Canaan. Noah was a husbandman; who indulged in too much wine, became drunk and lay naked within his tent. When Noah woke from his drunken state, he knew what his younger son (Canaan) had done unto him. Noah declares "cursed be Canaan, a servant of servants shall he be" (Genesis 9:25).

Throughout scriptures, homosexuality is always associated with sin. Remember in the twentieth century how the HIV virus had run rampant in places like Africa where homosexuality was being practiced? Unfortunately, there are consequences for certain lifestyles that do not conform to the laws of nature.

ADULTERY, FORNICATION, COVETOUSNESS ARE ALL SIN

Let's first look first at the house of God. If I'm a practicing adulterer, than I have no business condemning homosexuals. If I enjoy lying all the time and I will not repent, then you should not pass judgment on others until you get your life right before God. God hates adultery, God hates homosexuality. In fact, in God's eyes, all of it falls under the category of sin. Some of the more liberal opponents seem to suggest that God compromised his law by loving the homosexual. Let's be clear, heaven and earth shall pass away but his word forever abides in heaven. His word is immutable, it never changes. However, we have changed. Having said that, I realize that we need to admonish people based on love and not personal interests. On the flip side of the coin, do not allow people to pull out the discrimination trump card on you. Those that have knowledge should stand for righteousness without fear of reprisals, retribution or retaliation. It's sad to see just how many denominations are compromising the word of God today. Case in point: recently, during 2014, it was reported that the son of a president from a particular religious denomination, had openly confessed he was a homosexual. Subsequent to that revelation, many churches separated themselves from that alliance. Now is not the time to compromise the truth of God. Furthermore, "if you can't take the heat, get out of the kitchen". I don't care who calls "evil good", Jesus foretold us of the days when there would be divisions amongst Christians, fathers against worldly children. The implication may be that fathers would be accused by their sons of discrimination.

> "The father shall be divided against the son, and the son against the father; the mother against the daughter, and the daughter against the mother; the mother-in-law against her daughter-in-law, and the daughter-in-law against her mother-in-law."   --Luke 12:53

Instead of standing our ground for righteousness, we cave into popular public opinion in an attempt to avoid division, but I got news for you, if you're going to be all you can be for Jesus, there will be division. It speaks volumes as to the level of passivity that has pervaded rank and file religious leaders of the twenty first century.

FIRST GET THE BEAM OUT OF YOUR OWN EYE SO YOU CAN SEE CLEARLY

Jesus made it clear; we need to remove the beam out of our own eyes so that we can see clearly to take the mote out of our brother's eye. At first glance, opponents might cry out "foul play", but the reality is that there is a larger issue at stake here. Today, we hear statements from the liberal wing like "love never fails", and "Jesus fathered a child from Mary Magdalene". Moreover, if you refute it, then you are using inflammatory and discriminatory language. Look, I have the right to be involved in the affairs of my community and in the church at large.

Recently we've heard some politicians have a change of heart when one of their children revealed that he or she was a homosexual. These politicians then attempt to justify their ungodly doctrine on the merits of evolution. I think the statement was "I'm evolving." Truly, the latter infers that God is somehow progressive, and thinks like them. The same administration that, back in 2008, opposed marriage between homosexuals, now describes itself as "evolving". Context suggests that somehow the evolution of man infers the evolution of God. One thing is for sure, God does not evolve, for Jesus declared "I change not the same yesterday today and forever."

AGAPE V.S. PHILEO LOVE

Let's talk about love or better yet agape love. Christians are stigmatized because they believe that God hates homosexuality, and he does. More than ever before is Isaiah 5:20 being fulfilled that says "woe unto those who call evil good."

Look, there is a reason why biologically, men and women are attracted to each other, its part of nature. It's natural for a man to be aroused at the sight of his wife, but it's not natural for a man to be intoxicated with another man. I've heard during the elections in 2012 statements like "you should be able to love anyone you want to." At first glance this sounds harmless, but is it? Love is a powerful word, but what overtures does the word love have in the former context? There is a unique difference between the Greek words phileo and agape. Phileo is the love between brethren, but agape is unconditional sexless love between Christians. Any human being can practice phileo with another person because it does not require the Holy Spirit, but agape can only be understood when you are baptized in fire. What do politicians really mean about "loving anyone that you want to"? Christians are supposed to love everyone, but not sexually, to put it bluntly. Let's be honest, as the onset of a physical attraction between two men commences, naturally, the next step might be to engage in a sexual encounter with that person. Of course opponents will cry out homophobic, discrimination, and intolerance against Christians. Moreover, secular intellects like the ACLU typically concoct interesting language in order to thwart the righteousness of the Bible, represent God-haters in lawsuits and have made quantum advances towards atheism in our society.

I suppose if you're politically correct then you're not homophobic, but if you stand for righteousness you are. That said, no wonder some Christians are caving into the political pressures of this world.

SUBTLETIES OF HOMOSEXUALITY

I'll never forget the experience that I had as a teenager in my old neighborhood before I was saved. One day, I was visiting the house of one of my classmates. On this particular day, his older brother was at home and he happened to play the piano very well. Homosexuals, in general, appear to be quite normal at first glance, that is why the Saints need to operate in discernment. Since I enjoyed music, I was fascinated by his piano style. Little did I know that he was a practicing homosexuality during the 1970's. In fact, no sooner did I leave his house when he made a proposition that I meet him in the woods so that he could show me some things. Fortunately, I never ventured into the woods to find out what surprises were on the agenda. God sent his angels on many occasions to deliver me from destruction.

STUBBORNESS AND REBELLION

This brings me to a very important point about self-esteem, anger, bitterness and rebellion. On the secular side, one of the associates on the job is a self-acclaimed homosexual. His ability to change his mannerisms can be very deceptive, for one moment he is business oriented, and in the next utterly perverted. Again, unless you have discernment, you would not perceive the source of his subtle crafty nature. He has no problem boasting about an orgy that he had the night before. I discerned a deep-rooted bitterness in his life as well as an extremely stubborn nature. These two dysfunctions tend to be common factors among homosexuals. Let's be honest, we all have dysfunctions in life but each of us has learned to manage our own shortcomings in different ways. Often, homosexuality is nothing but a blatant display of rebellion towards society as a whole.

HOMOSEXUALITY IS NOT A GENETIC CONDITION

Look, let's cut to the chase, homosexuality is not a biological condition but a decision. No doubt that there tends to be some external feminine physical attributes associated with the demeanor of a male homosexual. One day while dialoguing with this co-worker with the unique sexual orientation, a curious thought entered my mind regarding roles. Interestingly enough, this individual claims that he both studied theology and attended service in the parochial school while he was an adolescent. Moreover, he has an acute hate for scripture and claims he is going to hell.

If two men decide to marry, which will be the wife? Although, opponents decry discrimination, at close observation, you'll notice one of the men attempts to play the female role but without the sexual parts. To their dismay, one may enlarge one's breasts, but you can't fabricate a womb to date. If you study female homosexual behavior, there is an inordinate lust for the female sexual parts in the relationship; one always tends to portray the female wife role while the other plays the masculine male role. How can you tell? Just look at the haircuts. Typically, one has long hair, and the other short hair. Quite bluntly, it's an attempt to play the role of a man and women. A man is just as much spiritual as he is biological. Not only is he a man genetically, but spiritually as well. This is a detail that homosexuals cannot emulate easily.

COMPROMISE IN THE CHURCH

In most cases, homosexuals want nothing to do with the Bible or God with few exceptions. We've all heard of the huge compromise taking place in the Episcopal Church regarding homosexuality. In fact, in 1976, the Episcopal Church pronounced it's acceptance of homosexuals in ecumenical positions of authority. Today, Episcopalian, Presbyterian, and Methodist liberal churches are all experiencing conflicts within their own ranks. Essentially, Episcopalian, Presbyterian, and Methodists are all offspring of the Anglican church of England. In general, no wonder England is one of the most liberal countries in the world.

Saint, as the homosexual community ran rampant in the Roman first century society, so are the people of the United States caving in to this liberal mindset of equal protections. It is a well-known fact that homosexuality was one of the contributing factors that weakened the infrastructure of Rome resulting in a collapse of the empire. In many ways our culture is similar to that of Rome. If you recall your history, upon creating the lower house, the framers of the constitution of the United States borrowed the concept from the Roman senate as a model.

MORAL DECLINE IN OUR SOCIETY

Today, homosexuals are a rising class in our society, gaining equal protections under the law. Like dominos, states are caving in one by one due the complexity of this moral issue. Not only are the lines blurred between heterosexual and homosexual, but now the defense of marriage act is under attack as well from the current administration. What are the implications to this immoral corruption in our society? First of all, it means the level of persecution towards Christians will proportionally increase on a scale of the likes never seen before.

THE SUPREME COURT DECISION

I found it humorous when proposition 8 was referred to the Supreme Court and the justices were arguing about the constitutionality of heterosexual marriage. How do you define marriage? Was the intent of marriage designed by God to procreate? Shall there be marriage requirements that ask the question as to whether two people are able to procreate? What happens after 50 when a woman enters menopause and can't procreate, should she still qualify? Unfortunately, the Supreme Court ruled that the lower court's judgment of marriage between a man and a woman would stand. In other words, California's vote on proposition 8 to preserve traditional marriage between a man and a woman was declared unconstitutional. As biblical prophecy is fulfilled, we slowly see a departure from the wisdom of our founding fathers who crafted the Constitution of the United States.

DETRIMENT TO ADOPTED CHILDREN

Perhaps the most disappointing gain made by proponents of the gay community is that children can be adopted by homosexuals. Without any data as to the negative effects of such adoptions, to date, courts refused to acknowledge that adopted children forced into that atmosphere have a real chance of practicing homosexuality themselves. In other words, there is an aberration between the lines of normal such that children will be raised with a dysfunctional concept of marriage. However, if on the other hand, you don't see the negative impact of homosexuality, then you're not inclined to condemn the placement of homeless children with homosexuals. I don't mean to be graphic but how does a child perceive two men, Joe & Moe, kissing with preludes to a sexual engagement? What are the lasting effects on children when they see both Les & Bian intimately grinding in their bedroom? It's unconscionable.

DISCRIMINATION AGAINST HOMOSEXUALS

Are Christians really discriminating against homosexuals today? According to God's word, marriage has been a holy institution from day one. The Bible does not say that in the beginning God created two homosexuals named Adam and Steve. I know that I engage in a little hyperbole, but the Bible declares that He created a male and a female named Adam and Eve. When you look at the women she was created to fit with the man for the purpose of procreation. Two women cannot procreate; neither can two men produce a newborn. In fact, if you put a male and female on a desert island, they would most likely procreate and proliferate into new class of people. On the other hand, if you put two men on a desert island, they would ultimately become extinct.

To redefine marriage as some secular institution is a blatant rejection of God's word for we know that Christ is the head and we are the body, moreover the bride without spot or wrinkle. If the Bible did not exist, I would acquiesce to our liberal opponents that we are discriminating against a class of people. However, that is not the case, the word is very clear regarding marriage between a man and a women. Marriage by its very definition suggests intercourse or intimacy between partners with the potential of procreation. Hence, I submit that declaring righteousness from a biblical perspective is not discrimination; but our mandate as the Saints of the Most High.

GREATER PERSECUTION LIES AHEAD

While a growing number of people convert to homosexuality, Christians are quickly becoming a minority class of their own. Observing the response from the Supreme Court reveals the level of corruption that has pervaded the highest offices of the land. If the will of the people in California upholding marriage as an institution between a man and a women was regarded as unconstitutional, it won't be long before legislation is passed that will force pastors to marry homosexuals.

Someday, you may go to jail for a hate crime if you mention the word homosexual to the wrong person. There may come a day when if pastors refuse to marry two men on demand, it will be recognized as discrimination by the civil courts regardless of what the ecumenical institution decrees. This may result in revocation of your pastoral license or 501(c)(3) when you stand by God's word. It is a foregone conclusion that someday, homosexuality will be legal in the United States as pressure mounts against the conservative states. At the end of the day, for many Americans, the emphasis is more about the number of votes and money rather than a God that protected this nation as a sanctuary since the Pilgrims landed at Plymouth Rock.

In my humble opinion, this chapter was not about a solution, but a wake-up call to the church. Nevertheless, in the days to come, we shall witness conversions from homosexuality to Christianity. As a result, many shall begin to live productive normal lifestyles because some bold men and women of God refuse to settle for less than the biblical standard.

Chapter 5

GOD'S PECULIAR GENERATION

One way to escape your enemies is to outlive them.
--Michael Biagioni

"It was hot that summer and the air conditioner in my car was not working. Essentially, I was broke and could not afford to have a mechanic repair my old car. Suddenly, the Lord spoke to me 'go upstairs and get your Tupperware container and fill it with water.' So, I went upstairs, found the Tupperware container, filled it with water and returned to the car. At the same time, I noticed the pastor of the church that I was attending getting out of his car and coming in my direction. Then the Lord said to me, 'pour the Tupperware container full of water into the air conditioner vents'. I was concerned that if anyone observed what I was doing they would think that I had lost my mind. I knew that I had to hurry because the pastor would be standing at my door any moment. After I finished pouring out the entire container, I started the car and turn the air conditioner on and set the fan on full. For the first time since I purchased the car, an ice-cold stream of air rushed out of the vents, man did that feel awesome. Suddenly, there was a knock on the window, it was the pastor. I opened the window and he asked me 'what were you doing?'

I replied and told him how the Lord had instructed me to get a Tupperware container, fill it with water, and pour it into the air conditioning ducts of the car, but to my surprise he shook his head in disbelief. I hoped that someone would believe that God truly was speaking with me and the pastor would share in my joy. I was looking for someone that would believe in me."

-- Prophet David Paul

I was amazed when Prophet David Paul related that story during a service one day in Hartford, Connecticut. Fact is, most leaders do not understand God's prophets. Unfortunately, some carnal leaders are actually intimidated with God's apostles and prophets. I've come to realize that there is a segment of Saints that are familiar with all the buzz words, can quote scriptures, but truly have not experienced any real supernatural events in their lives. Part of the underlying problem is related to the emphasis today on physical healing and prosperity. While there is nothing wrong with physical healing and prosperity, Christendom has somehow diminished many other aspects of the supernatural. You ask, are the unusual and unanticipated phenomena of the supernatural really necessary? I believe so. If not, then Jesus would never have performed so many unusual and odd miracles. Even Peter imitates the unusual of Jesus in the same manner when he walked on the water.

THE UNANTICIPATED AND UNUSUAL

Throughout history, God has raised up a bunch of very peculiar people as a spectacle to fulfill some very unusual assignments. I've got some good news for you; He's still in the business of raising up some Jehu's to perform all of His will. If there are false prophets, then God has authentic prophets. If devils exist then there must be angels. If sadistic men are allowed to commit genocide, then God must be preparing a Moses or Joshua to deliver His people. When God is at the center of reform, some things cannot help but be a little unusual. What would Christian culture be like without the unpredictable from God? The root of the problem can be related to a generation of leaders that have become complacent before God. We are no longer interested in the phenomenal and unusual, but now stuff takes center stage in the church. I believe the unusual, unexpected, the "suddenly's", are paramount to a thriving church that's under attack by political agendas. What then separates the Church of Jesus Christ from the other religions of the world? Is it not that we are a peculiar people, serving a peculiar God?

I chose this chapter because I felt that it is important for us to return back to our roots. As the church slips into laxity and retreat, suddenly, it becomes the norm for the next generation. We as pioneers and forerunners need to uphold the standards that have been laid down by our Judeo-Christian forefathers. Is not that what separates today's Saints from the rest of the world, the fact that we have intimacy with an amazing God?

To love Him means to be like Him. Jesus was the brightness of God's glory and the express image of His person. Jesus acted like God because He imitated God. Jesus watched the father and when His father raised the dead, Jesus raised the dead. When His father opened blind eyes, Jesus did the same. Paul writes in II Corinthians that if we are in Christ, we are new creatures. Everything old must pass away, and now all things are becoming new. Get ready for the unusual, unpredictable, amazing, and remarkable things that God has prepared for this generation.

Throughout the generations, God has raised up some unusual Saints. Many of us are unfamiliar with church history during the last 100 years. In order for us to be well rounded men and women of God, it's good to be informed about some of the pioneers that have run before us. Not only is it enlightening but encouraging that you may be the next Kathryn Kuhlman or an A. A. Allen to initiate a revolution and incite reformation amongst God's holy remnant. If you study the pattern of the different movements orchestrated by God over the last century, one can discern that God established these prototype Christians for our benefit, that we might believe and experience something phenomenal in the days to come.

Let me introduce to you some highly unusual people, if not outright strange, to say the least. They came from every walk of life, even different societies for the glory of God; men and women considered misfits and often rejected by mainstream religion. These are a generation of Saints, never truly understood by society, but chosen by God, and precious.

THE NINETEENTH CENTURY'S GREATEST

What I consider to be one of the foremost apostles of the nineteenth century is a man by the name of Smith Wigglesworth. Born in Yorkshire England in the late 1850's, Wigglesworth came on the scene during one of the greatest revivals of church history, the Faith Healing Movement. Society would never truly come to grips with what God had planned through the life of Wigglesworth. Wigglesworth exclaimed that he thought about God even as a child. Albeit his parents were not religious, God began to use him at a very young age. Smith Wigglesworth had two professions, songbird wholesaler and plumber. Wigglesworth often asked God to show him where the songbirds where hiding so that he could catch them for sale. Even at a young age, Wigglesworth had a keen sense of God's presence. During this period, a forerunner named William Booth established the Salvation Army. Unlike the pseudo organization of today in England, the Salvation Army actually was incorporated for the dissemination of the gospel of Jesus Christ. Soon, Wigglesworth became fascinated with their enthusiasm and the fire of the Holy Ghost.

WIGGLESWORTH FIRST MIRACLE

At one point, Smith Wigglesworth sought employment. Finally he was hired as a plumber. From childhood, Wigglesworth suffered from a hemorrhoid condition. During a service at the Salvation Army, one of the ministers told Smith that he could be healed. After a short prayer, Wigglesworth believed God, and was miraculously healed from the condition for the rest of his life. This would be the beginning that would set the stage for the legacy of Smith Wigglesworth. Being a man of faith, his basic tenets were love and compassion. He loved the lost and wanted to save the entire world. At first, Wigglesworth transported people that needed healing to the healing ministry, but this would set the stage for his own ministry.

THE DUNAMIS POWER OF GOD MANIFESTS ITSELF

Albeit Wigglesworth didn't seem to have confidence in himself, others perceived the glory of God resting upon him. On one occasion, Wigglesworth is asked to pray for a woman who is on her death bed at home. In desperation, he found another man who would travel together with him to the dying woman's house. Once there, Smith asked his fellow soldier to pray for the woman, but to his dismay, the woman's condition intimidates his friend causing him to pray in preparation for her death. After a period of exasperation, Smith told him to hush and then asked the husband to pray. Unfortunately, her husband had no faith while praying and Smith told him to "shut up" as well. Finally, in an act of utter desperation, Wigglesworth grabbed a bottle of oil, and while pouring the entire bottle upon the woman, Jesus appeared to him with a smile. Immediately, the woman sat up in the bed, suddenly declaring that she was completely healed. Since miracles were an unusual manifestation in the nineteenth century, everyone in the house that witnessed the supernatural were either paralyzed or in a state of shock for the entire day. These events would mark the beginning of Smith Wigglesworth's great ministry.

GIFT OF FAITH PUTS A DEMAND ON THE ANOINTING

On another occasion, he receives news that a woman just died. Nothing stopped him from completing God's assignments whether by foot, train, or bicycle. Upon arriving, Wigglesworth walks up to the bed, grabs the woman, pulls her out of bed, slams her up against the wall, looks the dead in the face and says, "you're going to walk today." Trembling and shaking, the dead woman revived and began to walk. Sometimes the faith of Wigglesworth was considered arrogant, reckless, and even brutal at times.

I've heard people say that if the Spirit was not moving in a meeting, Wigglesworth would move the Spirit. As the Saints of God, we need to learn how to access the glory of God in our ministries. Moreover, during the twentieth century, God restored the gifts of the Holy Ghost, but there is one thing lacking. Where is the glory? Walking in his glory is paramount to a greater manifestation of power. Can you imagine the limitless number of results that could occur if God's anointed people not only operated in the gifts of the Holy Ghost, but also walked in the presence of His glory? Unfortunately, most men in our generation with great anointing have learned how to operate in the gifts of the Holy Spirit without the glory of God.

After the turn of the nineteenth century, the fires of the Pentecostal movement were still burning. With the restoration of baptism of Pentecost came the new phenomenon of speaking in unknown tongues. Because Smith was desperate to experience everything in the Bible, this became a point of conflict between him and other acquaintances. Either Smith would compromise his passion or had to say farewell to some dead folk that were not interested in revival. Fortunately, Wigglesworth chose to speak in unknown tongues and the rest is history.

SPEAKING IN UNKNOWN TONGUES WILL COST YOU

During some of Smith's meetings, he would promote speaking in unknown tongues. He would inform the Saints that on this particular night, after receiving the baptism of the Holy Spirit, some would speak with tongues. As he prayed with unyielding faith, tongues would erupt all over his meetings. Not only did Wigglesworth promote unknown tongues but also promoted a new phenomenon called holy laughter. According to legend, during a service, a couple of workers, both father and son stated that they wanted to experience holy laughter. While one of them attempted to sit down, missing the chair, he fell to the ground. Likewise, his son missed his chair as well and fell to the ground in front of the entire congregation.

Since Smith was adamant about maintaining order in his meetings, it's not hard to imagine boisterous roars of laughter that erupted that evening after what seemed an unfortunate mishap. Or was it just a set up orchestrated by God for Smith Wigglesworth to experience a new phenomenon called, "holy laughter"? Nevertheless, a dozen people or more experienced this jovial spiritual phenomenon. Soon it became a part of the Wigglesworth tradition for holy laughter to break out like wildfire during a service. This wonderful move of the spirit is still taking place here in Tampa Florida at the renowned River Church hosted by Pastor Rodney Howard Browne. Few know that the holy laughter movement of the Spirit actually began during the early nineteen hundred.

After Smith Wigglesworth's wife passed, his crusades, especially in California, were so large he had to quit his job as a plumber. Not only were people healed but special miracles took place by his hands. During meetings, he would cut anointed handkerchiefs, give them to the people to take back to the sick and they were healed.

SMITH WIGGLESWORTH PERSONAL TEST

Look, when you are impacting such a large percentage of people, the enemy of your soul will not go on vacation. It's paramount for a warrior to be on guard for ambushes from the enemy. That is why it is quintessential for people to intercede for us when we are in a camp meeting. After several meetings, Smith experienced pain in his body. As a man of great faith, one that was instrumental in demonstrating the resurrection of the dead first hand, he prayed for himself. When the pain only seemed to get worse, the doctor informed him that he had kidney stones. This is a good lesson for all of us. When things change from bad to worse, it's not time to abandon God. Often, when things get ugly, people retreat from commitment in ministry. However, when you are at the level of Smith Wigglesworth, quitting isn't an option. Smith continued to preach and pray during bouts of horrible pain. There were moments when he had to excuse himself from the meeting so that he could pass a stone. According to some accounts, he passed as many as one hundred stones before God healed him completely. He never quit nor complained, he simply persevered while being a blessing. Many have studied this great man in an attempt to capture the essence of his anointing. His famous retort was simply, "only believe God.

WILLIAM BRANHAM GOD'S SERVANT

One of the foremost prophets of the twentieth century was a man by the name of William Branham. By man's standards, he was considered unlearned, but in the first century, the apostles would have embraced him as one of them since the Jews considered all of them to be ignorant. By biblical standards, men of God were considered peculiar in the world's view because they did not conform to the standards of that century educationally, theologically, philosophically, or otherwise.

Born on April 6, 1909, God was preparing to raise up a man with the same type of mantle as one of the prophets of old. The priesthood of the early twentieth century was hardly ready for what God had planned for William Branham. Without a doubt, Branham raised a few religious eyebrows during his time due to the manifestation of the supernatural that marked his ministry.

On the cusp of the Pentecostal Revival movement like Welsh and Evan Roberts, William Branham would shock the nation as a true prophet of God. Without a doubt, Branham was an authentic tribute to the first century as a prototype of his generation who was anointed with great grace and the apostolic witness of the resurrection of the dead.

So that Braham would not be influenced by the religious system of the day, God sent a whirling light to Branham's home to anoint him while he was a newborn child. William Branham himself documents the following events based on the story conveyed to him by his mother. Unlike Branham, many people today can prophesy, but have no tangible documented proof of a bona fide visitation from God. Without a doubt, from his youth, William Branham had a peculiar anointing resting upon him.

By virtue of the vow he made with God that he should never "drink, smoke or defile his body", Branham conducted a solitary life style. His life was consecrated and separated unto God from worldly pleasures. During Branham's calling, he received many signs from God. On one occasion while just a boy, his father told him to fetch some water. On the way back he sat at the base of a tree, suddenly, according to his own testimony, the wind blowing through the top of the trees spoke to him, "never drink, smoke or defile your body because I have a work for you to do when you are older." He would hear that wind and the same words while he struggled to run from God. Even his brother Edward died prematurely because he would not hearken to the voice of God. Don't ever think that God will not do something because of theodicy. We often try to defend God against objections of holiness, morality, evil and calamity. God is sovereign; he does what he pleases with whomever he desires according to Dan 4:35. While Prophet William Branham remained obstinate, tragic events continued to evolve in his life.

During surgery from a stomach illness, Branham became weak unto death. Again he hears the familiar sound of the wind in the trees speaking to him, and finally, while leaving his body, he asks God for help. God confirms the call on his life and Branham makes a covenant with God. Branham proposes that if God will send him back to earth, he will preach the gospel, and in the next moment he is sitting up on the operating table completely healed. I guess God made an offer that William Branham could not refuse!

But what was about to come next will raise religious eyebrows. Branham would have been our contemporary living in the 1930's. He truly was a forerunner of the prophetic office of the twenty first century. It's common knowledge amongst Fivefold believers that God completed the rebuilding of the office of the prophet towards the end of the twentieth century in which Branham was a forerunner. God continued to seal Branham's ministry with strange events that people had never seen before.

By 1933, Branham joined the ranks of John Calvin and was baptized in the Ohio River. While being baptized in the river, a strange phenomenon occurred, while in the water, a light came down from heaven causing Pentecostal paranoia amongst those waiting to be baptized. Many such events marked the ministry of William Branham.

KATHRYN KUHLMAN'S UNPARALLELED ANOINTING

As one of the foremost voices by the middle of the nineteen hundreds, Kathryn Kuhlman took America by storm. During a time of the great depression, America was in need of healing after

WWII. Not possessing any particular qualities, Kathryn was just a home girl from Concordia Missouri. Born in 1907, Kathryn Kuhlman was the apple of her father's eye throughout her life. He never would have imagined that his daughter would be in such great demand across the United States.

Attending a Baptist church with her father, Kathryn truly loved God from day one. Meanwhile, her mother was an anointed teacher at the Methodist church. Kathryn never adapted to her mother's church; in fact, she would joke about the methods implemented by man in religion throughout her career.

EVANGELISTIC TRAINING

When her sister Myrtle married an accomplished evangelist named Everett, Kathryn would earn her keep each day by maintaining the Parrott's house. Unfortunately, after a while, Kathryn witnessed the unraveling of her sister's marriage until she realized it was time to part company with Evangelist Everett. Meanwhile, Kathryn would continue to grow in wisdom and anointing though she was unaware of it.

Later on, Kathryn would move to Boise Idaho where she would preach her first message. Until now, Kathryn knew nothing more than the salvation message. One of her first messages would be preached at the Pool Hall of Boise Idaho. It was in Boise where Kathryn would discover the power of radio and begin one of her first broadcasts. People were drawn to her radio broadcast at a time when the nation needed healing. Kathryn developed a very unique theatric style of speaking which I think provoked curiosity among the people.

VERY UNUSUAL MOVE OF GOD

Kathryn had a very unusual style of preaching, in fact it was so anointed that her mother was drawn to a Kuhlman service one evening. It was in that service where the mother that never showed Kathryn any affection, came up to the front for prayer.

Although Kathryn was opposed to the methods used to save the lost, she did promote speaking in unknown tongues. As she placed her hand on her mother, what happened next would impact her life forever. Emma, the mother that never demonstrated any affection to Kathryn, was desperate for the baptism of the Holy Ghost. Suddenly, without warning, the most beautiful sounds erupted from her mother's mouth in the form of unknown tongues. It was that same anointing that would draw thousands in the future. She spoke in an almost prophetic tone, warning people both saved and unsaved of the end times. Kathryn never truly preached messages that empowered ministry teams, nor fire and brimstone sermons that would compel people to come to the altar. In fact, most people received healing at a distance and not by laying her hands on them. Kathryn in her many broadcasts would confess publicly that she always had a complex with her physical features. She even called her beautiful red hair "fuzz" that she could not control. Kathryn would say, "I have not talent, I have nothing to offer, all I have is love, if you can use that Lord, then use me."

AN ITINERANT EVANGELIST

Unmarried, Kathryn was completely devoted to Jesus. With a renewed excitement and only five dollars to her name she moved to Denver for no particular reason. Once there she found a radio station, and embarked in one of the biggest projects of her ministry. Instructing her team to find a building, Kathryn then promoted her services on the radio. Her voice would begin slowly, pronouncing each word, building mystery in her message. Her style of speaking was so unique, many have attempted to imitate it but failed. Within a short few months the building was filled to capacity.

At the pinnacle of ministry in Denver, she suddenly received news that her father was in an accident, and consequently died. Losing the only man that adored her was so shocking that she fell into a deep depression. Losing a father would have stopped the average evangelist dead in their tracks but not Kathryn; she seemed to develop a very strong personal character and thick skin as a result of this tragedy.

SUDDEN TRAGEDY

Nonetheless, in 1936, Kuhlman drew crowds each night in the order of 2,000 people. In addition to record-breaking crowds of people from around the world, she had one of the most influential broadcasts during the 30's. But sadly, her loss would not mark the end of Kuhlman's despair, in fact, at one point she decided to marry a handsome evangelist named Buroughs Waltrip. More often than not, some women tend to seek for a man that bears the attributes of a biological father, even contrary to the counsel of some of your closest acquaintances. Needless to say, she suddenly became aware of her error and her marriage ended in disaster driving Kathryn into seclusion for almost 8 years.

EVEN WITH ODDS STACKED UP SHE BOUNCES BACK

By 1946, Kathryn Kuhlman's tenacious character drove her out of the wilderness ready to fight, but she was not alone. During the twentieth century, she had the good fortune of joining forces with some of the greatest tent revivalists of her time. Kathryn's contemporaries included Oral Roberts, William Branham, Jack Coe, Gordon Lindsay, R. W. Schambach, Aimee Semple McPherson, and many more. In fact, Kuhlman had an opportunity to both meet and minister with many of the great men and women of renown in her day.

With the aftermath of WWII, the nation was now in need of healing. Fortunately, Kuhlman was the right person for the job. Heretofore, the thrust of Kathryn's message was simply salvation, but everything would change. I have no proof to back up this statement but I have read that one of Kathryn's favorite preachers was Evangelist McPherson of the Four Square denomination. I would even dare to say that some of the elements of her style of deliverance may have originated from McPherson. Kathryn commenced many radio messages with a very deep slow mysterious voice. People were simply mesmerized by her broadcasts. Radio became one of her greatest assets in the middle of the nineteen hundreds. Actually, her ministry was established between both the Pentecostal and the Latter Rain Movement. The Pentecostal Movement made great contributions to the restoration of Christianity including baptism by fire and speaking in unknown tongues. Shortly after, God ushered in the Latter Rain Movement which included deliverance, evangelism, praise and worship. Surrounded by many great mantles, Kathryn's ministry was ready to move to a new level. According to records, Kathryn's healing ministry was activated in 1947 when she began to hold meetings at the new Faith Temple. Seating some two thousand people, this became Kathryn's church where she gained great notoriety.

RADIO WAS ONE OF HER MOST IMPORTANT ASSETS

Arguably, Kuhlman's anointing drew some of the largest crowds on record in her time. As an evangelist, Kathryn enjoyed traveling to other states to preach where she would pack the house including Carnegie Hall in Pittsburgh. Later she would make Pittsburgh her permanent residence from where she would launch her national radio broadcast Some 50 broadcast stations transmitted her thirty-minute broadcasts, at least five days a week. Her voice reached out to places like Canada, including the overseas broadcasts that covered most of Europe. Her broadcast series was entitled "I Believe In Miracles." This radio broadcast helped catapult Kathryn into the arena of the big time evangelists.

Kathryn manifested one of the most unusual ministries of her time. Miracles manifest in auditoriums, opera halls, and theaters.

NOTABLE, REMARKABLE, MIRACLES

They came in droves from every corner of the earth, from every walk of life, and from all denominations. I've watched several of these miracle services. One in particular took place at Oral Roberts Mobee Center in 1974 and the other at Las Vegas Convention Center in 1975. A typical Kuhlman service commenced with a huge choir that praised the Lord before Kathryn came out to preach. She had a very graceful theatric style of flowing around the stage, almost dancing as she preached. Her voice sounded like an actor in a Broadway-style drama. That night, she referenced scriptures in the Bible but never truly read from the text. In front were rows of medical professionals that would witness miracles and sometimes certify individuals after they were healed. Suddenly Kathryn begins to point to the upper level seats with a word of knowledge that God was healing a certain type of disease. She intentionally never conducted an alter call with the intent of refuting the methods of main stream religion. Nevertheless, the Holy Spirit would begin miracles in the very seats of her audience. She claimed that she had not power to heal during the service. Yet people were jumping out of their wheel chairs, the paralyzed walked, blind eyes opened, cancerous tumors disappeared, and people believed. Many skeptics attended her services but left as believers. Many have attempted to imitate her graceful style and even emulate her anointing but failed. Later, she would exclaim that the secret of her huge success was simply the Holy Spirit. The Holy Spirit was tantamount to any other styles that she might have learned while watching other mighty Saints of God at that time.

HEALING MINISTRY OF ORAL ROBERTS

Born on January 24, 1918 in Pontotoc County Oklahoma, Oral Roberts claims to have heard God's voice over 23 times.

Ironically, Oral means "utter by the mouth" and yet Oral Roberts was tormented by stuttering while he was a youngster.

Unlike Kathryn Kuhlman, Oral Roberts was endowed with more of a hands-on ministry. Oral's unique style consisted of him sitting in a chair on stage and laying hands on people as they would come to the front of the auditorium. Knowing that he would minister to thousands on any particular evening, standing was not an option. Oral always believed that God was not the author of disease but used it so that he could be glorified. One thing we do know is that God can be the author of calamity.

"7I form the light, and create darkness: I make peace, and create evil: I the LORD do all these things."--Isaiah 45:7

Arguably God is not the source of sickness for Christians, but he did put disease on the Egyptians. I raise this side of the argument so that we don't walk in ignorance and the text does not require a lot of scrutiny.

"And said, if thou wilt diligently hearken to the voice of the LORD thy God, and wilt do that which is right in His sight, and wilt give ear to His commandments, and keep all His statutes, I will put none of these **disease**s upon thee, which I have brought upon the **Egyptians**: for I am the LORD that healeth thee."   --Exodus 15:26

HEALED FROM TUBERCULOSIS

Instead of saying "evil does not come from a good God", I simply say that God is sovereign and can do whatever He pleases according the counsel of His own will. Case in point, when Oral Roberts was a youth he was stricken with tuberculosis. His plans to be a lawyer and then someday the governor of Oklahoma were shattered. God had a different purpose for Oral Roberts. After seeing many physicians to no avail, the family took him to see an evangelist. On the way God spoke to Oral Roberts and told him that "after he was healed, he was to carry the healing to the nation." As the evangelist bound the foul tormenting disease, Oral experienced an electric shock go through his body. In the next moment he was able to take a deep breath without shooting pains in his lungs. Not only were his lungs healed but he stopped stuttering as well. God capitalized on this disease to catapult Oral Roberts into a healing ministry.

ORAL ROBERTS' FIRST MIRACLE

One of the most amazing miracles occurred while Oral Roberts was in his twenties. A motor had fallen on the foot of one of the deacons at church, named Clyde. When they arrived, Clyde was in excruciating pain. Blood was seeping from his shoe when Oral bent down to pray. Reality was that Oral did not know how to pray. After praying under his breath a few short words, when he took his hand away, the deacon stopped screaming. Amazed, the injured man jumped to his feet completely healed.

Oral, among others, believed in putting out a fleece to confirm God's word. Today, church leaders would say that we should not follow signs but Oral was not following a sign but looking for confirmation. As he arrived at the auditorium for his first healing service, he had asked God for 1,000 people. God exceeded his expectation with 1,200 Saints. Pandemonium broke out in that service and the power of God showed up and showed off. The manifestation was in agreement with Mark 16:20 "the Lord was working with them, confirming his word with signs and wonders." Oral continued to preach in Oklahoma and on one occasion he preached in Nowata. During this occasion, God's voice spoke to him "now you will feel my presence in your right hand, through my presence you will be able to detect demons, and you will have the power to cast them out."

GOD GIVES ORAL ROBERTS A SIGN IN HIS RIGHT HAND

This was one of the examples of the unusual ministry of Oral Roberts. Going forward, he would sense a presence, even a tingling in his right hand. With this same hand, he would put his fingers in the ears of a deaf boy, and for the first time, the boy began to hear. Soon God led Oral to Durham and purchased the biggest tent available. During the services in 1948, the police estimated that the crowd was in the order of 9,000 people.

Before Oral's healing ministry began, God gave him the parameters he would use for maximum results. The instructions revolved around the sign of his right hand. God told him not to begin a service unless he could feel his presence in his right hand. He described it as a throbbing power that began at the elbow down to his hand. Oral also learned that he could not control the power of God in terms of turning it on or off. When God was ready, he would feel the presence in his right hand. The sign in his hand gave him an unspeakable boldness when confronting diseases. Oral also felt hostile towards disease such that he would almost rush towards the infirmed to release them of their torment.

ULTIMATELY GOD IS SOVEREIGN OVER ALL THINGS

When the presence of God in his right hand subsided, he would then call for an offering. Roberts arrived at the crossroads of his life when he had to decide whether he would be in control or God. Since he could not activate the right-hand anointing at a whim, he discovered that walking by faith was the key to success. Many people are oblivious to the fact that even Jesus Christ had to walk by faith. Without faith we cannot please God, and the Father always testified that he was pleased by His son. On different occasions, great fear gripped Oral when the presence of God stopped in his hand. This anointing created both confusion and jealousy. Feeling obsolete, some contemporary ministers asked what they were supposed to do now that Oral had this type of anointing. One of two things can happen to the Saints when they come with desperation, either they receive a touch or they walk away depressed. Oral Roberts learned to have total confidence in the power of God's eloquent speech. Listen, you may know hermeneutics, homiletics, apologetics, and even expository preaching, but after you finish preaching then what? If people have come with a certain expectation, you must deliver the goods and that requires faith. Not everyone will be healed on a particular night and other people may receive varying degrees of healing, but faith is paramount to signs, wonders and miracles.

OVERCOMING A NEGATIVE ATMOSPHERE

Not all of Oral's crusades were initiated with enthusiasm and expectation. There was one in particular that he organized at Goldsboro, North Carolina, inside of a B-29 hangar. The huge arena could hold up to 10,000 people. As Oral's ministerial team of seven walked into that arena on the first night, they were anticipating a great service. Oral knew that God would confirm the word that he preached with signs and wonders however, he noted something unusual in that place. Since it was the first time a crowd of this size gathered for a healing service, Oral experienced negativity in the atmosphere. Each night, Oral's faith was bigger than the huge crowd of spectators that came to check him out. Albeit, there were large healing lines, nothing remarkable took place for four nights. By the fifth night, Oral realized that something phenomenal needed to take place to stir up this large group of unbelievers. During the healing line, Oral noticed a young boy with his mother. When the child and mother finally reached him, he discovered that the boy suffered from Perthes disease which results in an abnormal hip causing the leg to be shorter. Not only was Oral's reputation on the line but there were thousands that desperately needed salvation. God never failed

Oral; suddenly, he felt that presence in his right arm and then energy traveled down his arm through his hand that was on the boy's hip. "Be healed in the name of Jesus." Oral then asked Douglas if he felt like God had touched him. Of course, the response was "yes." He then asked little Douglas, "what would you like to do?" He replied "run"! "Run then." Suddenly, Douglas for the first time took off running down the aisle. This of course brought the multitude to their feet. Not only did this crowd of unbelievers rise to their feet, but people were dancing, shouting, and praising God in the aisles.

A SIGN FROM GOD

I'll never forget the time when my wife and I were visiting my son's mother-in-law, Matilda, at her house. She was celebrating her daughter-in-law Kiara's birthday party. Kiara was pregnant, but experienced uncertain complications in the pregnancy. That night while chatting at the dinner table, suddenly, Matilda fell to her knees praying with her hand on her daughter-in-law's womb. After a short silence, everyone was waiting to see what would happen next. Finally, I felt it was time to demonstrate God's character. I asked Kiara to stand up so that we could pray. I believed God would give us a sign for this unborn child. I felt the anointing fall over me and the angel of God was present. As I began to declare life to that fetus, suddenly, the baby began to kick in the womb. Family members placed their hands on the womb to feel the child kicking, perhaps for the first time. Unfortunately, after God stirred up the child in that mother, defying the laws of science, after few short months the child finally died. Of course, we were believing for more than just a kicking in the womb in response to the Holy Ghost. We wanted to see her deliver that baby girl, but God ultimately decides what the outcome will be. I must admit, the latter superseded the former, but I'll never forget how God stirred up a fetus to kick in her womb as a sign that the heavens respond to God's servants.

It's interesting that if you're a faith healer, and someone in your service does not get healed, you never see headline news that the evangelist is a "false faith healer". However, if you are prophet and presumptuously declare that the child will live, you are immediately dubbed "false prophet." Look, this kind of thing can destroy an individual if they are not strong. News will spread like wildfire that a baby has died, but no one really cares about what took place weeks prior when the fetus began to kick at the womb for the first time. You must understand that you have no power to heal, that if God does not perform a miracle, then the outcome will be death. Often, we judge the outcome of a particular event to determine if it meets our expectation. What If God heals someone and then they die shortly thereafter, can God be God?

SOME MISCONCEPTIONS

When you read the story about William Branham, it will cause you to question whether or not you're really called as a prophet. During the great Ohio flood, Branham's daughter died then his wife died. He arrived just in time to raise her from the dead, but she asked him, why did you wake me? Ultimately, Branham had to let his wife go to be with the Lord.

For this reason, we need to remain humble before God, never think that you have arrived yet. If you stumble, you're down for the count, and the odds are stacked up against you, maybe it's time for a rebound. You need to bounce back, Jack, make a new plan, Stan, don't be coy, Roy, just listen to me. Look, we are in a learning process, just like Oral Roberts when he was uncertain about his right-hand anointing. Even after Roberts was healed from Tuberculosis, it was a matter of months before he experienced a renewed energy in his body. It's not time to quit because of some negative fan fair. Get back up fighting, and remember one thing, whatever you do, do it with love and compassion. Oral Roberts developed an amazing love and compassion even for the unlovable.

TODAY WE SUBSTITUTE ELOQUENT SPEECH FOR THE ANOINTING

Have you ever seen some people pray? Some think that by quoting the entire Bible it will provoke God to move. When in reality, much of what we do is learned behavior from the 1880's Divine Healing Movement combined with the 1970's Word of Faith Movement. The previous "Word" generation passed its culture to ours, subtly suggesting that a plethora of "words" wouldi ultimately influence the outcome when we pray. This could not be farther from the truth. If truth be told, Jesus used very few words when He imparted wonder-working power. De facto, Jesus combined great wisdom with power when He healed.

> "[41] And He took the damsel by the hand, and said unto her, Talitha cumi; which is, being interpreted, Damsel, I say unto thee, arise. "   --Mark 5:41

Notice how Jesus simply utters "Talitha cumi" resulting in a bona fide resurrection. I am convinced that great "exousia" and dunamis rested on Jesus to perform great miracles. That is great authority and power. Jesus always knew how much to say, and what method to use. Each particular case demanded a unique set of words and methods. The next excerpt from the book of Mark reveals a very short declaration that would open a man's eyes:

> "[33] And He took him aside from the multitude, and put His fingers into his ears, and He spit, and touched his tongue; [34] And looking up to heaven, He sighed, and saith unto him, Ephphatha, that is, be opened." –Mark 7:34

Could you imagine if Jesus began praying, "Father in the name of Jesus, I ask you to cancel this assignment that Satan has put on this child of God, I take authority over this dysfunction because I know that in the glory everything is made whole, and for this reason Jesus was made manifest to destroy the works of the devil". Sounds familiar? Where we think that we must quote a litany of scriptures to move the hand of God or activate a miracle, Jesus simply declares "Ephphatha" meaning "be opened". Oral Roberts practiced this style as well, he never quoted long scriptures, but simple placed his hand on an individual and God did the rest of the work.

IMPATIENT GENERATION

Has anyone ever asked you to pray and while you paused for few moments to hear God's voice, the people around you became impatient due the differences of style? Then suddenly, they exploded with prayer as fast as possible that by the time God gave you some words, everyone was finished. It has become today's Christian culture. No one really knows why we do the things that we do because most are not concerned with traditions from one generation to the next. By that I mean repetitious prayers, dialogued speech, antics, and loud fast music, alter calls and so forth. Today Christians declare, proclaim, and decree many things but unfortunately; there is rarely a bona fide anointing in many churches. Some houses approximate showcase cinemas including dimmed lights, mirror disco balls, strobe lights, and pyrotechnics al compose today's meetings. The methodology of man today appears more important than God's methodology. We will not admit it but it is intrinsic in our approach to miracle healing. If we want to see God's glory again like the first century, we need to pray for God's wisdom and methodology towards alter calls, and the miraculous.

PECULIAR MEN AND WOMEN OF GREAT FAITH

Reading about some of the most inspiring charismatic figures of the last century helps create a trajectory line as to where we are going. Just when you think you have rationalized God, He suddenly takes an unexpected turn down the road. As we reflect on the many peculiar vessels that God has appointed, we realize that God is sovereign and that He works according to the counsel of His own will. We may not agree with an individual's character, personality, doctrine, or style but when God puts His seal of approval on a servant, we cannot deny it.

Heretofore, we have learned about the different movements, anointing's and mantels. For your benefit, I have created a short chart that combines some of the greatest revivalists and movements of Christianity. It's obviously not a complete list but a partial list. I challenge you to take the time and use the list I have provided as a template to build a more complete chronology of phenomenal men, women and events of our time.

GOD'S PECULIAR GENERATION

Date	Revivalist	Details
1521	Martin Luther	Reformation
1509	John Calvin	Founder of Calvinist Baptist
1600		Puritan Movement
1700		First Great Awakening 1700 - 1740
1703	John Wesley	Founder Methodist
1703	Jonathan Edwards	Calvinist Preacher
1714	Howell Harris	Welsh Calvinist Methodist
	George Whitefield	Methodist Preacher
1792	Charles Finney	Revivalist
1798		Second Great Awakening
1801		Cane Ridge Revival
1804	James W. Alexander	School Master
1824	Duncan Matheson	Itinerant Scottish Preacher
1857		Prayer Meeting Revival
1904		Twentieth Century Awakening
1905	Evan Roberts	Welsh Revivalist
1905		Pentecostal Revival Azusa Street
1905	William Seymour	Pentecostal Revival Minister
	Charles Parham	Father of Pentecost
1905	Smith Wigglesworth	Apostle
1905	Aimee Semple McPhearson	Evangelist – Key Note Speaker

THE SAINTS OF GOD

Date	Revivalist	Details
1947	William Branham	Notable Prophet
1947	Kathryn Kuhlman	Preacher with notable healing
1950		Latter Rain movement
1950	Oral Roberts	Preacher with notable healings
1967		Charismatic Movement
1970		Asbury Revival
1983	Prophet WV Grant	Eagles Nest Cathedral
1993	Rodney Howard Browne	Evangelist - Holy Laughter Revival
1993	Karl Strader	Carpenter's Church – Holy Laughter
1994	John Amat	Pastor Toronto Airport CF Blessing
		Campus Revivals
1995	John Kilpatrick	Pensacola Outpouring, Brownsville
2008	Todd Bentley	Third Wave of Glory, Lakeland Revival
		Evangelist – remarkable signs and wonders

Chapter 6

UNCOMMON MANIFESTATIONS

I often like to pray the following; "I am an uncommon servant, seeking uncommon communion, with an uncommon God". Late one afternoon, a small group of us were standing around in a circle in a Walmart parking lot worshipping, crying for fire to come down, open heavens and imploring God to send ministering spirits on assignment. I distinctly remember making the statement, "let there be fire from heaven" and suddenly there was a strong odor of a burning fire in our midst. Cerebral at times, I approached a car parked nearby searching for a burning electrical system or smell from the exhaust, but the smell diminished as I moved away from the circle. When returning back to the inner circle where we were imploring, crying and praising God, the odor increased again. The same thing occurred on another occasion letting me know that this was a tangible visitation from God.

Let me be clear, I do not follow after signs, but I do expect them in my meetings. Unfortunately, there are those that do not put much emphasis on the sign-gift ministry. Some leaders today unknowingly have committed a disservice to the Saints by denying the existence of signs in the twenty-first century. Fact is, some ministers have a sign-gift type of anointing to demonstrate before the world.

Understand that many Christians have even developed talking points due to a lack of revelation, spiritual growth, disinterest, intimidation, erroneous doctrine, or quite frankly, erroneous teaching from the church where they attend.

Come join me on a trip down memory lane as I describe some of the most phenomenal moments in the supernatural as each moment continues to be greater than the last.

SIGNS CONFIRM GOD'S WORD

Case in point, one day, my son brought a youth group to our house for an evening of praise and prayer. I distinctly remember promoting the sign-gift ministry.

I was explaining that God uses signs for several reasons, among which he confirms the message and or place where you are laboring. In the middle of my sentence, one youth countered me by quoting John 20:29 "Thomas, because thou hast seen me, thou has believed but blessed are they who have not seen but believed." The inference was that if you believed in signs, somehow you would not be blessed. It was more of a justification why few Christians, if any, experience signs in their ministry.

Let's be clear, Jesus was referring to those who had not seen Him but believed. If fact, immediately after Jesus gently rebuked Thomas (New Testament) that those who believed without seeing were blessed, He Himself sort of contradictorily continued demonstrating signs and wonders to all of His disciples so that they might believe!

> "[30]And many other signs truly did Jesus in the presence of His disciples, which are not written in this book: "
> --John 20:30

Look, there is a difference between the fruit faith, and the gift of faith. At our birth, we exercise the fruit faith to believe for salvation, but that's different from the gift of faith (1 Corinthians 12:9). When Jesus spoke to Thomas He was referring to the

Ephesians 2:8 type of fruit faith for salvation. Blessed are those who have not seen Jesus but believe that He is the Savior, that He shed His blood on the cross, that to as many that believed in Him without seeing, would have the gift of life. I have said, ad nauseum, that I do not need a sign to believe Jesus, but there are critical moments that I need a sign to confirm God's will or word in an area where I am ready to take a step of faith. Let's be honest, we make mistakes, but we don't want to waste our time believing for things that are not His will for this season. God can communicate to His children in an unlimited number of ways. One of those ways is by signs and wonders to confirm His word.

BELIEVING WITHOUT SEEING

As this doctrine proliferated and took on wings of its own during this complacent generation, many who desired to experience the sign-gift ministry were stymied by the erroneous scriptural interpretation of John 20:29. Moreover, Christians who were considered either a little too deep or simply believed God for this type of anointing were admonished by the words of that same young lady, "Remember, we walk by faith and not by sight." To be sure, every crowd has a nattering nabob of negativism ready to remind you of your limitations. You've heard the same quote and it stopped you dead in your tracks. But when you read the scripture in context, it is clear that He was talking about believing in Him with fruit faith not the gift of faith. Let me break it down. We use fruit-faith (Galatians 5:22) when we believe for salvation (Ephesians 2:8,9). However, that differs from the "gift of faith" (1 Corinthians 12:9) that produces signs and wonders.

One problem I have discovered is that many Christians believe everything that they hear without confirming their doctrine with the Bible. Unfortunately, we who aspire to be prophetic cut off our nose to spite our face. Look at this verse again:

"And many other signs truly did Jesus in the presence of
His disciples, which are not written in this book."
                                        --John 20:29

Why would Jesus just moments after He lectured Thomas
then turn around and demonstrate signs in the presence of His
disciples if it wouldn't be a blessing to them? Why not just tell
His disciples, "you've seen enough, just believe and you'll be
blessed?" No sir, signs shall always have a place in the kingdom
of God especially during times of eschatology. Saint, you need to
implore God for signs to accompany your ministry and then
stretch your faith to demonstrate His character. In fact, when your
faith becomes bigger than the signs or wonders, perhaps it's time
to beseech God for a new level.

MATERIAL THINGS VERSUS THE METAPHORIC

Another curious mindset occurs in our Christian churches
every day. We have no problem believing for certain things to be
"material" but other things are spiritual. I have no problem with
this philosophy. On the other hand, when I pray for healing, no
one is satisfied with a spiritual healing for their blood pressure or
spiritual prosperity. Can you imagine if God spoke through a
prophet that someone would become a spiritual millionaire? In
other words, no money in the bank, just spiritual play money. I
don't think so. We would demand that we get some real money,
not some spiritually deep funny money. You know the "Do, Re
Me" kind! Can you imagine if you needed God to create a new
lung, but I prayed that God create a spiritual lung? I don't think
that you'd want to be so metaphorical at that moment. No, you'd
want a tangible, honest to goodness lung to fill up with air, not
some spiritual metaphor. But we pick and choose what should be
tangible and what is intangible. No, the problem is that your
environment does not promote extreme faith. Jesus was reckless
in His faith, He was intense, focused, determined to fulfill the will
of His father at any cost, even His life. Jesus operated in the gift

of faith resulting in the demonstration of great power and authority. Pray,

> "Open my eyes to receive this revelation, related to the "Saints experience" of the first century. I believe you God for signs and wonders in my ministry."

Now trust Him. Tell God, I want the first century Saints experience. I will not settle for less. Now get ready for rejection and persecution, because believe it or not most people in church are going through the motions, rituals, and ceremonies of religion. For that reason, signs and wonders are few and far between amongst the Saints, but for those who are desperate, get ready for the Bible says that "the spirit and power of Elias" will come again. I believe that it is falling upon this generation of Saints to demonstrate the character of God.

Saint of God, don't let anyone diminish what God has revealed to you by His Spirit. Understand, not everyone is called to this type of ministry; nonetheless, there shall be signs and wonders from now until the end of Great Tribulation.

We can validate signs and wonders in the last day by taking a quick look at the book of Daniel 12:6. It appears that Jesus and Peter are not the only ones walk on the water during the tribulation period.

> "And one said to the man clothed in linen, which was upon the waters of the river, How long shall it be to the end of these wonders?" "that it shall be for a time, times, and an half; and when He shall have accomplished to scatter the power of the holy people, all these things shall be finished."   --Dan 12:6, 7

Most scholars will tell you that the words "time, times, and a half" imply the first 3 ½ years in Great Tribulation. The intention of this book was not to spend time discussing hermeneutics and eschatology, so it may require additional research on your own time.

As a sidebar, I also believe that the book of Daniel, which was sealed, is now being opened to the Saints of God as we speak. God never stopped marking important events with signs. Again, I personally don't require a sign to believe, but signs can confirm preaching, mark events, reveal His purpose, confirm approval, and stir up faith in desperate people.

The remaining portion of the chapter is a testimony of some of the most unusual events that have occurred in my life. It's not hard to imagine that signs similar to these were probably the norm for the first century Saints. I submit that signs should arguably be the norm for the Saints of God today. Let's proceed, shall we?

AN ANGEL SENT FROM GOD

Around 8 years old, I remember going to the local park in Cromwell, CT. To the best of my recollection, there was a least one other older boy playing. When I least expected it, without provocation, this older boy decides to knock me down, and then sit on my hands and chest. Unable to move I cried out to be released but to no avail, this older boy enjoyed his sadistic intimidation. Suddenly, I heard the voice of a man say "GET OFF HIM, NOW". When I looked up from the ground, I saw a tall man with dark hair looking at me. After the boy released me, I stood up and spun in a circle to locate the man to acknowledge his kind deed but to my dismay, the man was gone into thin air.

AN AUDIBLE VOICE

During hurricane Bob in 1989, my wife and I went to assist Don Walker and David Paul in a miracle service in Agawam, Massachusetts. My wife and I were assisting Prophet Walker during the camp meeting. During the morning service, Don Walker asked me to lead praise and worship for the evening service. We returned to this old dilapidated motel on Main Street in Agawam. After resting a while, suddenly I was startled when someone called my name. When I looked up, I saw no one but I realized that God called me by the name of "Michael" in audible voice. When I looked at my watch, if He hadn't called me, I would never have opened the tent on time for that evening's service. Thanks to God's voice, not only did we get dressed in time but I was able to start praise and worship for the first time.

TRUST ME SAID AN AUDIBLE VOICE

I'll never forget as long as I live the time when our refrigerator stopped cooling while living in a condominium in East Hartford, CT. It was 2000 at the time, and I was working for the Travelers Insurance Co. Being frugal, I decided to buy a used refrigerator. When my wife learned about my plan she was depressed. Neida wanted a new refrigerator, not a stinking used appliance with broken shelves and trays. Instead of arguing with me, she headed towards her bedroom. What happened next would change her perspective about God forever. As she passed through the threshold of the door, she neglected to turn on the light. Suddenly, an audible voice of authority said "trust Me." She was so frightened that she ran out of the room and asked me, "What did you say?" At the time I was washing the dishes and I told her "I said nothing". Watch this, God will make sure that you hear Him. As she returned to the room, God spoke audibly again, and said "trust Me." She did. We were able to buy one of the widest refrigerators on the market, so wide in fact that we had to cut at least one inch of the counter for it to fit. God is still speaking audibly but if you've never heard the voice of God don't worry. He has many ways of communicating. One thing about your Father, He loves to communicate. True, there are moments when you walk through the valley of the shadow of death, or you're in the wilderness for forty days and nights and hear nothing. God can speak to the Saints by an audible voice, vision, angel, Bible, preacher, prophet and a host of other ways. I usually like to spend three hours with God if possible. The first hour is to stop all the noise in my head. The second hour is a time of prayer, supplication, praise and worship. The last hour is a time of intimacy where God can open my eyes, show me a vision, or speak to me. Develop your own special time with God and be consistent. God is a God of order and consistency. Ask God to speak to you today, He can't wait.

WATER DROPLET

I'll never forget this as long as I live. When we heard about the outpouring 2008, we decided to take a trip down to Lakeland to soak in the anointing. I was in the upper levels at the Lakeland coliseum looking down at the service, when suddenly the evangelist shouted "what's happening?" Apparently, the people that were seated on the ground floor where they play sports were screaming. He then asked them if it was raining inside the building. When I heard that I knew it was my opportunity to experience the supernatural. I told God if it was raining inside, I wanted to feel the tangible rain. Suddenly, I literally felt one drop of water from above splashed on my lower lip. I knew than that when people are desperate, anything can come from heaven.

OPEN THE WINDOWS OF HEAVEN

On one occasion, I traveled to Malaysia in February of 2010. While preaching in Ipoh, a particular preacher name Patrick chauffeured me to a service. On the way I declared, let the windows of heaven be opened. On the following night, there was a sudden thunderstorm that flooded the streets. The water was so deep that it reached the door jams on the car we were in. He looked at me and said "do you remember what you declared yesterday?" He was surprised by the sheer volume of water.

LET IT RAIN

I can't remember why but one night I woke up and began to praise the Lord. It was around the 2008 time frame. Sometimes you just feel the anointing. While sitting on my bed, I lifted my hands and cried, "Let it rain." Honestly, I was not expecting anything unusual at that early hour, but what happened I'll never forget. Suddenly, there was a massive crashing sound on the roof. I was amazed that it did not wake my wife. I was in shock when it happened. I suddenly realized it was a huge volume of water that crashed on the roof. It appeared like God had positioned a cloud over the top of my house to drop rain upon my roof. Signs still are valid for those who believe.

AMANI, AMANI SHE CRIED

Again during that same time in 2008, I fasted three times every week, Friday, Saturday, and Sunday. I was accustomed to praying in my room for three hours on Saturday. One day while I was praying, a black woman from Africa appeared to me shouting "Amani, Amani." Later, I accessed the internet to try and understand the message. I found entries such as "power, powerful." Little did I realize that God was sending me to Africa in part vindicate the black man. This woman was simply preempting my trip to Africa in her native tongue. The angel of the Lord went before me and did wonderfully in those services.

MY TABLE WAS MARKED BY 54

While in Malaysia in February of 2010, my host asked me to prepare for a men's business meeting. Before I spoke, God healed a few people before the meeting. After the meeting, I was asked to come downstairs for brunch. At the time I was 54 years old. You won't imagine how God confirmed my trip, when I went to sit down there were some 50 chairs at the tables in that place. But one table had the number 54 to reserve my spot. What are the chances? I stopped trying to figure it out, instead I realized that when a man is ready to take a demonstrative step, putting his life in jeopardy, God is ready to confirm his actions with signs and wonders

A NOTABLE MIRACLE

My son Michael decided to join the National Guard in 2001 and then later trained at the Aberdeen Proving Ground in Aberdeen, Maryland. As the war escalated in Iraq and Afghanistan, my son was deployed to Afghanistan in 2002. For the first time, my wife and I were completely helpless with regard to his welfare, we were forced to trust God completely.

At the time, I was taking courses at ORU for a degree in church ministries. While studying, I decided to put everything aside for a moment to pray because we were unsure as to the welfare of our son Michael. While in prayer, the Spirit of God carried me to my son's outpost command tent in Afghanistan. I was able to see the top of his tent. They were known as the Nomad's, Co G, 104th Avn. During my trip to Afghanistan by the Spirit, I asked God to post an angel over his tent for protection. I know some would say, " this is what dreams are made of ". Listen, the reason that this has not happened to you in part, is due to the lack of revelation. We need to be schooled in an environment that embraces the supernatural and understands the purpose of angels.

ANGELS INTERVENE IN THE AFFAIRS OF MEN

After imploring God, I was at peace and returned back to the United States in the Spirit. Next moment, I found myself in the same place in my room before I had taken the trip in the Spirit. After my son completed his tour of duty in April of 2004, his platoon was given a hero's welcome at the National Guard hanger at Bradley International Airport. On a subsequent Sunday, the whole family was worshipping at Spiritual Life Fellowship church in Hartford. I distinctly remember that a prophet was asked to speak on this occasion. After he finished his message, he began to minister to the Saints. Suddenly, he called out "Michael". My son went forward to answer the call. The prophet then began to describe what he saw in the Spirit. "I see explosions in the air, I hear the chant of Islam, Allahu Akbar, Allahu Akbar, what is this that I hear in my ears?" My son replied, "it is the chant of Islam." Then the prophet said, "What is this sand I see at your feet, fire, and explosions?" Michael replied, "I was stationed at Kandahar, Afghanistan."

GOD PROTECTS HIS CHILDREN FROM THE ENEMY

Suddenly he shouts, "Oh my God, this is too deep for me, I see an angel posted at your command tent, as the RPG missiles are being fired by Al Qaeda, some are heading towards your coordinates." Everyone stood with shock and awe. Suddenly the prophet kicked into the air with his feet and said "Oh my God, the angel is kicking the RPG missiles away from your tent. I see him kicking missiles far away from your position." Michael then replied, "I can confer to those facts, one night we were laying in our tent, and we heard the RPG's coming in to our location, you could hear the sound of the engine, it was a horrifying sound." He continues, "but on this night, something strange happened, as the missiles approached our position, I was sure that we would become war casualties that night, but suddenly, the rocket engines that made a whistle-like noise simply became silent as though they were removed from the air. Later we heard those same RPG's missiles exploding in a distant location."

MICHAEL THE ARCHANGEL IS WORKING FOR THE SAINTS

Suddenly the prophet cries, "Oh my God this is too deep for me, your name is Michael, but I see another Michael also." At that moment I stood up and joined my son. But next was the most stunning revelation yet, the prophet said, "there are two Michaels but there is another Michael also." He was without a doubt referring to Michael the Archangel, who is my assistant when I preach the gospel. If you need some proof as to whether the prince Michael has any involvement with God's people, please read Daniel 12. And I quote,

> """[1]And at that time shall Michael stand up, the great prince who standeth for the children of thy people: and there shall be a time of trouble, such as never was since there was a nation even to that same time: and at that time thy people shall be delivered, every one that shall be found written in the book."   --Daniel 12:1

Angels, including the prince Michael, are intervening in our lives daily in various ways. Some angels protect, others come on assignment to push back the enemy, some rescue the Saints from perils, others touch barren wombs to produce prophets and great men of God. I would need to write an entire book just on angels since my previous sentence does very little justice to their divine purpose. When I went to Nigeria, Africa, in March of 2009 I actually relived a Bible story. Do you remember the women from Zarephath in I Kings 17:9?

THE WOMAN FROM ZAREPHATH

The story began at my home when fasting three days a week and praying for three hours each Saturday. On one particular Saturday of 2008, I suddenly had a vision of black woman in African dress crying "Amani, Amani." When I researched the meaning of the word Amani, it appears to be of an Arabic origin but used in the Swahili dialect. According to etymology the word means "desires, aspirations, and wishes". Some scholars define the word to mean "peace." God was setting me up for a trip to Africa, the hottest place on the planet.

After I had finished preaching in Ogoja, I boarded a jet for Legos Nigeria. In flight I declared "there must be more, it can't be over yet." My God it was hot all the time. It was so hot that the jets did not ever carry ice for drinks. All drinks on board were room temperature. When I landed in Legos, I discovered that my suitcase was ripped on the Aero Airlines. Disappointed that my clothing was dragging on the floor, I realized that no one really cared about my problems in Nigeria. As I stepped outside I flagged a taxi to take me to my hotel reservation that did not exist. My sponsor did not book a room for me after the revival meeting. I told the taxi driver to take me to the most expensive hotel in Nigeria near the airport. At the time Sheraton was a five star hotel for business men and movie stars. After a short trip, the taxi driver whose name was "Christian" charged me $40.00. From that point, I began to realize that people take advantage of tourists in foreign countries, but that was just the beginning of my travail. The security at this hotel was tantamount to a maximum security prison. Guards stood at every door and elevator.

As I approached the front desk, prices began to be revealed to me, something similar to $300-$400 a night. Finally, the front desk quoted me a price for a room, about $500.00 a night. Until now, a Nigerian named Tanko was my security while there, but I have to admit, I felt he was more a thief than some of the shady characters at the airport. Finally, I told Tanko "good bye, I'll trust the Lord."

The Sheraton was a maximum-security hotel, you could not move without being asked for your identification. The lack of sleep over the week started to accumulate, and I was tired, sleepy, and hungry.

Exhausted from the journey, I sat down in front of a representative of the Aero Airlines. I thought to myself, I think I'll complain about the suit case incident. Next moment, I heard God tell me, "get up and give her a testimony about the wonderful works I'm doing in Nigeria." I said to the Lord "I'm hungry, sleepy and that's the last thing I want to do."

I'VE BEEN WAITING A LONG TIME FOR THIS MOMENT

I sat down in front of her desk and began testifying about the trip to Nigeria. Suddenly she cries out "ooooooooooooohhhh" I've been waiting for this a long time." I began to tell her about the vision, how God had sent me to vindicate the Christian black man, and how His angel was appointed to help me during my trip. In conversation, she said her name was Ade. I thought to myself, look, God even sent me some help. What's the chance of her name being Ade? For a moment, it occurred to me that in 1 Kings 17, God sent the hungry prophet Elijah to a widow woman from Zarephath. After telling her about my mishap, she said "don't worry, I'll get you another suit case." Instantly, she put the ripped suit case behind her desk. At that moment, it was clear that these unusual events were occurring for two reasons. One, because travelling to Africa was a demonstrative act of faith and two, God sent me to pray for her father.

GOD'S POWER TOUCHES HER MUSLIM FATHER

After calling her driver we were off to her home to pray for her Muslim father who suffered a stroke. Prophesying into her life on the way, we finally arrived at her house. After a short trek up to the second floor, I was invited to sit down in a room and next to me was an older man. Suddenly, he changed the television channel to the largest church in Nigeria featuring a choir singing gospel music. I looked for faith in his eyes. It was time to ask the question, "do you believe in Jesus, son of God, that can heal you?" His response was a firm and determined, "yes." All three of us, as a three-fold chord, joined together in a short prayer. In a moment's time, virtue was released, heat and strength came, and I said rise and walk. Not only did he walk better, but he had a little gate in his walk for first time in years, slowly but surely his steps increased in speed. I said, "walk faster", but the final test was walking down stairs which he no longer was accustomed to doing. For the most part, he usually remained upstairs, but for the first time, he went down using both legs. Strength was imparted to the right side of his body. His daughter was experiencing tears of joy. At this point, I thought I was finished and we could get something to eat, but she had other plans.

GOD SET ME UP

"Now, pray for the rest of my family downstairs" she said. While we were upstairs her living room was filling with people, God had set me up for signs and wonders on that day. I began to read their mail, and prophesy to these somewhat complacent youths. God spoke details about each one and we were all amazed. I realized that you will pay a price for the anointing. Finally, Ade announces, "Let's eat now." She took me to a fast food restaurant where people just gawked at me, probably thinking these Nigerian women had found a rich white man.

HER PERSONAL LIFE BECAME AN OPEN BOOK

During the trip back to the Sheraton Hotel, God revealed many things about her past, present and future. God revealed to me details such as problems with relationships, and constant propositions by men. While they transported me back to the Sheraton Hotel in Nigeria, God revealed that the relationship that she was pursuing in England was not His will He also revealed that she enjoyed traveling, and she later disclosed that she would be making a trip to England that year.

After we returned to the Sheraton, I was reminded that there was no availability at the hotel. What may appear to be a problem in the natural presents an opportunity for God to be glorified. I decided it was time to improvise and found a nice reclining chair in the pool area. By this time, Ade had disclosed my personal problem to the entire hotel staff. As I slipped into a light sleep, suddenly I heard "sir." Startled, I thought, "now what?" The guard informed me that the hotel manager wanted to speak with me.

FIRST CLASS FAVOR

As I passed through the door, some six people were standing there staring at me. As I approached, the hotel manager introduced himself and said that he recognized that I was an evangelist and that he appreciated my work and sacrifice. What he said next confirmed God's sign of approval over my life. "We will take care of you with top security, and you're welcome to use our dining room free of charge and the cook will make anything that you want." We can also find a nice cushioned chair in the restaurant for you to sleep in, don't worry about a thing.

That morning, I felt like I was on golden pond. Not only was I pampered with complete buffet-style meal, but I had the entire dining room alone, and there was a cook at my beck and call. Shortly thereafter, Ade and her driver picked me up and brought me to the airport.

FINDING GRACE IN GOD'S EYES

Every person can state that God takes care of them to a different degree. Actually, no one can really say for certain to what degree God is involved in their life. It's more philosophical than real for some people who do not serve God. We often feel that since I am part of the human race, God is obligated to be my step and fetch-it man. I've got news for you, you're not that important unless you meet the qualifications of service unto God. In my case, the demonstrative act of flying to Africa moved God to give me favor in the eyes of men. Let's face it, nothing is free in this world, and the Sheraton Hotel was unaffiliated with the Aero Airlines. God gave me favor with "The Women from Zarephath." In short, God showed me His seal of approval for my commitment to His work in Nigeria.

THE HANDFUL OF FEATHERS

On December 31, 2010, I was asked to preach at a small church named Centro De Restauración Emanuel in St. Cloud., Florida. It was New Year's Eve, and I was going to share what I had seen for the New Year. We were standing on the left side of the church when I perceived an angel in the air hovering over the top of church members. It seemed like an eternity before they called me up to speak. After laying a foundation, I shared with the group that I had perceived that an angel had hovered over the tops of their heads before they introduced me. Although there was no unusual reaction from the people I continued to preach, when all of a sudden, a boy came running up the center aisle.

If you've ever spoken before a group before, you know that when someone comes running up the center aisle it could mean trouble. While he was approaching me I noticed something white in his hands. I asked him "what do you have?" He told me, "a handful of feathers." "Feathers", I exclaimed, not sure what he was talking about. He then stated in front of the entire church he found these feathers in the exact same spot where the angel had been hovering. Then he said, "These are angel feathers." My God, the angel actually left evidence behind that he was there. Suddenly, the pastor who was sitting in the back of the church stood up and shouted that "this wasn't the first time this has happened".

At that point, my mind was considering the evidence and wondering if there had been some garment failure in that spot, but no one that had attended that service had white feathers in their garment. It was without a shadow of a doubt, amazing evidence that angels do exist and are sent on assignment to help the heirs of righteousness.

As you can see, I believe in signs. From the beginning, God has always used signs to both confirm His word and validate His servants.

GOD CONFIRMED HIS WORD

For those who have been saved for any length of time, know that God has a numeric system. In fact, eight represents "new beginnings" in the Bible. It was 2008 when my wife and I realized it was God's will to stop renting and purchase a house. Anyone who was business minded knew that 2008 going forward were unusual times in the real estate market. At the time, I was negotiating a loan with a particular bank in Kissimmee, Florida. The loan officer at the time gave me an appointment to come in and complete a loan agreement. At the time, single family, one floor, three-bedroom houses priced around $200,000. In my case the owner was asking $208,000. However, due to the recession, some real estate values had dropped to almost half of the original asking price. I'll never forget the events that unfolded in the loan officer's office. I removed the Bible from my business bag and told him that "I was banking on my Bible for a miracle."

GOD ADJUSTS THE NUMBERS

He then grabbed his HUD HFA mortgage guide and said "I'm banking on my Bible." I said to myself, looks like a showdown, so I opened the Bible to Proverbs 10:22 and quoted the following verse "the blessings of the Lord maketh rich and he addeth no sorrow to it." He then stared at me long and hard. After inputting a few numbers, I said "let's tweak the numbers slightly for a new mortgage calculation." I asked him to calculate a new mortgage payment for $125,000, 5% interest, and a PMI of $55. What happened next will blow your mind. After he completed the calculation, he told me the monthly cost would be $1,022 and change. Suddenly it dawned on me that God had confirmed his word. The scriptural verse that I quoted was the same number as the monthly payment.

The Lord literally adjusted the monthly payment so that it would coincide with the scriptural verse. The loan officer was shocked and said, "This is the strangest thing that has ever happened in this office." When a man's ways please the Lord, He will give you a sign to endorse His approval. Not only did God demonstrate in that man's office, but I discerned that he had a drinking problem and was probably separated or divorced. Later, he actually confirmed that he was alone. Why does God do unusual things for His people? God will use anything to win your heart so that you will serve Him.

ELEVATOR RIDE TO HEAVEN

As you've probably concluded, God has not changed; He is the same throughout all generations. As the Bible records, amazing things occurred during the first century church. I believe that it is God's purpose to not only do similar things today but even greater things. Wherever I preach, I remind people that the truths of the Bible are just as valid today as they were 2,000 years ago. In biblical terms, theologians would call this a great awakening or reformation. One thing that God is restoring is teleportation. Some may call it translation, others may define it as "being carried by the Spirit." I truly believe that Saints are transported by the Spirit either physically or spiritually every day.

GOD IS PREPARING AN ARMY FOR BATTLE

It was a Sunday morning, and we were worshipping God. Being translated by the Spirit was something that I spoke on ad nauseum. Suddenly I have a vision of chariots, horses and soldiers standing in the midst of a dust cloud. As I saw the soldiers and spears, I knew that it had to be God's army. In the next moment, I experienced the sensation of an elevator ride into the air. It was so intense that I felt my physical body losing balance while standing. My natural body was losing equilibrium, and I began to feel dizzy as if I was on the runway taking off like a jet. Suddenly, in the next moment, I was in the clouds with the same soldiers, chariots, horses, and lances that I saw on earth. I remember that I could actually reach out and touch the clouds even though they were simply vapor. I was in a state of complete bliss. The only conclusion I can think of is that God is preparing an army for the end time revival when Jesus returns with His armies. I must admit, being there was just as natural as standing on the earth. I did not want to return again, but I realized that it was imperative to return so that I could testify of the vision.

THE EPIPHANY OF A WOMAN

One evening while praying, I was seeking the Lord regarding a host of things when suddenly there appeared a woman. Her arms were opened to hug me and she simply said, "I'm praying for you." Then the epiphany was gone. The experience that I had was actually biblical by nature.

> "And a vision appeared to Paul in the night; there stood a man of Macedonia, and prayed him, saying, Come over into Macedonia, and help us."   --Acts 16:19

We see that a man from Macedonia travels in the dimension of the Spirit to give Paul a message. Whether it was tangible or not has no importance, the purpose was to deliver a message. Travelling like this was common in the first century and throughout scriptures, for that matter. As knowledge continued to increase, so man has also evolved into becoming self-sufficient no longer requiring this type of phenomena which was common place in the first century church.

By promoting the truth, I am enlightening the eyes of your understanding, thereby giving you an opportunity to decide if the supernatural is right for you.

You can either travel physically to preach in another location or you can be carried in the Holy Spirit. One purpose would be to meet someone, deliver a message and then return immediately to the original location. God is also able to change time. He can accelerate time into the future, reverse time into past, or halt time all together. If you really think about, it, God is sovereign over the metaphysical world in which you live. Why are these principles so uncommon today? Many simply view God as a myth that makes a good bedtime story. Since our nation as a whole has rejected God, and turned to paganism, the next generation of children will suffer the consequences. Fortunately, throughout the generations, God has always preserved a remnant of hard core Saints that would not cave into coercion. As the Saints of God, we need the supernatural of God just like the first century. In fact, we need the glory of God more than ever before.

THE ANGEL IN THE CLOUD

If we want to experience the unusual, what I call the first century standard, we must be ready to get radical with God. Often God executes the complete opposite of what principled man would surmise. Why? Because He's God and can do whatever He pleases according to the counsel of His own will and does not have to ask permission. That leads into my next experience. In 2011, I remember being driven into the wilderness for six days to seek God. Because of the high incidence of mosquitoes, I was forced to sleep in the car at night. I was desperate to enter that dimension of the Spirit that our forefathers had become quite familiar with. Rising early in the morning, I prayed all day, continuing into the late hours of the evening.

Not only did I want to hear from God but I was seeking an experience with God's angels as well. On the sixth day, in the afternoon, I started my trek back home filled with excitement. As I was driving on I-4 towards Orlando, I happened to look up into the sky. There were very few clouds in the sky that day, but one big cloud in front of me. Now I am aware of the fact that people witness cloud formations that resemble different things but for a cloud to take the shape of something you were expecting is something else. There it was, the perfect figure of an angel flying ahead of me. I could tell that the angel had long white flowing hair and wings. I quickly looked around for any car passing me to determine if anyone else was seeing this angel. I realized this was the sign I was waiting for to confirm my time in the wilderness with God.

THE JAWBONE OF AN 18-YEAR-OLD

I must admit that when I was younger, I did not care very well for my teeth. Although my mother taught us sibling's good hygiene, I was always distracted with other things. With each visit to the dentist, the problem was exacerbated by improper maintenance. During 1998, I was seeing a dentist name Dr. Albert, a Jewish man. Ironically, I retained all 32 teeth although the bone was deteriorated. During each dental appointment, my 32 teeth with no caries would become the spectacle of the office. I capitalized on the fact that I had 32 teeth by telling the hygienists that I was blessed by God. Believe you me, they were a captive audience. In one subsequent appointment, Dr. Albert called me into his office. He informed me that I would require a procedure called "scaling" as soon as possible and it would cost something like $592.00. Then he stated that he "did not want to provide services to me as a primary care physician". The reason that he stated was that "he did not like the fact that I spoke to his staff about Jesus Christ". Within the next few minutes, he gave me the x-rays and sent me packing.

God opened the door for a new dentist name Dr. Katz, who was also a Jew by birth. Meanwhile, I decided that I would prepare an offering for $592.00 and offer it unto the Lord at our next church service. I did just that with joy. When I arrived at my appointment with Doctor Katz, I told him what happened.

Much to my surprise, Dr. Katz assured me that my experience with the other dentist was nothing short of bad policy and that he did not obligate any of his patients to undergo procedures with which they were not comfortable. After the new x-rays were taken, Doctor Katz measured the distance from the top of my gum line to the bone around my wisdom teeth. He said to me "Sir, I can't explain this but the bone around your wisdom teeth is that of an 18-year-old." I then gave him the testimony of how my wife had a dream that I gave $592.00 to God. He then asked me if he could share the testimony with his other patients. In addition, he asked me and my wife to go and pray for his mother who was dying of cancer. Look at God.

Without a doubt, I could write a book on unusual phenomenon and experiences that we've had from heaven. Let me make one thing clear, I don't need signs to believe that Jesus Christ is the Son of God. But the unexpected is part of our sign-gift ministry. I hope that these testimonies have inspired every reader to be desperate for the supernatural as well.

KING SIZE BED FRAME

Perhaps one of the most spectacular miracles occurred when we bought a new king size bed. There is no question that God had given us favor on the purchase of this bed. As you know, a new bed can be a rather large investment during these economic times, but we believe in the economy of heaven. Whether in tribulation or not, there is a storehouse in heaven that can't go bankrupt if you are investing. While the bed was on a lay-a-way plan, coupons from Mattress Barn offering a $300 discount on a king size bed and free delivery were sent in the mail. We took full advantage of that offer and financed the rest of the debt. However, our current bed frame would not adjust to a king size bed so we were obligated to purchase a new frame. They ranged from $49 to hundreds of dollars.

God spoke to me and said, "I'll help you convert that frame into a king size frame". What I did not realize is that I would need two pieces of angle iron about 72 inches in length. We decided to check out Home Depot for angle iron. Passing by the hardware section, we located angle iron in various shapes. I grabbed two sections not realizing whether or not I could utilize these lengths. The cost was $32 for all the hardware. Mind you God said he would help me with this project. I browsed the internet for the standard width of a king size bed which was 76 inches. The two new sections when put in place would have to provide enough width to meet the requirements.

To this day, I ask myself what are the odds of a store having the exact width necessary for a random project? I removed the old angle iron, fit the new pieces into place and amazingly, the total width was 76 ½ inches without cutting anything. Expect God to manifest a sign at strategic points in your life just to let you know that heaven is embracing your ministry.

PHONE CALL FROM GOD

One Friday evening on June 27, 2014, my wife and I were praying that God would open a door for us minister that night. I remember distinctly seeking a place to pray in my son's room while my wife prayed in the living room. It was about 7:30pm when I decided to sit at the dining room table. Suddenly, in the still atmosphere, the phone rang startling us both. "Hello" my wife said. Apparently, no one answered at the other end. Finally, she passed the phone to me hoping that I would deal with this anonymous caller. Because there was no response at the other end, I hung up the phone. What if someone was trying to reach me to minister I thought? I decided to return the call. After the phone rang several times, the call was answered but there was no human voice at the other end. Finally, I decided to call one more time, and this time someone with a deep voice said "hello". I responded to the caller by telling him that my wife and I were praying about ministering tonight. Then he responded by saying "who is this?" I responded Prophet Michael. With a slight hesitation in his voice, he declares, I going to a cell group tonight and you can come, I'll come and pick you up. Mind, you, I still have no idea who I was speaking with. Within minutes, he was outside waiting for us. I went out to meet him, suddenly I recognized him as a person that had attended our bible study several years ago. I asked him, "Did you call me?" He replied "no, I never called you." After we got into the car, he commented that his wife had asked about us two weeks prior. Just for the record I don't believe in a coincidence or causality for a child of God.

What are the chances of someone calling you at the same moment that you're seeking God about where you can minister. Furthermore, what would be your conclusion when the person insists that he did not dial our number? My only conclusion would be that God used his phone to call us so that we could be used for his glory.

Once we arrive we were greeted by our host and invited into the house. Little did I know that God had prepared that night for me to minister. Suddenly in that tiny living room I felt the fire of God shut up in my bones and I knew that I had to deliver what was in me. Let me tell you, the gifts of the Holy Spirit began to work in me captivating the hearts of that cell group. Apparently, the host of the house was a pastor and he simply yielded to the Holy Spirit. Never before have I seen God so succinctly make all the right connections and then a short time later, open a door to speak impromptu.

GOLD DUST FROM HEAVEN

It was May 23, 2014 and my wife and I were ministering at our first miracle revival crusade entitled "Sonido Celestial" (Heavenly Sound) 2014 at the Rosen Plaza Hotel in Orlando. Our host had set up 288 chairs for a powerful two-night service. The theme of the Crusade was "Equipping the Saints for warfare."

The first night I preached on I Kings 18:36 entitling the message "Let it be known this day that thou art the God of Israel." Essentially, it required fire to fall from heaven to turn back the hearts of Israel to God. On Saturday, the final night, God gave me the message "Training Prophetic Teams." Although we had a distinct move of God for two nights, it was nothing compared to what happen on Sunday. While contemplating God Sunday afternoon, I received a call from a pastor that wanted me to preach in her church that Sunday evening, little did I know that God was continuing the crusade a third night but in a different venue.

I had noticed a gold flake under my left eye and decided to leave it there until Sunday. On the Sunday service in that small church, some amazing things manifested that created shock waves. Since I've come to Florida, God told me to buy a bible in Spanish. Since I bought the bible, God loosed my tongue in the Spanish language. When the translator stood up to translate from Spanish to English, she had difficulty with my extensive vocabulary. Suddenly, she handed the microphone to my wife so that she could translate from Spanish to English. Although apprehensive, she began translating and I began to realize that this sign marked the beginning of Neida's ministry. Before I finished my message, I lifted my hands and said, "God let it rain gold dust from heaven." A few moments later, I noticed gold dust between my thumb and index finger in addition to the gold dust under my left eye. In fact after the service, several women approached me to show me the gold particles that had appeared on their faces. This was just the beginning of signs from heaven.

During that service, I saw this crippled black woman leave the service, but when I looked to the right side, I noticed that she was sitting in a chair again. However, I did not perceive the magnitude of the events that were about to transpire. Later, after the service, we were made to understand that she was the victim of a horrible stroke that left the right side of her body paralyzed. Suddenly, boldness arose in me and I told her, "not only will you look for a job, but you will get married." Never have I witnessed before, the face of a person filled with such joy. Furthermore, she had an utterly twisted right arm, and she dragged her right leg. I looked directly at her with the love of God and declared "I loose you from this infirmity" then I commanded her to walk. She began to walk to the front near the altar then stopped against the wall. Let me tell you, I've never witnessed the love of God manifested like this before. As she stood there, the whole church witnessed God healing her body. She lifted her left arm several times brushing her hair. At that moment, I stood behind the people so as not to be a distraction. Suddenly, the twisted right arm began to move, then, it flew up into the air then down again. The hand was now in a normal position as she attempted to touch her hair, as this happen, the people burst out with shouts and screams as this women touched her head with her right arm. Honestly, at that moment, I felt my eyes fill up with tears. It was absolutely wonderful.

In June, I met her again, and she told me that one night she got dressed to dance, and actually dance before the people during a church service. Saint, these types of manifestations were common place in the first century church. Unfortunately, the knowledge of how God's power works was lost during the dark ages of church history. But I've got some good news; God is restoring everything for this generation. So, get ready to witness God's glory in the days to come.

THE SAINTS OF GOD

Chapter 7

DEMONSTRATING
GOD'S CHARACTER

"Men that have hazarded their lives
for the name of our Lord Jesus Christ."
--Acts 15:26

Early one morning during the week while at my office, I received a phone call from Walmart. "Michael", the caller cried impatiently, "your wife Neida feels dizzy as if she is going to pass out, please hurry". As I ran from the office to start up the car, my mind was racing with different scenarios as to my wife's condition. While praying and confused, it seemed like an eternity before I arrived at the Walmart parking lot.

As I parked the car as close as possible to the door, God let me know that I was on time. It was not difficult to discern where my wife was due to the several co-workers that surrounded her like the apostles surrounded Peter at Antioch after he was stoned.

As I walked through the door, I was amazed to see the number people involved ministering to my wife until I arrived. We borrowed one of Walmart's motorized scooters to transport my wife to the car. Once in the car, we began to pray, she was without a doubt emergency-room material. Again, it seemed like an eternity to drive back home. Once at home she stepped down from the car, slowly entered into the house and went directly to bed.

THE SAINTS OF GOD

After a short prayer in our room, I decided that it was time to eat. When I opened the door to the fridge, I heard God say to me, "what are you doing?" "Your wife could end up at the emergency room at any moment and you're going to eat?" So begrudgingly, I closed the refrigerator door and headed to the living room, found some praise and worship by Kim Clement, and began to praise God. No sooner did I begin to praise the Lord, when I felt like it must be a demonstrative act, so I grabbed my staff. Before I knew it, I was shouting *Shabach*, and assuming posture of *Towdah* unto the Lord. For the first time that I can remember, I was ready to deliver a violent praise. What my wife was facing was big, so I concluded that my praise had to be proportionately greater. Although I don't dance demonstratively in church on a regular basis, I always regret not letting go and letting God be God in every area.

As I was shouting, thoughts pervaded my mind that perhaps the neighbors would hear me. I was concerned that someone might call the police because of the unusual amount of noise I was making in the house. My voice was at number 10 on the dial. Suddenly, I began to dance, and shout like a crazy man (bad grammar, good gospel). After 20 minutes I felt exhausted but I could not stop even if it killed me. Next moment, I heard my wife moving around, but I didn't stop dancing and shouting full volume. I danced and practically bounced off the walls with an air of violence, arrogance, immodesty, shamelessness, impudence, and cockiness. While intimate with God, I could feel the weight of His glory cloud coming down, His will being done, in heaven and in earth. I perceived heaven colliding with the earth when suddenly, my wife was standing there looking at me, but it was too good to stop. Now completely out of breath, my wife begins to dance and shout also.

The following represents Neida's own testimony:

"The bus left me off at Walmart when I started to feel a bit dizzy, but I continued to punch in. I knew I wasn't feeling well, and my hands were cold. As I started work, the symptoms of vertigo continued to intensify. I was forced to tell my co-worker that I was not feeling well, I am feeling dizzy and I cannot stand any longer. At that point they accompanied me to the bench to sit down while they continued to comfort me. I felt helpless, trembling, and could not move my head without losing consciousness. After a long period, Michael arrived and took me home. When I finally got into bed, we prayed and then my husband left the room. I was afraid of losing consciousness or dying in bed. Suddenly, I heard music from the other room. It was a powerful praise and worship music. After about 10 minutes, I smelled a strange fire coming into my room; it had a fragrance that I have never smelled before. It was a sweet smell mixed with fire that entered into the room. Somehow that odor, fire, fragrance, gave me the strength to sit up on the edge of the bed. As the burnt odor increased in intensity, I got up, and walked to the living room where my husband was in the middle of a violent dance to praise and worship music. As I walked into the living room, I felt a renewed strength, and as I praised God, all the symptoms began to diminish a little at a time. By the end of praise and worship, I felt as though nothing had happened to me. Instead of going to the emergency room, I went to the grocery store. I now know how much God loves praise and worship because He healed and restored me."

--Neida Biagioni

In my case, demonstrative praise caused uncommon demonstrative results. If I were to compare the first century with this century, it's apparent that first century Saints knew how to demonstrate the character of God.

See, you can operate in what I call the "gift of faith" which is different from the fruit of the Spirit faith referred to in Galatians 5:22. There is a difference between the character of God and the nature of God.

ATTRIBUTES THAT EXPRESS THE CHARACTER OF GOD

The gifts of the Holy Spirit are given severally according to the will of the Holy Spirit based on those who are desperate to demonstrate the character of God. These are divided into three categories - power gifts, revelatory gifts, and inspirational gifts.

Revelational Gifts
- Word of wisdom
- Word of knowledge
- Discerning of spirits

Power Gifts
- Faith
- Gifts of healing
- Working of miracles

Inspirational Gifts
- Prophecy
- Diverse kinds of tongues
- Interpretation of tongues

The gifts produce the character of God found in the following list:

- Power (Dunamis)
- Mighty works
- Glory clouds
- Great grace
- Walking on water
- Causing an axe head did swim
- Water gushed out of the rock
- Raising Lazarus from the dead
- Transfiguration in the mountain
- Disappearing amidst the angry mob
- Fasting 40 days and nights
- Dividing the Jordan and Red Sea

- Taken to heaven in a chariot of fire
- Returning sun dial back in time by 10 degrees
- Stopping time during the battle in the valley of Ajalon
- Accelerating time when Jesus saw Nathanael under fig tree

FRUIT THAT EXPRESSES THE NATURE OF GOD

The following list represents the nature of God which are the fruits of the spirit (Gal 5:22).

Fruits of the Spirit are these
- Love
- Joy
- Peace
- Righteousness
- Longsuffering
- Gentleness
- Goodness
- Faith
- Meekness
- Temperance

No matter how anointed you are, God puts a premium on the fruits of the Spirit. Not only was Jesus a prototype of the character of God but He also expressed the fruits of the Spirit or the nature of God. Love and compassion were expressed by mighty works. While we today express our love with money, Jesus expressed His love with power. While we have faith that God can use the doctor or money, the faith of Jesus required no intervention from man or money. Jesus utterly relied on the anointing, authority and glory to do the Father's bidding.

You can't truly express the character of God without tribulation. The anointed ones characterized in scriptures are always accompanied by tribulation. We petition God for power but refuse to walk through the valley of the shadow of death.

In the first century, there were "men that have hazarded their lives for the name of our Lord Jesus Christ" (Acts 15:26). Perhaps this is why the Bible declares in Acts 4:33 that

> "great power gave the apostles witness of the resurrection of the Lord Jesus and great grace was upon them all."
>   --Acts 4:33

Today, Christians typically are not true witnesses in Jerusalem like the first century apostolic team. To be a witness implies that you have power and demonstration. What is the witness all about? Great works witness that God has sent you to do His work; else, all we have is a handful of tracks. In the first century, death threats towards the apostles on a daily basis were the norm. I submit that very few today are willing to die for Jesus. We are more fascinated with $10,000 platforms filled with multi-media sensory overloads that draw big crowds than to be part of the anointed few.

By faith, I believe that one of the reasons that you are reading this book is because you're not satisfied with the status quo. You're desperate and you want something more. God has more, *only believe*, all things are possible to them that believe.

While in the early church their senses were stimulated by the Holy Spirit, today, the senses of this generation are stimulated by a visual sensory overload of lights and sounds. Moreover, as the first century Saints were moved inwardly by the Spirit, today's believers are being compelled visually outwardly by dramas, multimedia, state-of-the-art sound effects, and the big screen. It's a sham; no wonder groups like Islam command so much attention in today's world.

Did you know that Muslims now have their own radio broadcast in Kissimmee, Florida? Not only that, but they chant on the radio in Arabic, drawing people because of their enchanting melodic tones, mesmerizing the multitudes of ignorant people. "allahu akbar" is becoming commonplace in the USA.

Today, democracy in America affords its people the luxury of making ignorant statements that are just foolish. One pastor in particular said, "I don't have to warfare and fight because God will take care of me."

While this is true, at the same time he is walking in denial, when in reality, many Christians are being beaten physically. Just look at the statistics of female Christians that are beaten and abused by God-hating men. In Isaiah 54:17 the Bible declares

"¹⁷No weapon that is formed against thee shall prosper;
and every tongue that shall rise against thee in judgment
thou shalt condemn."

THE PRINCE OF THIS WORLD CAN TOUCH YOUR FLESH

What most "word" preachers won't tell you is that satanic weapons can touch your flesh and the flesh of your loved ones. Many make blunt irresponsible statements about divine protection until they've taken a good beating. Factually, after a weapon formed against you has touched your material things, it cannot prosper. When I say "prosper" I mean that it cannot fulfill the intended purpose of your destruction. In fact, this is where God enters the picture. Remember when the Bible says the following:

"So shall they fear the name of the LORD from the west,
and His glory from the rising of the sun. When the
enemy shall come in like a flood, the Spirit of the LORD
shall lift up a standard against him."   --Isaiah 59:19

That is why we need to understand how to war in the Spirit as well as how to skillfully use our weapons of warfare. Men like Philip and Stephen in the book of Acts were familiar with demonstrating God's character. Not only was Stephen anointed with the Holy Ghost but as he approached death for the Lord's sake he witnessed open heavens while being stoned.

"And the saying pleased the whole multitude: and they chose Stephen, a man full of faith and of the Holy Ghost, and Philip. And Stephen, full of faith and power, did great wonders and miracles among the people."
--Acts 6:5, 8

"But he, being full of the Holy Ghost, looked up steadfastly into heaven and saw the glory of God, and Jesus standing on the right hand of God, and said, Behold, I see the heavens opened, and the Son of Man standing on the right hand of God."   --Acts 7:55, 56

Finally, Steven is martyred at the feet of Saul of Tarsus. Just as a side note, the stones did not directly kill Stephen, just as the cross was not directly responsible for the death of Christ. Both of these men "gave up" the ghost, in other words, when it was time, they said, "now it is finished."

THE BIBLICAL STANDARD

In the first century, there were certain norms in operation that God is restoring for His Saints today. Philip was a man accustomed to demonstrating God's character. Not only did he have great grace and favor over his life, but he had a very unique connection with heaven by virtue of the angel who spoke with him.

"And the angel of the Lord spake unto Philip, saying, Arise, and go toward the south unto the way that goeth down from Jerusalem unto Gaza, which is desert. 27And he arose and went: and, behold, a man of Ethiopia, an eunuch of great authority under Candace queen of the Ethiopians, who had the charge of all her treasure, and had come to Jerusalem for to worship"   --Acts 8:26, 27

Then the Spirit said unto Philip, "Go near, and join thyself to this chariot" (Acts 8:29). Understand, prior to this moment, Philip had never known this man from Ethiopia personally but by the Holy Spirit. Being fully equipped, Philip was prepared to supply every need that this eunuch might have by demonstrating God's character. Let me make one thing clear, you must be filled with the Holy Ghost to demonstrate God's character.

> "But ye shall have power after the Holy Ghost has come upon you, ye shall be witnesses unto Me both in Jerusalem, Judea, and in Samaria, and unto the uttermost parts of the earth."   --Acts 1:8

Not only does Philip baptize this man in water, but when they came out of the water, the Holy Spirit transported Philip to Azotus to preach the gospel and witness the power of God.

> "[39]And when they were come up out of the water, the Spirit of the Lord caught away Philip, that the eunuch saw him no more: and he went on his way rejoicing. "
> --Acts 8:39

Both being transported from one place to another and angelic visitations represent the norms of the bible. Biblical characters including Enoch, Ezekiel, Jesus, John, and Paul the apostle, all experience this to a varying degree. Some were taken, caught away, transported, or translated, all representing gravity-defying elevation by the Spirit. All these events illustrate the dunamis power and character of God.

TODAY'S IMPOTENT CHURCH

Progressively complacent, lax, in retreat and steeped in traditionalism, many Christians simply do not believe that the apostolic doctrine is for today. Such are called cessationists. Unfortunately, many in the church have a "form of Godliness but deny the power thereof" (I Tim 3:5).

It's unfortunate that after 492 years of restoration, evangelism has been relegated to simply handing out tracks and telling people

"Jesus loves you." Moreover, church leaders have put more emphasis on a "secret coming" of Christ instead of equipping Saints for assignments, and becoming a powerful church to face its enemy Satan during tribulation.

Building Mega-churches became more important than reformation and the "times of restitution of all things"(Acts 3:21). Over the last 43 years, movements such as the 1970's "Word of Faith movement", have created a generation of prosperity junkies. As a result, many view the scriptures through a narrow prism, mitigating the sovereignty of God. Moreover, extremists have made statements similar to "God can't interfere", "He'll never oppose your will", "calamity could never come from God", and "the Holy Spirit is a gentleman". Statements like these and similar, all tend to taint the truth with carnality.

Did you know that all scripture is given by inspiration of God? Although verses like Romans 10:8-10 are effective in the salvation of a soul, scriptures cannot be understood without the baptism of the Holy Ghost. Man has a very small perception of spiritual matters. Therefore, the Bible was not written for ungodly men but the church.

Each generation follows the previous in what I call "learned behavior". Why do we do these things?

DEBUNKING SOME MYTHS

The following lists represent some myths that were not true in the first century culture:

- Jesus made altar calls or prayer lines for salvation
- God will never cause calamity or create darkness
  --Isaiah 45:7
- Jesus asked His followers to repeat the sinner's prayer
  --Rom 10:10
- Jesus demanded that the unredeemed confess His name openly
  --Mt 10:32,33
- Jesus coerced or manipulated believers using the rapture doctrine   --1 Thes 4:16, --2 Thes 2:2

- Apostle Paul suggested that before "The Day of The Lord", the earth would become one big happy planet
- Paul described himself as a free moral agent, "I get saved when I decide", or "I can quit God at any time "   --Phil 1:13
- God will never violate my will   --Gen 20
- God is incapable of putting sickness upon (wicked) men in the Bible   --Num 12:10, --Deut 7:15

How can we demonstrate the character of God if we continue to walk in humanism and propagate these myths?

TIME FOR A NEW MINDSET

During this time of restitution of all things, our mandate should be to restore a first-century Christian cultural mindset. As the Holy Spirit withholds the full manifestation of the man of perdition, God is restoring the church back to a formidable state. Unlike former generations, I believe that the "glory days" of biblical proportion are here for another "great awakening."

Scripture underscores that Christian Saints should not be just "hearer's only" but doers, or better yet, demonstrators of the character of God. For years, the body of Christ has walked in passivity and weakness, but our charge as a new vibrant generation of Saints is to empower believers according to Acts 1:8 "ye shall have power after the Holy Ghost has come upon you."

LOVE MIXED WITH PASSIVITY

While the church at large limits the love of Jesus to a passive posture, we need to remind believers that God is both a man of war, and a roaring lion out of the tribe of Judah. We need to empower this new Elias generation to do more than just tell sinners "Jesus Loves You" but we must begin to demonstrate God's character again. Truly, that is what this current wave of glory is all about.

Our mantra should be "don't just tell people Jesus loves you but demonstrate it with His power." Again, we need to advocate to this generation that the kingdom of God is not just in "word or tongue" but power and great exploits.

While in the last days, as many depart from the faith giving heed to seducing spirits, we need to draw a clear line of demarcation in the sand between Christianity and other cults of this world with notable remarkable signs and wonders.

During the middle ages, God's manifest presence in the glory cloud was displaced by traditionalism. On the other hand, restitution which denotes a series of revivals, demands a shift from traditionalism to truth, passivity to boldness, retreat to "warfare praise", drowsiness to revival, and from the doctrines of men back to the 1st century standard.

THE THIRD WAVE OF GLORY

As the Day of Christ approaches, we have witnessed unusual things that men have never seen or heard of before during this millennium. One evening during 2008, I was attending what was dubbed the Lakeland outpouring in Florida. While up in the bleachers of this huge coliseum, I heard people crying out down below on the main floor near the stage. Suddenly, Todd Bentley asked the people who seemed to be in a euphoric state, "is it raining inside the coliseum tonight?" Until then, this was the kind of revival that I had only read about, but now I was experiencing it firsthand. I beseeched God, "if it is raining inside the coliseum tonight, I want to feel the physical, tangible rain drops." No sooner had I spoke than one drop of cool water splashed onto my lower lip, and in that moment I knew that unusual things were manifesting in that place.

RETURNING TO OUR FIRST CENTURY ROOTS

The church needs to get back to its grassroots and advocate that all believers need a fiery baptism of the Holy Spirit which shall empower them to be witnesses both in "Jerusalem, Judea, and unto the uttermost parts of the earth."

Granted that faith works by love (Gal 5:6), love is not a substitute for the character of God. In fact, every great work that the Master performed was based on love and compassion. However, the love of Christ was not passive but demonstrative. Jesus may have been meek, but He wasn't weak. When in Matthew 15:33, Jesus saw the multitudes, He said, "I have compassion on the multitude, because they continue with me now three days, and have nothing to eat: and I will not send them away fasting, lest they faint in the way." Did He command His disciples to take up a collection to buy bread? No, He took what was in their hands, mixed His love and compassion with the power from heaven and made miracle wonder bread. Jesus always expressed His love and compassion in many ways including opening blind eyes, raising the dead, changing water into wine, or commanding Peter to walk on water.

My beloved brethren, we are overdue for a stirring of the gifts of the Holy Spirit in the body of Christ. Any idea how we might advocate believers to demonstrate God's character?

The following is not intended by any means to be an exhaustive list but I believe the Saints should:

- Conduct miracle healing services
- Demonstrate the prophetic
- Recognize and activate Fivefold leaders
- Restore the standards of Jesus Christ
- Impart and activate spiritual gifts
- Carry the fire of God to the desperate
- Equip the Saints as the bride to restore former generations
- Impart knowledge of the glory of the Lord
- Advocate the development of apostolic prophetic teams
- Send heavily spiritually armed teams to the cities to demonstrate the character of God

Since the Lakeland Outpouring ignited in 2008, the fire has been contagious. I therefore assert that during the "times of restitution of all things" (Acts 3:21), God has been equipping His Saints for the coming tribulation period.

A CONTAGIOUS FIRE

Like on the day of Pentecost, the fires of revival are being ignited all over the earth. As the fifth principal of Christ is restored during the Saints age, the dead shall be raised.

With warfare praise, this Elias generation will recover that which the enemy has robbed from God's people. So, what separates this generation from the previous? Is it not that we should be demonstrators of God's character?

RESTORING FIRST CENTURY STANDARDS

As first century standards are restored, we are seeing the tangible glory-cloud of God coming down. From the Latter Rain to Faith-healing of the 1800's, Holiness to the Pentecostal Azusa Street in 1906, God continues to restore His church. During times of restitution, companies of Apostles and Prophets are being raised to perfect the Saints and bring unity. As the "little horn" of Daniel labors to wear out the Saints, God's Fivefold leaders will meet in the theatre of battle for showdowns against the dragon, beast and false prophet. For this reason, I believe the bride of Christ needs to be in peak performance until Yeshua returns again in Revelation 19:11.

THE FIRST CENTURY VIS-A-VIS THIS GENERATION

What are some of the major things that we can expect in the days to come?

This is not by any means an exhaustive list.

- Outward display of power during the Saints age
- The spirit and power of Elias resting on this generation
- Power will validate a true witness of God   --Acts 1:8

- We shall enter into other men's labors
- After encounters with the anointed, Saints like the woman at the well will operate in power evangelism teams
- Men like Philip will suddenly be promoted into Fivefold office
- Apostolic prophetic teams shall emerge similar to Paul & Silas, Elijah & Elisha, Moses & Joshua
- Love and compassion will proceed dunamis power and gifts
- The seal of God's approval will rest on the Saints of God followed by miracles, signs and wonders
- Just as the apostles, so too shall our lives be in constant peril of death when we refuse to deny him (Acts 15:26)
- More Steve's and Philip's will be raised up and filled with faith and the Holy Ghost
- Just as the first century did not hand out tracks, "silver and gold have I none" but they put their money where their mouth was with power to change circumstances
- We shall discern between those that served God and those who do not from a distance with no name tags (Malachi 3:18)
- By revelation we shall experience divine help from heaven in the form of power, angelic visitations, and the Holy Ghost
- As Philip was translated "by faith", and Enoch was translated and did not see death, so shall many of the Saints
- Great power will give the Saints witness of the resurrection of the Lord during tribulation (Acts 4:33)
- Great grace shall be on the lives of this generation
- Power evangelism will create uproars and late breaking news that will be noised abroad wherever the Saints gather
- Strange things, unusual things, things that have never been seen or heard of before will occur
- Special miracles, the shadow of Peter, handkerchiefs from the body of Paul
- We shall be balanced with unconditional love, compassion of Christ and power to demonstrate
- As angels delivered the apostles from prison when they prayed and worshiped, so shall there be angels on assignment for us
- As Peter looked death in the face and commanded resurrections so shall the Saints of God (Hebrews 6:2)

Not only was Jesus boldly intense but He was extremely focused and determined to complete His assignments. Next time you're faced with an opportunity to stretch your faith to the limit, consider saying the following while ministering to another: "if thou canst believe all things are possible" (Mark 9:23). However, there remains another level. Stretch your faith by making the following declaration to another person and then add something to the end of the sentence.

"If though canst believe, I believe God will..."

Just one caveat, certain things will require fasting and prayer in order to reach a new level of anointing. But it never ceases to amaze me when I've actually heard people say that some believers fast to manipulate God. It's obvious that when these folks fasted and prayed, nothing unique every happened, so they attempt to discourage anyone else who was tired of the status quo because miserable likes company. When you reach a plateau in your ministry where your faith is bigger than the results, perhaps it's time for a new dimension in the glory.

DEFYING GRAVITY AND TIME

Previously, I mentioned the experience that Philip had with the eunuch. As they were come up "out of the water, the Spirit of the Lord caught away Philip, that the eunuch saw him no more: and he went on his way rejoicing. But Philip was found at Azotus: and passing through he preached in all the cities, till he came to Caesarea" (Acts 8:40).

When governments tell you that you can't get a passport or visa to preach the gospel, you will need additional tools in your arsenal. One of these is teleportation in the Spirit. Notice Philip is translated from one place to Azotus. I believe that in the days to come, when governments deny you documentation to travel, you will be translated right to your next assignment in a moment's time.

After the dark ages, for the last four hundred and ninety two years, history reveals at least thirteen major moves of God. During that time, God has begun to rebuild the old waste places, raise-up the former generations, and desolations of many generations.

BALANCE BETWEEN FRUIT AND THE POWER OF GOD

Most biblical scholars will agree that the Protestant movement revived the gift of salvation, Puritan movement restored water baptism, Holiness movement restored sanctification, and the Faith Healing movement restored divine healing.

Today, the church at large has become very efficient at expressing the fruits of the Spirit including love, joy, peace, longsuffering, gentleness, goodness, faith, meekness, temperance: against such there is no law. Moreover, we are the most generous nation in the world, but when dealing with powers and principalities, most Saints are not equipped to war against the prince of this world (Revelation 12:17).

One of the principles of Christ that God has begun to revive is "the resurrection of the dead." While in Lakeland in 2008, I witnessed actual resurrections from the dead during the outpouring. During this global event, God TV connected the revival to the rest of the world. On particular nights, people were encouraged to call into the revival regarding someone that had recently died. As we stretched forth our hands to pray, praise reports continued to filter into the service throughout the evening. Verifiable bona fide resurrections were being reported around the world.

God wants his Saints to do more than just preach "Jesus loves you", but we need to be doers of the word, not just have faith without works, but be demonstrators of His character with great grace on our lives. I will repeat this ad nauseum, Saints, we need to be demonstrators of God's character because faith without works is dead being left alone (Galatians 2:20).

So what is power evangelism? Most people reading this book can relate to evangelism from different perspectives, i.e. when Jesus commissioned the twelve and sent them out with power. Since the seven churches in Asia Minor were reduced to ruins before the Turkish Empire, some 1,400 years has past. The living prototypes that could teach evangelism were lost in the ruins. Although evangelism was restored in the 1950's, the knowledge from a practical standpoint of how the first century evangelized was still lacking. Moreover, evangelism of the twentieth century has been conducted with a more passive methodology than in the time of Apostle Paul.

POWER EVANGELISM

While the restitution of evangelism has resulted in the salvation of the lost, the day has come for a new dimension of evangelism that more closely conforms to the Book of Acts. Power evangelism is precisely what it sounds like; it's not just witnessing with tracks, but it is demonstration of God's character. For that reason, the kingdom of God is not eloquent speech of man's wisdom but demonstration and power.

> "8But ye shall receive power, after that the Holy Ghost is come upon you: and ye shall be witnesses unto me both in Jerusalem, and in all Judaea, and in Samaria, and unto the uttermost part of the earth."   --Acts 1:8

In the previous scripture, we see a one to one relationship between power and witness. Fact is, you can't be a witness without power, because power validates being a witness, not the reverse. In other words, with the power of the Holy Ghost you are a witness, but without the power what shall people witness? When we put a demand on the anointing and "dunamis" power is manifested, it is a witness that we are the Saints of God. Dunamis is defined as dynamite, explosive power.

Power Evangelism can effectively express the character of God when we:

- Train prophetic teams of power evangelists
- Teach Saints how to discern between the saved and unsaved
- Impart the anointing of the gifts of the Holy Ghost
- Continue the mindset of restitution of all things
- Expect angelic visitations anywhere that you are
- Advocate the power of resurrection of the dead

Get equipped to reap the fields which are white and ready to harvest (John 4:34-38).

RELIVING THE BOOK OF ACTS

Over the next generation, I believe that the book of Acts will establish the standard of expectation for the Saints of God. Essentially, I believe that the Book of Acts bears witness of the acts of the Holy Ghost, more than the works of the Apostles. God effectively established a proven model that we can use so that we will be effective in preaching, teaching and confirming His word. As our prototype, Jesus established a paradigm after He was resurrected by many infallible proofs. Like Jesus, we as the Saints of God need to provide infallible proofs as well as a testimony that God sent us on assignment. Telling the unredeemed man that "Jesus Loves You" without bona fide proof is limited in effectiveness. We need anointing to demonstrate before this world.

If we are going to "reenact" the book of Acts, then we need to be restored back to a first century mentality. Before demonstrating God's character at the local venue, let me suggest some critical points:

- Strive to use detailed accurate words in order to hit the main artery quickly. In the days to come, this anointing will be a premium as Christian Saints face greater principalities and powers in the kingdom.
- Set up a training camp at the local church for impartation and training seminars. Prepare the Saints to carry the anointing to other venues. In fact, the anointing is far too good to keep for yourself.
- The paradigm of Jesus was simply to preach, teach and then demonstrate the works of God. At the end of each session, allow people to flex their spiritual muscles by prophesying one to another.
- By analysis healing was only part of the ministry of Jesus. His sign-gift ministry ran the gamut from raising the dead to walking on water. Jesus was a phenomenal student because He learned by watching and then imitating His Father from heaven.
- No question that faith works by love, but we must be careful not to mix our love with passivity and complacency.
- Look for opportunities to ask God, "What's coming next?" God loves to speak so simply. Ask Him to show you how you can be a blessing to a leader, "Aint", or another Saint.
- I believe the day has come when Christian Saints who are anointed and trained will not have to ask questions such as "what is your name" or "what are the most pressing issues in your life" but will discover their secrets by the Spirit.
- Ask God to speak to you, ask Him for a secret, detail, and name, be accurate. Let the power of God work through you after you share the love of God
- If they can't believe you for your words, let them believe by your works

- Let God show you who to speak with, not everyone is ready for a flyer. Have something fresh to say about what God is doing today.
- Be prepared to deal with those who are God haters. Be expecting the miraculous, amazing, and outrageously unusual.
- Make sure that you send your angels ahead of you first before you demonstrate the power of God (Rom 1:16)
- Change your mindset regarding tribulation. Remember, in Revelation 7:14 John saw a great multitude coming through great tribulation dressed in white robes. In order for the gentiles to put on white robes washed in the blood, they first need a preacher. That's you my friend.

Just like our prototype Jesus, we should all strive to exercise our anointing in one form or another. Granted not everyone is at the same level, but that just means that you've not seen anything yet and there is more to come.

Maybe God will disquiet your spirit and you will talk to your leader about training classes to demonstrate the character of God. Perhaps you might want to take the basis of this book to create a seminar on establishing prophetic teams to be deployed in your community. You may have noticed that your methods have brought a modicum of success and you're desperate to get back to first century norms with respect to the power of God. Beloved it is no coincidence that you are reading this book, God is speaking to you right now.

THE SAINTS OF GOD

Chapter 8

THE PRICE OF OBEDIENCE

" ⁵ Then Zedekiah the king said, 'Behold, he is in your hand: for the king is not he that can do anything against you.' ⁶ Then took they Jeremiah, and cast him into the dungeon of Malchiah the son of Hammelech, that was in the court of the prison: and they let down Jeremiah with cords. And in the dungeon there was no water, but mire: so Jeremiah sunk in the mire."

--Jeremiah 38:5, 6

As a prophet of the Lord, Jeremiah truly paid the price because he was obedient to the voice of God. At first glance, we see the glitz and glamour of being called from the womb. Often there is the thrill of delivering a package to diplomats on God's behalf. From the outside, it seems existential like "Hakuna Matata", you know "it's a problem free philosophy, no problems for the rest of your days." Unfortunately, it could not be farther from the truth; when you serve God, you're going to pay a price. Jeremiah was anointed to foretell the future regarding the coming captivity of Jerusalem by King Nebuchadnezzar. God used the prophet to deliver a clear message to Zedekiah that if he surrendered to the Babylonian princes only then would he be saved. Unfortunately, Zedekiah was just a puppet king in name only with no real power.

In fact; it was the Chaldean princes who wielded the true power of the kingdom. Obviously, God allowed the princes to cast Jeremiah in the dungeon. Make sure that you are aware of the consequences of the anointing before you ask, "for the gifts and calling of God are without repentance" (Romans 11:29). Look past the surreal imagination of your biggest dream and understand the price you'll pay when you get it.

PREPARE FOR REJECTION

As Jesus demonstrates the power of God outside of His own hometown, people are astonished. Sadly, upon returning to His village as the Christ, most of His family members were embarrassed of Him. Let me warn you, this type of anointing is not for everyone, especially those whose self-esteem is based on the opinions of others.

Persecution during tribulation goes along with the territory. There are different callings and different levels of anointing. When Jesus left His hometown of Nazareth, in their view, Jesus was just a carpenter from Galilee. While He is going, His family, friends, and neighbors heard by word of mouth what appeared to be diluted gossip about Jesus.

JUST A CARPENTER

As Jesus returned to His own country, He began to teach in their synagogues. No sooner did He arrive than rumors begin to circle around town. Many Jews begin to question His divine nature and genesis by saying

> "from whence hath this man these things that even such mighty works are wrought by His hands? Is not this the carpenter, the son of Mary, the brother of James, and Joses, and of Juda, and Simon? And are not His sisters here with us? And they were offended at Him. But Jesus said unto them, a prophet is not without honor, but in his

own country, and among his own kin, and in his own house. And He could there do no mighty work, save that He laid His hands upon a few sick folk, and healed them."   --Mark 6:1-5

SUFFERING AS A PROPHET

As a prophet, you will suffer libel, slander, scandal, and ridicule. Can you imagine the risk Jesus took on the way to the house of Jairus? The daughter just 12 years old died, but Jesus told the ruler of the Synagogue, "be not afraid only believe." According to tradition, the Jews hired people to mourn for the deceased child. Not intimidated by death, Jesus asked the drama queens why were they crying and stated that "the damsel is not dead but sleepeth." Of course, when they heard that, they laughed at Him exceedingly. Rejection was prominent in the life of Jesus. One minute the multitude was in awe, and the next they were plotting to kill Him.

> "39 And when He was come in, He saith unto them, why make ye this ado, and weep? the damsel is not dead, but sleepeth. 40 And they laughed Him to scorn, and He took the damsel by the hand, and said unto her, Talitha cumi; which is, being interpreted, Damsel, I say unto thee, arise. And straightway the damsel arose and walked; for she was of the age of twelve years. And they were astonished with a great astonishment."

Being rejected and ostracized comes with the territory.

YOU MUST PAY A PRICE

If you can't endure rejection, perhaps you'd better think twice before you step into a Fivefold office. Not only does rejection come with the territory but often times prophets are rejected by their own people. Ever wonder why after meeting someone for the first time, they don't like you? Jesus wrote the book on the subject of rejection and humiliation. On the cross He declares to His father, "forgive them for they know not what they do."

> "²⁵But this cometh to pass, that the word might be fulfilled that is written in their law, they hated me without a cause."   --John 15:25

JOHN THE BAPTIST IS BEHEADED FOR RIGHTEOUSNESS

Not everyone will pay the same price. In the case of Jesus, His verdict was death. For this reason, many Christians today will not walk in righteousness like John the Baptist when he informed Herod that it was not lawful to have his brother's wife Herodias. In today's society, standing for righteousness is neither politically correct nor very popular. In fact, John the Baptist lost his head for the sake of Jesus Christ.

> " ²⁵And she came in straightway with haste unto the king, and asked, saying, I will that thou give me by and by in a charger the head of John the Baptist. ²⁷And immediately the king sent an executioner, and commanded his head to be brought: and he went and beheaded him in the prison "   --Mark 6:25, 27

Jesus constantly lived under the threat of death on a daily basis. Why? One reason was due to jealousy; in fact, others simply hated Him without a cause.

> " ³⁷I know that ye are Abraham's seed; but ye seek to kill Me, because My word hath no place in you."--John 8:37

Did you ever start a new job and discover that one of your co-workers does not like you for no apparent reason? It is noteworthy to mention that trials and tribulations build character in the life of a Christian. As Jesus endured tribulation, so shall we have tribulation in this world. Sometimes those of your own household can be your greatest enemies. Although the Pharisees were of the lineage of Abraham, they wanted to kill Jesus. The Pharisees were a religious sect that preserved the Law of Moses during 70 years of Babylonian captivity. They were the lawyers of His day. Where the Pharisees were a prototype of an intellectual, Jesus would have been the prototype of a spiritual man.

Due to their unbelief in the Son of God, Jesus argued with the Pharisees that their father was the devil. This in turn created an air of self-righteous indignation, ultimately sealing His fate. Probably the single most condemning act of blasphemy occurred when Jesus told the Pharisees "Before Abraham was, I am." These words incited a rage in these men that provoked them to commit the most heinous crime of all time.

When you're married to Christ your problems don't simply cease, in fact, they've only just begun. Doctrines especially within Christianity can set you at odds with certain groups. Case in point, when Paul stood in the midst on Mars Hill in Athens, to preach on the resurrection of the dead, all the philosophers mocked him.

" [32]And when they heard of the resurrection of the dead, some mocked: and others said, We will hear thee again of this matter. "   --Acts 17:32

In his treatise to the church at Corinth, Paul certified that while the Saints were reigning like kings, God had appointed the apostles unto death. When you are a Saint of God, you will be made a spectacle unto the world, angels and unto men.

"Being defamed, we entreat: we are made as the filth of the world, and are the off-scouring of all things unto this day."   --1 Cor 4:13

Not only is there a price tag for obedience but there is a payoff too. Paul draws a parallel between the fellowship of his suffering and the power of his resurrection. Not only did Paul affirm that he would attain unto the resurrection of Christ but that he would inherit resurrection power. As I've stated ad nauseum, the dynamite power of Jesus was based on His love and compassion for men. Jesus had both the power to destroy this temple and then raise it up again in three days. Any man that is buried in the likeness of His death will also experience the likeness of His resurrection while on earth. Furthermore, resurrection power works in us to resurrect our dead hopes and dreams.

THE GREATEST FAST IN SCRIPTURES

" [3]Wherefore have we fasted, say they, and thou seest not? wherefore have we afflicted our soul, and thou takest no knowledge? Behold, in the day of your fast ye find pleasure, and exact all your labors. [4]Behold, ye fast for strife and debate, and to smite with the fist of wickedness: ye shall not fast as ye do this day, to make your voice to be heard on high. [5]Is it such a fast that I have chosen? a day for a man to afflict his soul? Is it to bow down his head as a bulrush, and to spread sackcloth and ashes under him? Wilt thou call this a fast, and an acceptable day to the LORD? [6]Is not this the fast that I have chosen? to loose the bands of wickedness, to undo the heavy burdens, and to let the oppressed go free, and that ye break every yoke? [7]Is it not to deal thy bread to the hungry, and that thou bring the poor that are cast out to thy house? When thou seest the naked, that thou cover him; and that thou hide not thyself from thine own flesh? [8]Then shall thy light break forth as the morning, and thine health shall spring forth speedily: and thy righteousness shall go before thee; the glory of the LORD shall be thy reward."   --Isaiah 58

Once upon a time, I was helping someone in the music department while they sought another musician. During one service, the leader touched on our personal ambitions such as wanting gifts, anointing, office, title etc. Suddenly, he shocked me by saying "some of you think that you can manipulate God with fasting."

FASTING IS THE HIGHEST CALL OF SACRIFICE

Now, since I'd been around the block before, I knew that slogan came directly from one of our favorite television evangelists. Albeit not true for everyone, have you ever noticed that leaders who make assumptions that fasting is manipulating God all seem to have had miniscule results while fasting themselves?

It runs the gamut, those that don't speak in glossolalia refute unknown tongues, those that have never experienced an outpouring contradict today's outpourings, those who have not experienced mighty works discourage those who are impassioned to have the first century Saint's' experience.

Some of the greatest moments with God occurred during a long fast. Not only will extreme fasting take you to another dimension of intimacy, but unusual things begin to happen during meetings. In the first place, uncommon fasting moves the hand of God because we are denying ourselves nourishment. In fact, to the American Medical Association, a 40 day fast would represent the initial stages of death. Look, great grace rested on Moses that empowered him to fast 40 days. Moses did not live by bread alone but by every word from the mouth of God. I'm talking about living in the glory zone.

THE ENDS JUSTIFIES THE MEANS

Moses walked in the glory of God. In the glory, food, sleep, self-satisfaction, all are unimportant. During the narrative of Exodus 33, we find Moses focused exclusively on receiving from God. No doubt that there is a close relationship between mighty works and fasting. Fasting will usher you into the glory of God faster than any other means. I dare to say that fasting is a means to an end, namely entering God's glory realm.

I remember when the Lord spoke to me and informed me that some of these fasts would feel like death, so it was important to walk in faith. During a meeting at my house, I received a phone call from a precious Saint in another state. During our conversation, I actually could smell fish cooking in her kitchen. When I asked her, she gleefully screamed that she was cooking fish just before she called me. Friends, there is no substitute for fasting no matter what some prominent leaders will have you believe.

NOW IS THE TIME FOR RADICAL FAITH

As I had so eloquently explained in a previous chapter, that there is a clear difference between faith as a fruit of the spirit versus the gift of faith. Even after I had fasted 3 days each week for several years, the Lord announced a 7 day fast with liquids only. Look, just when you think that you have sacrificed enough, God wants to take you a little higher. I for one do not believe that fasting is manipulating God. I've heard this unconscionable argument before, and just dismissed it. Listen, God wants you to enjoy life, but also He's looking for demonstrative faith. Sometimes you just have to do something that is radically out there, outside of the mainstream to get God's attention and ultimately move in your favor.

As a leader, I've been desperate to experience manifestations of the first century. Even at the inception of my birth, I constantly attempt to provoke God with reckless acts of faith. During the early years around 2001 when I did not have a public ministry, it was during the winter up north around when God challenged my faith. Of course, I believe in the foolish things that confound the wise and prudent. God instructed me to walk outside through the snow in a certain direction as if I was going to preach the gospel. I got dressed, grabbed my ministry business bag, went outside, and simply walked in the knee-deep snow in the direction that He showed me.

THE PRICE OF OBEDIENCE

OBEDIENCE IS BETTER THAN SACRIFICE

Although I have failed God on different occasions, without a doubt, obedience is better than sacrifice. On one hand it's easy to be mesmerized by the glitz and glamour of a prophetic ministry, but the reality is totally different. I remember a particular service that was concluding on a Sunday afternoon in March of 2014. As you know, Pentecostal services can last for hours. The pastor had just finished preaching in the book of 2 Kings Chapter 6. The narrative begins when the sons of the prophets had grown to such an extent that the place they were staying was too narrow or, in other words, too small. They informed Elisha that they were going to pack up and move to Jordan. Before leaving each one had cut down a timber to carry to Jordan for the next building project. The pastor literally brought an axe to church to demonstrate cutting different branches. Each time he grabbed a branch, he gave it a name like pride, disunion, rebellion, limitation, independence and so forth. Each item metaphorically was a hindrance that had to be cut in two to make way for expansion in ministry.

After he opened the altar for prayer, the pastor's wife suggested that we join together to pray for the pastoral family. Prior to that moment, I knew God spoke to me and said "do not prophesy in this church." Next moment, one woman stepped forward to pray and exhort the pastors. I decided to remain behind the group in order to avoid prophesying to the pastors. At that moment I kept my eyes closed on purpose as to make no eye contact. No sooner did God admonish me not to prophesy when the women began to call for me unawares. Suddenly, someone struck me on the arm and when I opened my eyes the whole church was staring at me.

A DEFINING MOMENT IN MINISTRY

The brother that had struck me then said to me, "they are calling you". When I looked forward, the woman that had prayed for the pastors was frantically signaling me to come forward. It was evident that she wanted me to give the pastoral family a word but God told me "no". This was my defining moment, would I be swayed by the crowd or would I be obedient to God. Usually when you're asked you to pray, typically the answer is "ok".

I quickly turned to the man standing beside me and said "God told me not to prophesy in this church". It was probably one of the most embarrassing moments, I presume, for some people, not to mention the fact that I had overtly said "no" in front of 50 people. There have been moments where even my wife has been embarrassed by my actions.

I knew that at that moment, to some people, my defiance was acceptable, but to others, I had made some enemies. I found out the hard way, if you're going to lead by example, not everyone will be happy. You can please some of the people all of the time, all of the people some of the time, but not all of the people, all of the time. Being obedient will provoke enemies in the area of ministry.

When I had looked up again, the prophet that was standing beside me was then called to exhort the couple. When he finished he walked over to me perhaps expecting to hear a word from God, but I told him that the Lord had forbidden me to prophesy. He then confirmed that great things were about to break forth for me in ministry, and that I had to be obedient to God even if it cost me friendship with others.

A TEST OF TENACITY

It was a Sunday in October when I was asked to preach at a Spanish church Iglesia de Dios Misionera in Orlando directed by Dr. Amesty. Prior to the service a prophet by the name of Samuel grabbed the hands of my wife and me and prophesied "I see little girls all around you." You can imagine what my wife was thinking at that moment, "no way". I have to admit, I was not thrilled with the prospects of that prophesy as well.

Shortly thereafter, I simply put it on the back burner and continued building our ministry in Kissimmee, Florida. While at home, I think I was in the kitchen, and suddenly the doorbell rang. It probably was the late afternoon when I answered the door. Upon opening the door, a brother in the Lord was standing some distance away. I said "Hello, God Bless you". He responded, "hey, how are you Evangelist Michael." To make a long story longer, he said to me, "my family has no place to live." What I did not realize was that the rest of his family was out of sight on the driveway. Suddenly, three girls appeared behind him as he was speaking to me. Suddenly, a resounding prophetic word came into my mind about the little girls all around me. What I didn't know is that I was about to step into one of the most interesting experiences of my life.

BEING A DOER OF THE WORD AND NOT A HEARER ONLY

If truth be told, I am a man that wanted to experience bigger than life bible stories in the twenty-first century. Let me explain. If Jesus changed water into wine, I wanted to experience it. If Jesus walked on water, I wanted it. If Jesus fasted for 40 days and nights, I wanted to experience that also. In other words, I wanted to relive the bible literally. During this period, I would undertake great fasts before the Lord. One day during this season of fasting, I made a statement to the Lord that I wanted to experience Isaiah 58:7:

> [7]Is it not to deal thy bread to the hungry, and that thou bring the poor that are cast out to thy house? When thou seest the naked, that thou cover him; and that thou hide not thyself from thine own flesh?

This scripture combined with the prophetic word was my confirmation that God had sent this family. One error that we make when yielding to God is that we believe if I submit to His will, there will be no negative consequences. On the contrary, every trial by obedience builds character for the assignments that lay before you. I believe we are in training for something more challenging each time.

FORSAKING ALL FOR CHRIST

At this time my son was still living with us, so I had to yield my office so that this family could have some privacy. I think that as human beings we often live in a world of fantasy. We attend a crusade hosted by a name brand preacher. On the outside, we see this high profile, highly polished evangelist that simply appeared on the scene for a revival service. We don't care to imagine the type of challenges behind the scenes in his own private life. Our tunnel vision only allows us to see the glitz and glamour of an anointed vessel. Let me tell you, my life was fully exposed during those two months that they stayed with us. Everything that was hidden was brought out into the light. The mystery of the Man Of God, the prophetic anointed vessel was unveiled and all that remained was humility.

FAITH WITHOUT WORKS IS DEAD BEING LEFT ALONE

When Isaiah talked about the real fast of God, "⁷Is it not to deal thy bread to the hungry, and that thou bring the poor that are cast out to thy house?" What is not said is the most interesting part. Remember, that family had a lifestyle, and we had another lifestyle. I remember saying to myself, if Isaiah described that the fast of the Lord was more than just afflicting my soul, then God would provide the grace to be successful. Probably the most difficult part was that the children never experienced a stable environment for a period of time, but they were not to blame. The fast of the Lord was more than afflicted our soul, and thou takest no knowledge" but God wanted "to loose the bands of wickedness, to undo the heavy burdens, and to let the oppressed go free, and that ye break every yoke." In other words faith without works is dead. A Christian could fulfill the Mosaic law of fasting and be a hypocrite at the same time. Another way to say it is love without works is dead.

BE SURE THAT GOD HAS SPOKEN BEFORE YOU OPEN YOUR DOOR

Even thou we struggled, I was determined to pay a price for obedience. A word to the wise, do not bring someone into your house without direction from God because it potentially could devastate your marriage. Our marriage has survived the test of time, so we were ready for that higher calling. All I can say is that I am glad that I was able to help that family on their journey to perfection.

I know that I have mentioned this, but it bears repeating, never try to prove that you are somebody in the Lord. Let me be blunt, if you are an apostle, then defend your ministry like Paul, but don't attempt to exercise your gifts, work wonders or miracles before an unbelieving acquaintance because more often than not God will not substantiate your ministry. Our job is not to prove to others that we are the "real McCoy", our job is to touch the desperate with His power.

DON'T TRY TO PROVE TO ANYONE THAT YOU'RE ANOINTED

Let me be clear, there will come a time to demonstrate the anointing in order to be a witness of Him that sent you. A valid scenario would be when all the skeptics have come to watch you fail but God uses you to work a miracle right before their eyes. There is a season for everything. Be patient, some of the greatest miracles occurred amongst a simple minority of people. Just remember this one thing, "lest God builds the house, they that labor, labor in vain that build it". One of my favorite scriptures is:

"A man's gift maketh room for him, and bringeth him before great men."   --Prov 18:16

EXTREME FASTING IS NOT FOR EVERYONE

Don't let anyone stymie you through implication that you're manipulating God when you fast. I don't care how high up the ecumenical ladder they have climbed! On the other hand, if you suddenly decide that you want to be the next modern-day Elias and God has not called you, it doesn't matter if you fast 40 days; God knows what's best for you.

AN AMAZING PROPHET TO SAY THE LEAST

One of the most amazing stories of sacrifice can be found in Luke 2:36-38. I'm referring to the prophetess Anna during the Roman occupation. Luke describes Anna as being of a great age, yet she is making the ultimate sacrifice.

"36 And there was one Anna, a prophetess, the daughter of Phanuel, of the tribe of Aser: she was of a great age, and had lived with an husband seven years from her virginity; 37 And she was a widow of about fourscore and four years, which departed not from the temple, but served God with fasting's and prayers night and day."
--Luke 2:36, 37

Every time I read this story about Prophetess Anna in the book of Luke chapter 2, I get blessed. There must have been a special grace upon prophetess Anna that empowered her to fast day and night in the temple. Somehow, I feel that she fasted with just water during her time of fasting. My wife for example will not fast more than one meal a day. We all have a threshold of tolerance that limits our ability to fast. Anna was ordained to fast because she would play a very important role in the life of baby Jesus. She was a true Jewish prophetess that was waiting for Jesus to come.

> "³⁸And she coming in that instant gave thanks likewise unto the Lord, and spake of him to all them that looked for redemption in Jerusalem."   --Luke 2:38

Fasting and prayer facilitates intimacy with God. Fasting is tantamount to a dying process of our physical body while our spirit is being enlightened to hear God more clearly. In essence, fasting is germane to opening the windows of heaven for a unique experience. Anna was rejoicing for the day to prophesy over baby Jesus. Because she was consecrated unto the Lord, and was not distracted by a husband, she gave very concise and accurate prophetic words. Everything in the kingdom of God has a price tab except salvation where Jesus paid the price for you. As Saints of God, we may pay the price of an apostle or prophet but we can't pay the price for salvation.

CONTRARY TO PUBLIC OPINION FASTING IS NOT MANIPULATION OF GOD

While ministering on the phone to a woman in another state, I could see fish frying and I could actually smell its odor. This was a season when I was fasting each week, three days a week. I continued great fasts between 2008 and 2010. Personally, I walk in a different anointing while fasting. As I was ministering to this woman, I asked her about the fish that I could smell over the phone. She informed the group that she was cooking fish on the stove. Listen, one way to draw nigh unto God is during a fast. Fasting will cost you everything. Don't forget that the grace of God will cover you during long fasts. Make sure that you check with God before you begin a long fast. In my opinion, fasting activates the anointing, increases discernment, opens your eyes to see upcoming events, and biblically enhances intimacy with God to enter into the Holy of the Most Holies.

WALKING IN HOLINESS

Walking in holiness will cost you everything. As you put off the old man, jettison the old tired conversations, experience renewal of your mind, and put on the new man, then you can walk in true holiness (Eph 4:24).

You will experience moments that for no reason, people will simply disdain you even if you're innocent of wrong doing and have not offended anyone. I would draw a parallel to John the Baptist that reproved Herod when he said, "it's not licit for you to have your brother's wife Herodias."

Today, many Christians will not assume that posture of holiness for fear of rejection or retaliation. Unlike many today, first century Saints "hazarded their lives for the sake of Jesus Christ." In fact, one of the biggest fears some people have is fear of beheading but Islamofascists like ISIS. We fear what we do not understand, and truly most people don't understand the militant mindset of Islam.

If truth be told, today many Saints would not be good contestants for the award-winning television series "Fear Factor". We are bold in word, but weak in bodily presence. The apostle Paul was not only bold in letter, but also mighty in presence. For that reason he did not visit the church of Corinth with esoteric eloquent speech but with infallible proof that the kingdom of God was in "power and demonstrations."

WATCH OUT FOR PROPHETIC STUMBLING BLOCKS

When you begin to walk like John as one that has knowledge and preach righteousness during tribulation, it will establish a clear line of demarcation in the sand between you and the world.

Simply put, people will reject you for no reason at all. Therefore, be careful that you do not allow yourself to fall into what I call a "prophetic sink hole" denoted by a paranoid complex where we think that everyone hates us.

Jesus warned his disciples in (Luke 6:22, 23) that during tribulation period, that they would have to pay the price of obedience.

> "Blessed are ye, when men shall hate you, and when they shall separate you from their company, and shall reproach you, and cast out your name as evil, for the Son of Man's sake. Rejoice ye in that day, and leap for joy: for, behold, your reward is great in heaven: for in the like manner did their fathers unto the prophets." --Lk 6:22, 23

One might say it's faith alone; I say when you blend faith and fasting, God will shock you. There will be a measurable difference in the level of anointing when you deny yourself. Fasting and prayer are quintessential when seeking direction from God and to move His hand in a certain area. Not only will it help to increase your intimacy with God, but it is also healthy for your body. It never hurts to shed a few pounds from time to time. Unfortunately, some of us inadvertently say "yes" to God's calling before we count the cost of obedience. We see how Moses fasted before God as he was transitioned into the realm of God's glorious presence.

In order to move to a new level in your ministry, be prepared to pay the price by fasting and prayer.

THE SAINTS OF GOD

Chapter 9

ACTIVATION FOR PUBLIC MINISTRY

"² As they ministered to the Lord, and fasted, the Holy Ghost said, Separate me Barnabas and Saul for the work whereunto I have called them. ³ And when they had fasted and prayed, and laid their hands on them, they sent them away. "   --Acts 13:2, 3

Throughout scriptures, God has established a prototype for activating his servants for public ministry. Some activations occurred by virtue of a master–student prototype relationship where God transfers anointing from one generation to the next. By and large, activations today can occur during a revival meeting, discipleship training, conference or a seminar class. It is also evident that God has divinely connected anointed team members at a particular time for a specific purpose.

Activation for public ministry typically begins after the student learns how to be a servant under other men. Some examples include Moses & Joshua, Elijah & Elisha, Barak & Deborah, and Paul & Silas, just to mention a few.

Anointing with oil or laying hands upon the next leader was the paradigm that God established in the Old Testament. When the apostles laid their hands on a servant, essentially, they were imparting an anointing from the Holy Ghost.

Hence, at Antioch, both Barnabas and Saul were consecrated or set apart to work in their evangelical apostolic calling.

Prior to punishing Moses for his disobedience, God commanded Moses to lay his hands on Joshua before all Israel. If we were to contemporize his calling as a Fivefold leader, he might be considered a prototype prophet-apostle of the Old Testament. As a prophet, Moses therefore certifies the call and anointing upon Joshua whom appears to be in line as the next deliverer of Israel. This is evident from the fact that after Moses has departed from the sanctuary, Joshua remains behind to soak up the residue of the glory of God. Just as Moses, Joshua falls under the banner of prophet-deliverer who abides in the tabernacle of the wilderness.

After a short cursory snapshot of scriptures, we find adequate scriptural justification for impartation and activation of the Saints in order to operate in the Holy Spirit. Paul frames it up by writing 1 Corinthians 12:31, "But covet earnestly the best gifts: and yet show I unto you a more excellent way." Covet suggests a burning passion for endowment that would enable a Saint to express the love and compassion of Christ by means of demonstrative signs, wonders and miracles. Yet before an activation seminar can actually begin, we need some revelation regarding His eternal plan for this age. Just continuing with "business as usual" posture will not activate the Saints to face off with the rulers of darkness.

THERE IS A PURPOSE FOR THE ANOINTING

By revelation, the eyes of your understanding can be opened to see that God is restoring all things in preparation for a great conquest of His kingdom. More eloquently, the kingdom of God is suffering violence. God is in the process of reviving a fruitful and powerful church that is ready to wage war with the beast and the false prophets in the days to come. In Daniel 7:18, we read that "the Saints of the most high take the kingdom". Not only do they take the kingdom, but they also possess the kingdom.

According to biblical prophecy, each day, the Saints should be repossessing the kingdom of God. Not only in the United States but also in Jerusalem as well. Not only will the Saints need the anointing, but most of all the revelation as to what God is about to do amongst the nations. We are anointed for a purpose according to Luke 4:17 who makes it crystal clear why the Spirit of the Lord anointed Jesus:

> [18]The Spirit of the Lord is upon me, because He hath anointed me to preach the gospel to the poor; He hath sent me to heal the brokenhearted, to preach deliverance to the captives, and recovering of sight to the blind, to set at liberty them that are bruised, [19]To preach the acceptable year of the Lord." --Luke 4:18

The anointing empowers the Saints to preach the gospel, heal the brokenhearted, preach deliverance, recovery of sight to the blind, liberty to the bruised, and preach the acceptable year of the Lord. As a Fivefold team leader, while praying, you might lay your hands on one of your trainees. Spontaneously, the Spirit of the Lord might fall on them anointing them and empowering them for a variety of purposes.

IMPARTATION

In a team approach, the objective is to train and then impart the gifts of the Holy Ghost. The word impartation is synonymous with transferring something from one to another. As we have mentioned before, transferring an anointing occurred from the Old to the New Testament. After an impartation, ministers can prophesy, discern, give a word of knowledge, speak in tongues, exercise the gift of interpretation, and much more according to the will of God.

All too often, for a short season, we find ourselves in an environment that has not maintained pace with the restorative moves of God over the last 492 years. It's unfortunate that those that have a calling seem to view training as waste of time similar to Israel that wandered in the wilderness. This in fact can occur because a leader lacks revelation or is not ready to chart a new course according to God's purpose.

DON'T NEGLECT THE GIFTS FROM HEAVEN

Look, let's make a reality check, every ministry places emphasis on the particular area in which they believe fulfills the great commission. For example, some develop a deliverance ministry fashioned by the 1950's deliverance evangelism marked by mass meetings, healing and deliverance. Still others put emphasis on a salvation ministry, while others emphasize missionary work. Each one of these components needs to be part of the New Testament church makeup.

Unfortunately, many of these ministries morph into passivity, where I feel God is shifting us from passivity into violence. One of the mindsets in Christendom that runs rampant today is "I don't have to fight mentality". That's because many passive, lax Christians would rather take to flight instead of fight. Look, I understand that there is a time for peace and a time for warfare, but when I look at the Saints today, it appears like most are walking blindfolded in passivity. People are dying prematurely, the family nucleus is divided, our focus seems to be on prosperity, and apparently, no one truly has insight as to the spiritual state of the church. Although the signs of the times are evident, many appear to be oblivious because we are more comfortable practicing safe religion. Some people frequent church for all the wrong reasons. At times it's more about the cares and riches of this life than being a servant of the Lord.

While a new wave of glory sweeps the land, America at large is in trouble due to apostasy. We need an awakening before it is too late. For this reason, I want you to be activated so that you can be everything God has purposed for your life.

PASSING THE ANOINTING TO THE NEXT GENERATION

There are plenty of paradigms in the scriptures regarding impartation, anointing, and activation. Many have an anointing but remain inactivated for many years until they get connected to the right person. Personally, I believe that we need to identify leaders that can help put our anointing into action. Not only those who teach the word, but who after teaching will both demonstrate the anointing and then later, send their students on an assignment to exercise their gifts.

> "¹And Elisha the prophet called one of the children of the prophets, and said unto him, Gird up thy loins, and take this box of oil in thine hand, and go to Ramothgilead: ²And when thou comest thither, look out there Jehu the son of Jehoshaphat the son of Nimshi, and go in, and make him arise up from among his brethren, and carry him to an inner chamber; ³Then take the box of oil, and pour it on his head, and say, Thus saith the LORD, I have anointed thee king over Israel. Then open the door, and flee, and tarry not. ⁴So the young man, even the young man the prophet, went to Ramothgilead."--2 Kings 9:1-4

The former passage is what I call a prophetic training prototype. Prior to Elisha, the prophet Samuel established a school of the prophets. Evidently, the tradition continued decades later which is evident when the author of 2 Kings calls the student "one of the children of the prophets". Apparently, Elisha had imparted an anointing into an inexperienced student that was ascending among the ranks. Not only does he pass to him the anointing oil, but delivers unto the student a prophetic message. When you're obedient unto God, He may use you to raise up the next deliverer, the next apostle, or the next prophet. It's imperative that we become men and women of action, not just eloquent preachers.

Elisha trained, activated, and sent out his students to exercise their spiritual muscle.

WE'VE COMPROMISED THE ANOINTING

At one point I discussed what I call substitutions for the truth in today's church culture. Cases in point, at one time, Christian Saints were compelled internally by the Holy Spirit. Today, we are stimulated by a multimedia sensory overload from altars transformed into sound stages back-dropped by large screens. At one time, churches featured anointed preachers who could stir up the heavens, but today we've substituted them for motivational speakers. Back in the heyday, the dead were virtually raised; today we tell people "be quickened from the dead."

Paul admonished Timothy not to neglect the gift that was in him, which had been given to him by prophecy, and the laying on of the hands of the presbytery (1 Tim 4:14). Albeit many are gifted, yet they still need a presbytery to lay hands on them to stir up the gifts of the Holy Ghost. In the book of 2 Timothy 1: 6, Paul reminds Timothy, whom he had anointed, to stir up the gift of God that was in him. Perhaps at this moment in time the gifting or anointing seems dormant in your life. Find a way to fan the flames, re-kindle the fire, stoke the embers, and stir up the gift that is in you.

BUILT UPON LOVE AND COMPASSION

Today, God is holding people accountable for carnal behavior. What value has the anointing or a Fivefold office without the fruits of the Spirit?

"²And though I have the gift of prophecy, and understand all mysteries, and all knowledge; and though I have all faith, so that I could remove mountains, and have not charity, I am nothing. "   --I Cor 13:2

154

The love and compassion of Jesus were expressed by raising the dead. The fruit of the Spirit is tantamount to speaking with the tongues of men and angels. Without charity, we are as a sounding brass and tinkling cymbal. We are commanded to covet the best gifts, but Paul said that there was a "more excellent way." We should have a burning desire to represent God in the earth and at the same time manifest the fruits of love, joy, and peace toward mankind.

FAITH WITHOUT WORKS IS DEAD

On the flip side of the coin, faith mixed with passivity is dead. I don't diminish the fact that we need to express our love through charitable acts of food and clothing, in fact, my wife and I have helped a bunch of folks in this area. However, works are more than just food and clothing. It's curious to note that Jesus never mixed money, gold or silver with His love and compassion to produce food and clothing for the poor. The love and compassion of Jesus was mixed with dunamis power from heaven which transformed water into wine, multiplied loaves and fishes. Activating the gifts in your life empowers you to be a reproducer under the anointing. Contagious fire spreads when it comes in contact with combustible material. As a fire, you ignite others to imitate Jesus. As I have said ad nauseum, we need to demonstrate the character of God, not just be hearers only of the word.

EXERSIZE YOUR SPIRITUAL MUSCLES

What I am about to say may raise eyebrows, but just like a weightlifter needs to train for a show, so do the Saints need to train to perfect their gift. Some sixty years ago, during the charismatic movement, many leaders were skeptical as to validity of restoring the gifts of the Holy Spirit. If you were baptized in fire and spoke in unknown tongues you were considered to be a fanatic. In the book of Corinthians 14, Paul admonishes the church to practice prophesying one at a time. Not only should we

155

learn how to prophesy, but practice the prophetic so that others will be comforted. I am aware of the risks allowing some of the Saints to prophesy with a microphone. People will make mistakes but that does not imply that they are false prophets. If you'll be honest, everyone has been guilty of a Freudian slip of the tongue or has been presumptuous at one time. Moreover, if all may learn and be comforted, the word "learn" by its definition suggests failures will occur.

> "[11]When I was a child, I spake as a child, I understood
> as a child, I thought as a child: but when I became a man,
> I put away childish things."   --1 Cor 13:11

Notice how Paul acknowledged that each Saint must submit to a growing process during their Christian life. You must crawl before you stand, stand before you walk, walk before you run, and at each level, there is a certain degree of uncertainty.

ON THE JOB TRAINING

Be careful not to fall into the guilt syndrome. We first need to train with our brethren before we can jump into the action. I also believe that we can self-train anywhere we travel. Did you know that your gifting will work outside of church? For example, when I am in a public place, I ask God to speak to me about a person. Sometimes while standing in line at the bank, I will ask the Lord "which teller will serve me?" At times we will hear a name, or some detail about a person we are going to meet or that is standing in line. Faith is the key that helps you step into the supernatural. By faith, you step out into the unknown where the secrets of God can be found. God can give you a word of knowledge, a prophetic word or both.

> "Having then gifts differing according to the grace that
> is given to us, whether prophecy, let us prophesy
> according to the proportion of faith; Or ministry, let us

wait on our ministering: or he that teacheth, on teaching; or he that exhorteth, on exhortation: he that giveth, let him do it with simplicity; he that ruleth, with diligence; he that sheweth mercy, with cheerfulness." --Rom 12:6

Just a note, there is a difference between the fruit faith, and the gift of faith. The fruit faith can be understood by our salvation experience. Paul writes in Ephesians 2 that "by grace ye are saved by faith". Faith is required for salvation as well as prophesying. No one was exempt of having faith. Not only did Abraham believe, but Jesus exercised faith when he demonstrated God's glory. I believe Jesus operated in the gift of faith required for an outward display of God's power.

PROPHECY BEFORE ACTIVATION

Sometimes Saints tend to get ahead of the game when they experience a little anointing. A good example is when Peter asked the unidentified spirit he saw walking on the sea "bid me to come unto thee". He did not step out of the boat until the presumptive "spirit" said "Come" (Matthew 14:29). Later, the authenticity of the voice is confirmed when Peter puts his foot out and the waters sustain him. Likewise, Paul admonishes his son Timothy to fight a good war according to the prophecy that went before him. Now understand, I am not implying that you should be so spiritually deep that you are no earthly good. Most great men testify of humble beginnings before their visibility increased on a national basis.

> "This charge I commit unto thee, son Timothy, according to the prophecies which went before thee, that thou by them mightest war a good warfare" --1 Tim 1:18

Prophecy often precedes activation for ministry. Some scholars believe that these were prophecies given to pioneers of the Old Testament. I believe Paul prophesied directly to Timothy, and later he stirred up the word that was in him. Sometimes it seems like the fire has gone out. Six months have gone by and no one has invited us to preach. The word of prophecy is forthcoming to prepare the recipient for what God has purposed for their life. Often God will send another person to confirm the prophetic word that we received from a leader.

Before we go forward, I need to clarify one thing about impartation and activation of the gifts, although we desire the best gifts, we must remember that the selfsame Spirit divides to each person severally according to his will. I believe the Holy Spirit can give each Saint several gifts according to our level of desperation. Even though you don't operate in the gifts yet, that does not imply that God will not activate the gifts at a later date. Don't let the devil convince you that the default of a twenty-year delay of God's promise implies an automatic "NO". How many have heard other Christians saying, "you missed your window of opportunity, because if God were to open the door, he would have already done it already"? Sound familiar? Likewise, we don't have a much influence regarding our Fivefold calling inferring that obedience is not a determinant factor. On the other hand, disobedience can surely put a program on pause. Once you know the position that God wants you to occupy, press towards it with all of your might.

MOMENTS OF IMPOTENCE

> "Then the fire of the Lord fell and consumed the burnt sacrifice, and the wood, and the stones, and the dust, and licked up the water that was in the trench (1 Kgs 18:39).

After this amazing display of power, Elijah rounds up all the 450 prophets of Baal, takes them down to the brook Kishon and executes them. It has not rained in the land for three and half years when one day Elijah declares to Ahab to "get up, eat, and drink" because I hear the abundance of rain. While Elijah prayed for rain he sends his servant up to the Mediterranean Sea to look for a cloud of rain.

While it rained, the hand of the Lord rests upon Elijah and he runs before Ahab's chariot to the entrance of Jezreel. When Jezebel receives news that Elijah has killed her prophets, she makes a decree that the prophet of the Lord will die by the same time on the next day. When Elijah is informed that Jezebel will take his head off, he runs for his life.

After God manifested such great signs and wonders through Elijah, why would he suddenly fear for his life? Look, after God has used you powerfully, there will come a moment when you feel un-anointed and rejected by other people. Under the anointing you may feel invincible, but out in society, your just one of us common folk. Ever felt disappointed because things are not panning out according to the prophetic word?

> "¹And Ahab told Jezebel all that Elijah had done, and
> withal how he had slain all the prophets with the sword.
> ²Then Jezebel sent a messenger unto Elijah, saying, 'So
> let the gods do to me, and more also, if I make not thy
> life as the life of one of them by tomorrow about this
> time.' ³And when he saw that, he arose, and went for his
> life, and came to Beersheba, which belongeth to Judah,
> and left his servant there"   --1 Kings 19:1-3)

After destroying 450 prophets of Baal, why would an idle threat cause him to retreat in fear to the mountain of God? Somehow in his own mind, his anointing diminished because Jezebel threatened his life.

PERSONAL INADEQUACY

Even after someone has laid hands on you and you've been activated for public ministry, there are times when you feel inadequate as if no one really appreciates you. There is a time and a season for all things. Similar to a tree that changes during the four seasons, so is God preparing you for greater things.

I remember a season when I literally waited six months for an invitation to preach. As you can imagine, we try to reason with God as to why he should give us favor. Have you ever said, "God I'm at such an age or what did I do wrong?" In the meantime, God is severing connections, taking away every object of jealousy, casting down vain imaginations, allowing people to humiliate you, demanding all your resources, and at the end of the day, you feel none the better. Let me revisit one point, if there is one thing that causes jealousy, it's when a person or object assumes a position in your life that is reserved for God alone.

Regarding objects of jealousy, many times our human nature will attempt to hold onto people for as long as possible. For some it's their hour to move on but we refuse to let them go. You need to learn how to hold them, or fold them. You need to say "I am glad when they were sent and glad when they went." Even though it's contrary to your nature, the presence of some people may be keeping you from being promoted. Because you're of the opinion that without sister Boo, you can't make it. Ever wonder just how you made it this far without brother Gasbag? Look, it's not God's will for us to have other dependencies but Him. Mentors are fine at birth, but should not be venerated as gods. Some mentors, without expressly saying so, assume the position of God in the mentor-disciple relationship.

I can recall during my own training, I once thought that frequenting every service, participating in every outreach, traveling to every service, cleaning every spill, occupying every position in church, denying every family member, attending every meeting, vacuuming every floor, kissing everyone's ring, getting in every prosperity line, and attending weeks on end of revival, would somehow get me in the pulpit faster. Guess what? It never did. Why? Because one, timing is critical, and two, God demands that we exercise ministry for the right reasons without hidden motives or agendas of any kind.

A Final word: get trained, covet the best gifts, receive an impartation, receive the anointing, and find someone that can activate the anointing that's in you. Once a man has received the gift, now it's time to minister the same one to another as a good steward of God.

THE SAINTS OF GOD

Chapter 10

PROPHETIC APOSTOLIC FIRE TEAMS

"And God hath set some in the church, first apostles, secondarily prophets, thirdly teachers, after that miracles, then gifts of healings, helps, governments, diversities of tongues. Are all apostles? Are all prophets? Are all teachers? Are all workers of miracles? Have all the gifts of healing? Do all speak with tongues? Do all interpret? But covet earnestly the best gifts: and yet shew I unto you a more excellent way."   --1 Cor 12:28-31

FIRST THINGS FIRST

First, let's establish the framework of prophetic team ministry so that you may understand the urgency of unity, and working together. Moreover, if we emulate a first century prototype prophetic team approach it will produce leaders that are more effective and productive. It's not a coincidence that God created a Fivefold ministerial team in the book of Acts consisting of the apostle, prophet, evangelist, pastor and teacher. I will attempt to demonstrate in this chapter that God is placing an anointing on this type of team ministry approach to evangelism.

From the beginning, God established the power of the team approach. The first prototype team is found in Genesis 1:26 when

Moses writes "And God said let us make man in our image, after our likeness". Since the two words "us" and "our" are plural, biblical scholars recognize that these pronouns to infer the Father, Son and Holy Ghost.

TRI-UN BIBLICAL HOME-TEAM

Hence, these pronouns illustrate that the plurality of God's divine nature existed from the beginning. Furthermore, these pronouns establish a biblical model of a team whose members work together throughout the scriptures. One of the advantages of this celestial team is unity which we shall explore in depth in this chapter.

Unlike other forms of literature, the Bible maintains perfect agreement between all 66 books. For instance, in John's prologue Chapter 1 he writes:

> "In the beginning was the Word, and the Word was with God, and the Word was God "   --John 1:1-3

In the Greek, Logos in Christology means the Word, discourse, logic, or reason which refers to Jesus Christ, the living Word. The doctrine of Logos establishes the typology of the Trinity, Father, Son, and Holy Ghost. The Word was in God and the Word was God shows perfect agreement in type and gender. In essence although the Word was in God and God was God, it also is Jesus, the Word made flesh.

A perfect illustration of a biblical team is in the Book of Matthew 3:16,17:

> "16And Jesus, when He was baptized, went up straightway out of the water: and, lo, the heavens were opened unto Him, and He saw the Spirit of God descending like a dove, and lighting upon Him, 17And lo a voice from heaven, saying, This is My beloved Son, in whom I am well pleased."   --Mt 3:16,17

Today, many followers of cults such as Arianism, Docetism, Nestorianism, and Unitarianism, don't believe that there are three distinct manifestations of the God-head. Some believe that Jesus was just a man and not God in the flesh. Fortunately, Matthew debunks these myths in the previous passage as evidenced by Jesus being in the water, the Spirit descending like a dove, and the sound of an audible voice from heaven all manifesting simultaneously. This typology suggests a celestial team that is tangible to mankind. Each member of the triune God has a particular purpose which is germane to the creation. As one of the tenants of faith, Matthew admonishes the Jewish dispersion that a man must be baptized in the name of the Father, Son and Holy Ghost (Mt 28:19).

But the most tell-tale sign that underscores the Trinitarian doctrine is the following verse:

> [7]For there are three that bear record in heaven, the
> Father, the Word, and the Holy Ghost: and these three
> are one. [8]And there are three that bear witness in earth,
> the Spirit, and the water, and the blood: and these three
> agree in one."   --1 John 5:7-8

There is perfect agreement between all team members of the trinity. While Jesus glorifies the Father, the Holy Ghost glorifies Jesus. Teams in general provide unity, security, and power in agreement. This prototype team from heaven gives impetus to the development of Fivefold teams in preparation for evangelizing the nations.

MINISTERIAL FIRE TEAM

Today more than ever before, the church needs to mirror the Fivefold ministry of apostles, prophets, evangelists, pastors, and teachers. I like to call them the apostolic prophetic fire team. Actually, fire team is a military word referring to the smallest functional unit of six men that could be dispatched on any given mission and have all the resources available for success. As God had equipped the primitive church with Fivefold leaders to perfect the Saints, so should we strive to implement this type of team in our churches today.

What happens if we only have a pastor? Each Fivefold leader of the team has a specific purpose to implement in the kingdom of God. Albeit today, many leaders carry double mantels, i.e. apostle-prophet, or prophet-evangelist, the pastor's mantel was not designed to operate alone.

While a pastor will nurture his flock as it goes through growing pains, the prophet may express his or her calling by fore-telling the future, while the evangelists may operate in creative miracles.

Although a prophet could effectively offer counseling to a Saint, in most cases, it would not be his or her strongest suit. While a teacher could essentially evangelize the community, teaching the word would be more consistent with the particular calling of that office.

While a church may do well with only a pastor and elders, the other four offices are necessary to complete the "perfecting of the Saints, work of the ministry, and edifying of the body of Christ." In fact, I submit that in the days to come, more often than not, it will be the prophets who will bring unity between the fathers and the sons before the coming of the Day of the Lord.

BUILDING PROPHETIC FIRE TEAMS

Over the last 10 years, I have been involved in developing apostolic-prophetic teams in Kissimmee, Florida. Our vision focuses on one of the biblical principles that had been dormant over the last 492 years, but finally restored in the last century and that is evangelism. Restoration of this particular aspect of the Bible once again enabled us to be witnesses in Jerusalem. Today, in my opinion, the ultimate team will execute "power evangelism." Power evangelism is somewhat a new team approach where leaders train those called to be apostles, prophets and evangelists. An ideal leader for such a team should be an apostle or a prophet. Team members may be spiritual hopefuls who want exposure to the gifts of the Holy Ghost. I would like to discuss some of the advantages of the ministerial team approach in the next few pages.

FIRE TEAM-WORK

In times past, we attempted to evangelize on our own and discovered that we were unable to maximize our effectiveness because we did not understand the dynamic of a team approach. Perhaps an example of a first century prototype team leader would be Jesus, who was the head prophet-apostle over His apostles. I would call this an apostolic prophetic team. When Jesus ascended He left behind gifts unto men which are the apostles, prophets, evangelists, pastors and teachers.

Amongst many of the characteristics of a team approach is strength, security and comfort. As one of the wisest men in biblical history, Solomon reveals that when establishing teams, "two are better than one", just in case a brother falls.

UNITED WE STAND DIVIDED WE FALL

In numbers there is great strength.

"Two are better than one; because they have a good reward for their labour. [10]For if they fall, the one will lift up his fellow: but woe to him that is alone when he falleth; for he hath not another to help him up. [11]Again, if two lie together, then they have heat: but how can one be warm alone? [12]And if one prevail against him, two shall withstand him; and a threefold cord is not quickly broken."   --Ecc 4:9-12

1. Reward

When we team-up to accomplish a common goal, the reward comes when if one falls, the other will have strength to lift him up. In a team setting, when the apostle is weak the other four can lift him up.

2. Supply

What one team member possesses, he can supply to the others that lack in a team setting. In a power evangelism setting, while one is praying, others can be interceding for the individual receiving prayer.

3. Support

Not only can a prophetic team be very effective in touching people outside of the team, but a well-oiled team machine is able to edify, comfort and exhort within itself. Look, some of the best moments I can remember is after intercessory prayer when the team began to minister one to another under the anointing.

4. Practical application

For years we have been conditioned to believe that discipleship training is the cornerstone of Christianity. One caveat, after you get your certificate, then what? The next dimension in building teams is practical application that goes beyond handing out tracks which in my opinion have been relegated to antiquity in this century. Today, more than ever before, people are demanding to be submerged in tangible glory of God.

5. On the Job Fire Team Training

Unlike the former years of exclusive discipleship training, today we both train disciples and then put their training into action in a prophetic team setting. For example, there needs to be a rifle team leader that is mature in his office that can lead a team of twelve members on different missions.

Probably a five-member fire team is the most effective and light weight. Teams develop tactics to deal with satanic power outside the walls of the church. With the understanding that we pray for angelic support and back up, teams discuss a plan of how to put into play the instructions learned in discipleship training. But first, team members must understand that "ye shall have power after the Holy Ghost has come upon you and shall be witnesses in Jerusalem" before the team can be deployed. Just as there are ranks in the military so are there ranks in the prophetic team setting. Now instead of just talking about raising the dead, this twelve-member team can actually put their love and compassion into action by raising the dead, opening blind eyes, and exercising the gift of knowledge.

6. Security

Perhaps one of the most important aspects of the prophetic team is protection. During the years of the World Wide Wrestling Federation (WWF), a wrestling match included tag-teams, two wrestlers on the same team who would stand back to back protecting each other from a rear assault with a metal folding chair.

Look at the Marine Corp's rifle fire-team prototype, having six men each with M-16 automatic weapons consisting of a fire team leader, assistant fire team leader and 4 riflemen in a triangular formation. Though they take casualties, the team can effectively complete the mission because of good control of protecting one another. Sometimes the Saints experience casualties but the team is able to sustain itself because of the anointing in the team members.

When we stand together as a team, when one is attacked, the collective team comes together to pray for the wounded soldier. When they drag Paul's body out of the city, the disciples make a circle of protection around him. Because of the great grace over Paul's life, not even the stones were a game-changer.

"[19]And there came thither certain Jews from Antioch and Iconium, who persuaded the people, and having stoned Paul, drew him out of the city, supposing he had been dead. [20]Howbeit, as the disciples stood round about him, he rose up, and came into the city: and the next day he departed with Barnabas to Derbe."   --Acts 14:19, 20

UNITY AMONGST THE SAINTS

If there is one very important fact that I can't stress enough that would be unity amongst the Saints. After selecting team members on the first week, I would suggest that new team members intercede while the lead apostle or prophet demonstrates the character of God. In this way, as a prophet in training (PIT) gains wisdom observing the mature leader. Then, when you least expect it, the mature squad leader may give you an assignment to take a prophetic word with a box of oil and anoint the next leader/ deliverer of Israel.

Can you imagine the Marine Corps prototype fire team under attack and there is no unity amongst the rifleman? Most likely someone on the team will get wounded by his own team member. There must be an established communication and synergy among team members. While in training, perhaps you don't know how to use your weapon but someone on the team can train you in the mission field. When the prophetic fire team works together, we can do more collateral damage to the Devil Satan's kingdom.

"One can put one thousand to flight and two can put ten thousand to flight"   --Lev 26:8, --Deut 32:30

EXTREME FAITH

One of the gifts and a fruit of the Spirit is faith. I believe that there is a difference between the faith exercised by mankind and the gift of faith which is extreme faith. As an intense apostle-prophet, Jesus operated with extreme faith. In fact, everything that

Jesus did was extreme. By nature, He was intensely focused on fulfilling the law of God at any cost. As I mentioned earlier, everyone can walk in faith which is a fruit of the Spirit but not everyone can operate with the gift of faith. An expression of extreme faith might be when the Sprit drives a Saint into the wilderness to fast for forty days.

Regarding fasts of long duration, I had a friend who decided to fast for 40 days without proper guidance. By the grace of God he completed the fast but ultimately had to be taken to the hospital because his veins collapsed. My recommendation is to first check with your leader to determine if it is the hour for such an extreme step of faith.

When the gift of faith is in operation, people will witness unusual miracles that defy the laws of nature of this world. Extreme faith can manifest in many forms including giving radically, dancing with violence, or participating in resurrecting a dead ice-cold cadaver.

While in a parking lot, our prophetic team began to praise God and shout "let fire come down from heaven". Suddenly, a burning fire literally manifested in the middle of us producing a distinct smell that I will never forget. The prophetic team needs people that walk in that dimension of the Spirit so that they can see His glory. In the last chapter of the book I talk about living in His glory. As a prophetic team, we need to, as the Bible exhorts in Isaiah 61:4 "build the old wastes, they shall raise up the former desolations." We need to rebuild what was lost in the first century.

FAITHFULNESS

Before we can be productive, we first need to express faith which is a fruit of the spirit. Often, we make statements with our mouths that we have no intention of keeping or are too weak to complete. Moses writes in Deuteronomy 23:21:

"When thou shalt vow a vow unto the LORD thy God, thou shalt not slack to pay it: for the LORD thy God will surely require it of thee; and it would be sin in thee."

The vow is a covenant with God that you agreed to keep. For example, we tell a Saint, I'm going to help you on this team because God sent me. But as soon as the cares of life and the deceitfulness of riches show up at our doorstep, suddenly, we have every excuse under the sun, such as "it's too late, I can't make it, I am not feeling well", and a host of other excuses because you were not able to pay the price. Great anointing historically required a great price. I'll talk about the cost of obedience in another chapter.

Often, our society today idealistically searches for that one special talented person. On my own secular job, I never had time to be the most talented because of my commitment unto the Lord. On the other hand, regarding faithfulness, I strived to be second to none. Hence, on occasion, my boss would call me, "old faithful." In fact, we expressed our extreme faith leaving everything behind in Newington, Connecticut, to move to Kissimmee, Florida. Although our income is less than before, we've been able to do twice as much with less. We've even had to trust the Lord without health insurance at times. Early on, we determined to give God His cut of our harvest first, regardless of how loud the creditors screamed.

Learn to be faithful like the good and faithful servant.

" [20]And so he that had received five talents came and brought other five talents, saying, Lord, thou deliverest unto me five talents: behold, I have gained beside them five talents more. [21]His lord said unto him, Well done, thou good and faithful servant: thou hast been faithful over a few things, I will make thee ruler over many things: enter thou into the joy of thy lord."
--Mt 25:20,21.

I will never forget the day when a man from Pakistan name Pastor Sohail Jacob called me to ask for a charitable gift for his orphans. Albeit I never knew Jacob, I sent a gift of $300 to Pakistan. Later, Pastor Jacob called me from the United States where he was attending a seminar for pastoral development and church planting. He explained that he needed another $100 to take care of expenses he incurred in America. I responded by sending another $100.

FAITHFULNESS AND HARD WORK PAYS DIVIDENDS

One day on the job, exhausted from ministry and also people calling from the outside, I noticed my boss had come and deposited something on my desk. I did not really pay much attention to it, but as I looked, I noticed that it was cash. At the time, the CEO of the work place new nothing about my personal life other than the fact that I was in ministry.

Upon a closer inspection, I found 4 fresh crispy $100 bills neatly stacked where he put them. I've learned to work hard and walk in extreme faith in ministry for it pays dividends.

"For a dream cometh through the multitude of business and a fool's voice is known by multitude of words"
--Ecc 5:3

You will never fulfill your vision or dream unless you are involved in a multitude of God's business. Let's face it, these principles work among the heathen, that's why there are a good number of multi-millionaires in America. Can you imagine how much more we could accomplish with God's help? By the way, did you know that God gives travail to the heathens to heap up wealth for the righteous?

In the first century, Jesus trained 12 disciples to continue the work after he was resurrected. As I previously mentioned, the first team in the first century consisted predominately of apostles, but then Paul writes to the Ephesians expanding the team to five different offices:

> "11 And He gave some, apostles; and some, prophets; and some, evangelists; and some, pastors and teachers; for the perfecting of the saints, for the work of the ministry, for the edifying of the body of Christ"
> --Eph 4:11.

FIRST CENTURY FIVEFOLD FIRE TEAM LEADERS

I might note that Philip who was filled with the Holy Spirit was anointed by the apostles to take care of the Greek widows. Just as soon as he became faithful in the small things by caring for them, God suddenly used Felipe to show his dunamis power. When we are faithful, scripture declares that "a man's gift makes room for itself and bringeth him before great men" (Prov 18:16).

Later we hear that "Philip the evangelist" is transported by the Holy Ghost from one place in the desert to Azotus to preach the gospel. I believe that we should both pray and expect some of the same things to happen on future assignments. Especially, we should petition God to usher in His glory and confirm His Word while you are ministering.

A prophetic team can be composed of called-to-be apostles, prophets, evangelists, pastors, and teachers. Each team should have an anointed evangelist filled with the Holy Ghost to demonstrate the concept of power evangelism. Listen, Saints don't need a title, just obedience and desperation for His presence. Look at the woman from the well of Samaria; after Prophet Jesus finished reading her mail, she became a powerful evangelist at Samaria without a title.

Every organization should have an established order, for we know that God is a God of order (1 Cor 14:40). Likewise, team members must be willing to be trained by watching and praying in tongues, while others are ministering.

174

DIVINE ORDER

If we let all things be done decently and in order, hence our mantra will be "He is a God of order." Just as there are different branches in the government, including executive and judicial, so are there unique offices in the apostolic-prophetic fire team.

No matter how mature an individual is, regardless how anointed you may be, we all need some kind of covering. Just as the twelve disciples had a covering, we should be covered by a proven leader that can discern things that we can't perceive.

PROPHETIC TEAM ACTIVATION

Jesus did not just equip and train His would-be-apostles, but He also imparted His Spirit into them. The difference between discipleship training today in the twenty first century and the training of those disciples is that every doctrine that Jesus spoke, He provided practical application, so they could develop into the appointed apostolic team before He ascended. He taught, trained, equipped, and imparted the anointing and authority they would need to face the big demons.

> "[21]Then said Jesus to them again, Peace be unto you: as my Father hath sent me, even so send I you. [22]And when He had said this, He breathed on them, and saith unto them, Receive ye the Holy Ghost. "   --Jn 20:21, 22

Not only did He breathe on them to receive the Holy Ghost, but He activated them to fulfill their calling in ministry. Prophets generally are equipped to breathe on the Saints to impart an anointing. A proven prophet may also lay his hands on a Saint of God to ignite a certain gift of the spirit. Since the biblical standard was impartation by the laying on of the hands, your fire team members will also need an impartation and activation to perform as one well-oiled machine. In the book of Acts, the team concept was well implemented by the Holy Ghost.

In the first century church, we read in Acts 13 that there were apostles and prophets in that place. As they ministered unto the Lord and fasted, the Holy Ghost consecrated these men into apostle-prophet teams.

"²As they ministered to the Lord, and fasted, the Holy Ghost said, separate me Barnabas and Saul for the work whereunto I have called them. ³And when they had fasted and prayed, and laid their hands on them, they sent them away." --Acts 13:2, 3

"⁴⁰And Paul chose Silas, and departed, being recommended by the brethren unto the grace of God. " --Acts 14:40

As I've mentioned before, apart from the prophet Samuel, Jesus led the ultimate apostolic team recorded in the bible. Each day He taught His disciples many times through demonstrations of mighty works. True, they often were hardened in their hearts, similar to a little child who does not seem to be paying much attention to his or her parents but is soaking up everything. Not only did Jesus amaze the doctors of the law with His rabbinic knowledge of the Old Testament, but Jesus was without a shadow of a doubt a demonstrator of God's glory. Although it was not a prerequisite, the 12 apostles had firsthand knowledge of the mighty works of Jesus. They observed His approach and the unusual methods that He implemented to bring about a determined result. Not only did Jesus demonstrate how to walk on water, but Peter wanted to imitate the master. In fact, Peter did not even know who the spirit was that was walking over the water. They had never witnessed anyone walking on the water. When the apostles heard Jesus say, "It is I, be not afraid", at that moment, Peter wanted to experience the glory of the Christ. For that reason he said "if it be thou, bid me to come unto thee" inferring that he was not sure if what appeared to be a spirit was Jesus. Albeit Peter had faith and had heard the voice of the master, he remains unsure until he steps onto the water and the glory sustains him without sinking.

Now it was time to send them out as a team. On different occasions, Jesus sent his disciples out solo so they could practice what He taught them with the ultimate objective of saving the souls of men.

"He sent them out by two and two" --Mt 10:1, --Mk 6:7

On that note I must pause a moment. In reality, most men today have heard about Jesus Christ with the help of multi-media. You would be hard pressed to find someone that never heard of the name Jesus in every language under the sun. Not only are most men aware of Christology, but many have both attended service at one time and read a verse or two in the Bible.

When prophetic apostolic fire teams evangelize their country more often than not, team members may discover quite diversified roles. While some are sharing the gospel, others may be ministering restoration, while others may help to rededicate the lives of those who once had some type of relationship with God in the past. For that reason, I feel that the evangelical track used today to save by fear is not as effective as it was let's say 50 years ago. Although we need to use media, the emphasis should not be on literature but power evangelism.

First and foremost, fire teams must be filled with love and compassion just as Jesus expresses His love by virtue of mighty works. When Jesus evangelized all of Galilee, He expressed His love and compassion by raising the dead, by opening blind eyes, by being transformed in the mountain, by walking on water, and by changing water into wine, just to mention a few.

" 19Go ye therefore, and teach all nations, baptizing them
in the name of the Father, and of the Son, and of the
Holy Ghost: --Mt 28:19

At the dawning of April 2014, I had acknowledged the realization that although I gained a modicum of success in ministry, I did not understand how to express the love and compassion of Jesus towards others. I was tired of being at the same level in ministry for so long and I made a resolve to implore God to teach me the love of Jesus. Particularly, I was determined to learn how to experience the love that Jesus expressed when ministering to men.

THE LOVE OF GOD

By in large, most of us understand the mechanics and the theology of ministration but more often than not we don't minister with the same love and compassion as the Lord. Nevertheless, in the Spirit, I believed that God was going to show me the motive by which Jesus ministered to His people.

On that same note, I'll never forget the experience that I had on the April 6, 2014, while ministering to a group in Kissimmee, Florida. During the previous month, I had met a Hispanic minister name Evangelist Pedro in Walmart. Later, the Evangelist came to attend our weekly bible study at our home. On the following week I received a phone call from Pedro inviting me to preach at a miracle service hosted by his church group.

After I had spoken for about 45 minutes, we began to move under the unction of the Holy Ghost. God truly showed off during that service, but what occurred before the people departed was probably more significant to me than in man's eyes. I will never understand why God seems to leave the best for last.

"[10]Every man at the beginning doth set forth good wine; and when men have well drunk, then that which is worse: but thou hast kept the good wine until now." --Mt 2:10

Regarding the gifts of the Holy Spirit, God does not reveal all the secrets of his people during a service, hence some people will walk up to me and ask me to pray about a particular need in their life. At the end of this service, a young woman whispered in my ear, "I have a drug addiction problem, and I want to be free." At that point service was basically over and people began to mingle. It became necessary to move our ministerial team from the large room into the kitchen area where it was quieter. As usual, I prayed, but then I said to God, "Show me your love this time while I'm praying." When I prayed, something saturated me from heaven. I asked her, "Did you feel a physical touch from heaven?" She replied "Yes." Then I asked, "When you leave this place, do you feel a desire to use a drug? Please be honest with me." She then replied, "I am not sure". I felt the miracle was not yet completed. This time however, before I prayed, in my heart I knew that if this woman was not healed today that she might perish in her iniquity.

LOVE DELIVERS A GIRL FROM ADDICTION

We prayed again. I felt the love of Jesus filling my heart and burst out into tears. I felt slightly embarrassed by my reaction which was out of control. When I gained my composure, I asked her, "When you leave this place, is there a physical desire to use narcotics, please be honest with me?" But this time she replied, "I feel no desire to use narcotics when I leave this place". Immediately I realized that love did that, not Michael.

I was not aware at the time but God had not completed the transformation in me yet. One rainy Tuesday afternoon on April 8, 2014, while at home balancing the checkbook, a friend called me to help him renew his corporation with the State of Florida. It was about 7:00pm upon leaving my house, and I had not noticed that my dog Pepi had slipped out through an open door in the garage and was now exploring the neighborhood on his own. One big problem, he had diminished eyesight putting him at risk of getting lost. After helping my friend Jesus at his home, we decided to hand out flyers in advance for our upcoming miracle revival service that would take place on May 23- 24, 2014, at the

Rosen Plaza Hotel. My wife usually gets out of work at 9:00pm so we headed towards Walmart to pick her up. After we picked her up, I dropped Jesus off at his house and went straight home. Much to our dismay, when I opened the door to our home, Pepi was not there. My wife said to me, "Ok don't play now" thinking it was a practical joke but unfortunately, the dog was gone.

After searching the neighborhood, we realized that something had happened to him. I decided to go to Walmart and buy poster board and red paint to make a large sign. It was 2:00am in the morning when I finished placing three signs on our street. On the next day, my wife asked me to go to the animal services department. I filled out a missing dog report and showed them a picture of Pepi. On the way home, when the loss of our dog became a reality, my eyes were filled with tears. Even though I had faith that God would resolve his disappearance, it still was difficult. When the tears began to flow, the Spirit of the Lord said to me, "That is love!" The tears were a result of love and compassion. I got it, finally. Can you imagine the effectiveness of ministry if one could feel that kind of love towards God's people? Then God said to me, "Now it's time to find Pepi"

LOVE BRINGS PEPI BACK HOME

After I arrived home, I set out on my bike determined to find the dog. Somehow, I knew God had set me up. I knew God would help me somehow. After a short tour around the neighborhood, I returned back home. I felt distracted and did not want to pray. But finally, I got down on the mat and began to pray. No sooner did I hit the floor, but the phone rang. Normally, I don't like to answer the phone when I am praying but I felt, based on the situation that I should. A very delightful woman at the other end of the line asks me, "Did you lose your dog?" I replied "Yes." Then she said "I know who has your dog, her name is Karen Gaff, and I can imagine that you guys must be worried sick over the dog. Karen is going to call you at 3:00pm today." Sure enough at 3:15pm,

Karen called me with a gleeful voice. She brought the dog to my house immediately. Pepe was fed, washed, groomed, and half asleep in her arms.

TIME FOR A NEW DIMENSION IN MINISTRY

God spoke to me and said from now on, "You will minister to people with the same love that you felt when your dog had gone astray." God used my dog to teach me perhaps one of the most important lessons in the bible, love. God let me know that when I ministered with the love and compassion of Jesus, our ministry would move to a new level of anointing.

I have a passion to transport my team wherever I go. Whenever I am invited to preach, I enjoy taking my team with me so that they can exercise their anointing. As we are invited, our team is introduced to the pastor. After I finish preaching, I invite the team up to the front with me, and then release them to minister at the very seats of the Saints. The problem with altar calls is that it has become a method to ascertain whether people are being saved, healed or delivered. Often, it is used to wrap up and justify the end of a service. We assume that just because we have an altar call, that it must be how the Holy Spirit is moving at that moment. I believe in the effectiveness of an altar call but it does not justify the means to an end. Although it has become part of church culture, we need to return back to the first century prototype model of letting the Holy Ghost move in that direction. Instead of just another routine so that someone can feel justified by conducting an altar, the best method would be when we are directed by the Holy Ghost to conduct an altar call.

With the team approach, team members will receive guidance by the team leader as well as direction by the Holy Spirit to understand the disposition of God's will at any particular moment. Inasmuch as the first century church operated with great grace over their lives, likewise team members will also get an opportunity to stretch their faith while ministering in the theatre of battle. Of course in any setting, people will make mistakes, make assumptions, and be presumptions, nevertheless, that is the essence of training.

Whenever my prophetic team travels with me, after I have finished preaching, I will ask the team to approach the front, and then release them to minister. At that point, the Holy Spirit can lead them to minister to anyone according to the direction of God. Whether the first or the last row in the house, God will touch people wherever they are sitting. Based on our experience and that which we have witnessed, I believe that we are in the middle of one of the greatest movements that put the Saints of God at the forefront of the battle.

TEAM PROTOCOL AND RULES

Each week there should be a different assistant leader who will take turns leading the group at each outreach. I personally feel there is great value in maintaining formation. Discuss with your team leader the importance of staying in formation together as a formidable fire team. Pray for angelic assistance before you move into position. Pray in the Holy Spirit (unknown tongues) and strategically move in unity. Before you approach a potential candidate, ask God for the details, like name, rank, and serial number. Exercise extreme faith, ask God for razor sharp details, something that will convince the person that God has sent you and you're not a psychic.

- Teams should work together ministering as a team
- Begin each outreach praying together, expecting God to show up and show off
- Pray in tongues, watch in the spirit, stand together in unity, be ready to stand and fight
- Raising the bar requires fasting and prayer
- Ask God to open your eyes, be accurate and hit the jugular with razor sharp details

JUST A FEW SETBACKS

When you make a mistake, it is called "learning". It is inaccurate to call someone a false prophet when they spoke presumptuously. From a biblical standpoint, a false prophet is not one who is inaccurate, but a false prophet is one who leads believers to follow another god that is not Jehovah. I would say that if someone is inaccurate, then the receiver would know that God has not spoken and that prophet-in-training could be taught a more excellent way.

When you prophesy, or speak a word of knowledge, the tendency is to give more than God has spoken. It is part of human nature to want to fill the mold. Probably one of the hardest things to do is speak what one may consider trivial words that are accurate from God instead of delivering a dissertation. If the word is "thus sayeth the Lord, I am with you in this valley of the shadow of death" than deliver the package and move on.

Learn to be reckless in your faith, move to the extreme in some area where you are struggling, whether it be alms, praise, worship, dance, fasting, travel, Jericho marches, walking out your land, carrying a staff, fasting 3 days a week, or whatever would be extreme for you. Saints, as a prophetic fire team, we need the glory of God like never before, truly that is what is missing in ministry today.

> "For the earth shall be filled with the knowledge of the glory of the LORD, as the waters cover the sea."
> --Hab 2:14

Unbeknownst to many Christians today, in the coming days we will have to fight on two fronts. Not only do we fight in the theatre of battle to save a soul, but as the remnant we must be equipped to fight against the dragon's offensive attacks. I explain in another chapter why God has restored the Fivefold ministry.

Let's be honest, when the USA goes to war, it needs good commanders and generals to lead its military. Likewise, the body of Christ also needs some apostles, prophets, evangelists, pastors, and teachers to plot strategic courses of action that will be game-changers as to winning the battle.

EQUIPPING CHRISTIAN SAINTS IN TRIBULATION

In 2 Kings 9, we see how that time after time, God used Elisha to reveal to the king of Israel battle strategies discussed at high-level meetings in the enemies' command center. God used his prophet to reveal the secrets discussed only by the chief of staff in the Syrian war room. Likewise, apostles and prophets will reveal the strategic planning of the dragon and beast before the Saints are ambushed.

> "They feed the woman in the wilderness for a thousand two hundred and threescore days. 3 ½ years and she is nourished for a time, and times and half a time."
> --Rev 12:6, 14

> "And the dragon was wroth with the woman, and went to make war with the remnant of her seed, which keep the commandments of God and have the testimony of Jesus Christ." --Rev 12:17

Seed represents Christ, but by faith we are brethren, heirs, joint heirs of Christ (Rom 8:17). Notice that the word "seed" is not plural but singular which is Christ (Gal 3:16). Hence the "remnant" of her seed, or her offspring, must be Christians or spiritual sons that come from the seed (Christ) of the woman. But remember, no natural Jewish son of his bloodline came forth from his bowels producing a remnant, only spiritual sons that were washed in His blood.

TRAINING AND EQUPPING SAINTS FOR TRIBULATION

War denotes a fight, but to fight you need generals, captains, and sergeants to give directions, draw up strategic battle plans, and to speak Rhema words into your life.

During tribulation, in order to war against the dragon found in Revelation 12:17, Christians will need prophetic Fivefold leaders that will:

- Perfect and equip the Saints for peak performance, perfect the Saints, the work of the ministry, edify the body
- Demonstrate how to minister the gifts of the Spirit
- Bring unity during tribulation
- Impart fire and the Holy Ghost
- Stir up the gifts that lay dormant
- Reveal the battle plans of the enemy
- Edify the body of Christ
- Impart gifts, activate and instruct prophets and apostles
- Promote the resurrection from the dead, the fifth foundational principle
- Bring revival to desolate waste places, demonstrate God's character, and teach
- Lead showdowns against false prophets and antichrists

THE ANOINTING

Quite definitely, apostolic prophetic fire team members will need the anointing. Perhaps least understood, by far, one of the most important aspects of Christology is the anointing. Jesus commences His public ministry by declaring, "the Spirit of the Lord is upon me, because He hath anointed me to preach the gospel to the poor"(Luke 4:18).

The word anointing is derived from the Hebrew word H8081 *Shehmen* which is derived from the Hebrew H8080 *Shaw man* meaning to shine, grease, perfumed, olive oil, and ointment.

In a BIB101 course, the student will learn that Christ is derived from the word H4899 *mä·shē'·akh*. From this root is the word H4886 *mä·shakh'* meaning to rub with oil, i.e. to anoint, to consecrate.

The word H4899 *mä·shē'·akh* which is derived from H4886 means anointed, usually a consecrated person (King, Priest, Saint), the Messiah, anointed one. Literally, the name of Christ means *Maw-Shee-akh* "the anointing". There are other derivatives associated with anointing, like the word in Greek G218, *Aleipho* which derived from H3045 meaning to oil with perfume, anoint.

A word that you don't often hear in church today is H5545 *Chrisma* derived from H5448 meaning an unguent or smearing, endowment, chrism of the Holy Spirit, anointing, and unction. Jesus read in the book of Isaiah 61 that the Spirit of the Lord was upon Him, in other words, that He was anointed with oil that was consecrated for the mission. Jesus was consecrated or separated unto God for a divine purpose. As the Son of God, He was a man of Charisma with the endowment to draw a great crowd.

THE ANOINTING EQUIPS US TO DEMONSTRATE

In addition, as a prophetic team, we need the anointing to:

- Preach the gospel to the poor
- Heal the brokenhearted
- Preach deliverance to the captives
- Recover the sight of the blind
- Set at liberty them that are bruised
- Proclaim the acceptable year of the Lord
- Proclaim the vengeance of our God

The anointing rested upon Jesus to effectively minister to poor, blind, captives, bruised, and brokenhearted. As an apostolic prophetic fire team, each member needs an impartation of the anointing upon them by a Fivefold leader, preferably a prophet.

Today, God is taking the apostolic prophetic team to a new dimension of His glory for I believe that it's time that we appoint unto them that mourn in Zion, but we need power.

TEAMS APPOINT UNTO THEM THAT MOURN

In the name of Jesus we can appoint unto them that mourn in Zion 3 things:

- Beauty for ashes
- The oil of joy for mourning
- The garment of praise for the spirit of heaviness

We cannot go into the theatre of battle unequipped and unprepared to face principalities, powers and wickedness in high places.

KNOW THE HOPE OF YOUR CALLING

Everything said to date is a moot point if a Saint does not have a revelation of their calling. You may have thought, "I don't feel as though I am called as a prophet or apostle". That is perfectly fine. Perhaps you feel your calling is intercession, the ideal prophetic fire team would need intercessors praying while they contend with the forces that be. Perhaps you have the mantel of a teacher but you're not sure how you fit into an evangelical team. Look, although you've not had the experience yet, perhaps the Lord might inspire you to create a seminar course on prophetic team building that will move the church to a new dimension of God's glory. Often, a move of God or a revival begins with a revelation.

"That God may give unto you the spirit of wisdom and revelation in the knowledge of Him; the eyes of our

understanding enlightened, that ye might know what is
the hope of your calling."   --Eph 1:18

Look, personally, I am tired of "business as usual". I'm not
going to sit around waiting for a "secret catching away" while
enemies like Islam prepare for war with the Saints. Just like in the
days of old, as God completes restoration of the church, there will
be showdowns between God's team, and the devil's team. Read I
Kings 18:22. If there were false prophets in the Old Testament,
then surely there will be false prophets in the New Testament.

> "²⁴For there shall arise false Christ's, and false prophets,
> and shall shew great signs and wonders; insomuch that,
> if it were possible, they shall deceive the very elect."
>   --Mt 24:24

Not only are we responsible for lost souls, but we are also
responsible to fulfill our divine destiny. God wants a robust,
vibrant bride at maximum capacity that is not afraid to hazard her
life for Jesus Christ.

WARFARE PRAISE AND WORSHIP

Someone may ask, what is the relationship between being a
witness, and warfare praise? There is a unique synergy between
the favor of God and praise and worship. I believe we should
conduct warfare praise before each endeavor.

Before arriving to minister at a particular location, the team
leader should initiate praise and worship to help produce a
determined outcome for the service. If it is a parking lot at a mall,
the team can praise and worship God before getting into their fire
team positions.

Without a doubt, high praises bring down strongholds in a
Kairos moment. Know the opportune moment to give God a
Shebach meaning to adulate, adore or a demonstrative praise right

before a strategic move in ministry or perhaps to have a matter revealed (Dan 2:23).

"⁵Let the saints be joyful in glory: let them sing aloud upon their beds. ⁶Let the high praises of God be in their mouth, and a two-edged sword in their hand. ⁷To execute vengeance upon the heathen, and punishments upon the people. ⁸To bind their kings with chains, and their nobles with fetters of iron. ⁹To execute upon them the judgment written: this honor have all His saints. Praise ye the LORD. "   --Psalm 149:5, 6

Since we are a prophetic team of Saints, then we should capitalize on the weapons of warfare that God has provided.

SHOCK AND AWE ARE COMMON DURING TRIBULATION

Not only shall prophetic teams be effective during tribulation, but God is sending some help. Did you know that the Bible is filled with symbology during tribulation; in fact, there are two witnesses that will come down from heaven and prophesy one thousand, two hundred, and threescore days. This period represents a span of roughly 3 ½ years.

" ³And I will give power unto my two witnesses, and they shall prophesy a thousand two hundred and threescore days, clothed in sackcloth. ⁴These are the two olive trees, and the two candlesticks standing before the God of the earth. "   --Rev 11:3, 4

With the seal over the foreheads of the Saints some will have a chance to witness the shock and awe of these two witnesses. As a prophetic team, we are supposed to receive power after the Holy Ghost has come upon us, and we shall be witnesses here first.

One thing that is never mentioned in church is that the Dragon kills the two witnesses for three days. I suppose that if that was the end of the story, then there would be room for sorrow, but there is some glory behind this story. See, God always has the last word and whatever He allows, He allows it so that He might receive all the honor, glory and praise. Just when the inhabitants of the earth are slapping high-five's, boasting, mocking and laughing, then came the third day. It was a sad tale on a day traveling to a village called Emmaus when the disciples were discussing the death of Christ, but while everything appeared hopeless, suddenly Jesus showed up. Just when the God-haters think they have the last hand, God pulls the trump card and raises them from the dead, a feat that the devil cannot perform.

> " [10]And they that dwell upon the earth shall rejoice over them, and make merry, and shall send gifts one to another; because these two prophets tormented them that dwelt on the earth. [11]And after three days and an half the spirit of life from God entered into them, and they stood upon their feet; and great fear fell upon them which saw them. "   --Rev 11:11,12

The two witnesses work in tandem, as a team, with one goal in mind, to exercise the power of God to convince ungodly men that they need to be saved. Let these two anointed ones be a model of the effectiveness of working together as a team. Our teams should emulate the power and demonstration of these two witnesses

Above all, as a team, make sure you shout onto God, speak in unknown tongues, invoke His spirit, and ask for open heavens prior to executing your assignment.

Chapter 11

TRIBULATION
V.S.
WRATH

> *" I John, who am also your*
> *brother and companion in*
> *tribulation"*   *--Rev 1:9*

In 1959, during 8 years of Soviet occupation in Romania, Pastor Rickard Wurmbrand , a Jewish convert to Christianity, was tortured in a prisoner of war camp. In his prison 13 feet underground, from 5:00am until 10:00pm, Russians chanted anti-Semitic propaganda into their ears such as "communism is good, Christianity is stupid, and no one believes Christ." In this hellish underground prison, hundreds of Christians could not hear any noises from the surface. In fact, the guards wore cloth shoes so that prisoners would not discern when they entered or departed.

TRIBULATION OUTSIDE OF DEMOCRACY

After some 8 years, most Christians could not remember any Bible verses or even remember how to read and write. Wurmbrand recounts some of the methods of torture that were inflicted upon Christians.

In one instance, during 4 days, fellow Christians were tied to crosses, placed on the ground while prisoners beat them to death. After their bodies were beaten, mutilated bodies were disfigured, the crosses were elevated so that the prisoners could now bow and worship these Christ's on the cross.

In another episode, guards forced open the mouths of prisoners and poured 3 tablespoons of salt down their throats and they were forced to sit on the ground with no water for what seemed an eternity.

Wurmbrand describes other methods of torture that included large groups of Christians sitting on the floor for hours without being able to move. If you closed your eyes or even leaned over to rest, you were beaten.

Not only does pastor Wurmbrand tell a ghoulish story but in 1966, during his testimony before the US Senate in Washington, he removed his shirt to show the world his torture-ridden body. Under the Geneva Convention Article 5, torture was against international law but that did not stop his persecutors.

What the Senate saw that day shocked the committee; massive deep depressions all over his torso where large chunks of flesh were ripped from his body including below his waste. Russians used hot irons, bars, and sticks to antagonize and coerce prisoners to reject Jesus Christ.

DEFINITION OF BIBLICAL TRIBULATION

Democracy in the USA shelters most believers from the atrocities that are being committed against Christians in the Middle East. While protected by our military here in the USA, it's easy for opponents to declare that the tribulation days according to scriptures have not begun. One of the greatest deceptions among biblical scholars today is the doctrine of tribulation, great tribulation, and wrath of God in the Bible, more specifically the book of Revelation.

From a biblical standpoint, tribulation refers to the suffering of God's servants in scriptures. Jesus made it clear that in the world we the Saints would suffer tribulation but be of good cheer (John 16:33). Likewise, great tribulation is arguably an extension of tribulation but at a more intense level. I also assert that tribulation in general, refers to a time of persecution of the Saints. Many today have bought into the argument that it is a time of tribulation of ungodly men. Certain schools of thought erroneously teach that tribulation is a consequence for those that reject God.

When the scripture refers to tribulation 98% of the time, it comes from the Greek G2347 "thlipsis" meaning:

1. Pressing, pressing together, pressure
2. Oppression, affliction, tribulation, distress, straits

In fact, in more than 98 percent of scriptures, tribulation refers to the persecution of believers, or Christian Saints. Matthew reveals that the days of great tribulation should be shortened for the elect's sake so that man might still be saved (Mt 24:21,22). In the same context, Matthew doesn't even mention god-haters. Ostensibly, tribulation means to rub together, or polish. Most scholars know that historically, God has always allowed His chosen people to be tried in the furnace of afflictions at the hands of unbelievers. Shortly, I will cite some scriptures to demonstrate this point.

THE SAINTS IN TRIBULATION

In the book of Revelation, the word *thlipsis* is used four times referring to the suffering and persecution of the Saints of God, not unbelievers. As I noted in former chapters, that while Christian Saints have experienced tribulation during a 7 year period, ungodly men will be judged. Notwithstanding, scholars of the scriptures understand that although unbelievers die during tribulation, they are not the ones that are being tested.

At the opening of the chapter, I conveyed a true story about a pastor named Wurmbrand. Invariably, he is an example of a Christian who suffered tribulation by means of torture. It actually sounds ridiculous to attach the word "tribulation" to someone who has purposefully committed sinful acts against humanity and God. People that commit acts of genocide against a race of people are not recompensed tribulation but sentenced to death. Furthermore, if great tribulation is an extension of tribulation, then while the Saints are persecuted, unbelievers will be judged and sentence. In fact, believers are the ones that are tested during great tribulation at the hand of the beast, dragon and false prophet. Moreover, when you read Luke 21 you will discover that he is writing to gentile believers who are suffering during tribulation.

A CHRISTIAN SUFFERS IN TRIBULATION

While conducting an underground church at the inception of Communism in Romania, Richard Wurmbrand was kidnapped by Communist Russia and taken to an underground prisoner of war camp. In this scenario, while the guards were perpetrators, he was persecuted. Not only did he experience tribulation underground by his torturers, but he experienced angelic visitations as well.

Perhaps while living in this country, it's not easy to relate to tribulation unless we speak metaphorically, but please show me in the book of Revelation during the 7 years of tribulation, where ungodly men are being tortured day and night.

I'm sure that opponents would agree, not all things in the book of Revelation are literal but many things have a symbolic meaning. Conversely, anger, great wrath and vengeance is reserved for ungodly men that shake their fists at God each time a plague, disease, or death is released from heaven.

Contrary to public opinion, Christians experience tribulation from the persecution of the beast or ungodly, unrepentant men.

TRIBULATION V.S. WRATH

Tribulation of Christian Saints has already begun in the form of the trilateral union, one world system, political correctness, homosexual agenda, American Civil Liberties Union (ACLU), Mohammed's Islam, removal of Christian traditions in America, and the demise of the protection of marriage act to mention.

TRIBULATION HAS ALREADY BEGUN

I was shocked the day I read the following headline in the daily news, "Does the Army consider the Tea Party and Christians a terrorist threat?" It's unfortunate like so many other prominent events that have occurred in USA history, including *Roe vs. Wade, Pearl Harbor, Assassination of John F. Kennedy, Columbine High School, Virginia Tech and same-sex marriage that* Christians tend to be asleep at the wheel while persecution unfolds right before their eyes. Apparently, the mentality today is likened to "pie in the sky in the sweet by and by". The signs of tribulation are occurring all around us. Case in point, just recently, I was reading an article from a leading conservative news media that occurred on October 23, 2013, that stated:

> "Soldiers attending a pre-deployment briefing at Fort Hood say they were told that evangelical Christians and members of the Tea Party were a threat to the nation and that any soldier donating to those groups would be subjected to punishment under the Uniform Code of Military Justice."

It's hard to imagine that this occurred on the very base, Fort Hood, where a Muslim by the name of Nidal Malik Hasan, a U.S. Army major and psychiatrist, carried out a terrorist attack killing 13 soldiers and wounding 30 others? The article continued by saying:

> "On the very base that was the site of mass murder carried out by a radicalized Muslim soldier, it is

astonishing that it is evangelical groups that are being identified as a 'threat'."

Can you imagine the US military coercing soldiers not to donate to Christian organizations? Christian soldiers are losing their religious liberties under this administration in 2013. Without a shadow of a doubt, there is a blatant bias in America against Evangelical Christians, but, when dealing with Islam, people tend to walk in denial turning a deaf ear. In my opinion, Americans dread the sight of Islam, but despise what many label as intolerant Christians. Unfortunately, America did not truly understand the nature of terrorism until it targeted the twin towers in New York, on September 11, 2001, the epitome of American prowess.

It's a travesty that even the President of the United States has a problem with the term Islamic Terrorists, preferring the term enemy combatants.

Apparently, the 44th president is poised to change times and the laws in favor of secular humanism. What is the impact of these negative opinions towards Christian Saints? You guessed it, tribulation and persecution from the government towards a single religious group at an unprecedented level. It's interesting that the liberal news media will make discrimination towards homosexuals headline news but when a Christian cries discrimination, it's almost like we deserve it. Truly we shall witness hate crimes against Christians in the very near future. Laws will be amended to control the language used during a sermon claiming discrimination. Get ready to be incarcerated if you're not politically correct while preaching the gospel.

DAY OF VENGENCE OF OUR GOD

Great Tribulation is defined as the mounting of warring factions of ungodly men against Christian Saints beginning as evident in Rev 12:17 where the system-beast makes war against the "remnant of her seed" meaning the seed of the woman. Part of the remnant is Christian Saints. War refers not just to persecution but the threat of death to anyone who does not worship the beast's one world system. The day of vengeance of God is mentioned in many places in scriptures.

> "2To proclaim the acceptable year of the LORD, and the day of vengeance of our God; to comfort all that mourn."
> --Isa 61:2

> "5Behold, I will send you Elijah the prophet before the coming of the great and dreadful day of the LORD: "
> --Mal 4:5

If there is one area where most theologians agree it would be the period of time where God pours out His wrath on unbelievers. Moreover, many schools of thought agree that the day of God's wrath commences in Revelation Chapter 16 when the angels prepare to pour out His wrath. Hence, from Chapter 16-19 we see the wrath of God poured out upon the beast, the horn, the false prophet, and the dragon or devil.

> "11And I saw heaven opened, and behold a white horse; and He that sat upon him was called Faithful and True, and in righteousness He doth judge and make war."
> --Rev 19:11.

The King of Kings and the Lord of Lords, in battle dress, with a two-edged sword out of His mouth, has just arrived to execute vengeance flanked by old and New Testament Saints at the end of tribulation.

Just prior to the appearing of the white horse, all the saints are gathered to celebrate the marriage supper of the Lamb.

> "9And he saith unto me, Write, Blessed are they which are called unto the marriage supper of the Lamb. And he saith unto me, these are the true sayings of God."
> --Rev 19:9.

Now that the Saints have been caught up in the air to meet the Lord, God can begin to deal with the remaining Gentiles. Many of the Old Testament Saints that came out of their graves to witness at Jerusalem were already resurrected on the day of His resurrection.

In many ways, God is unlike many Christians today. Even during the day of vengeance, God gives ungodly men a last opportunity to repent. Yet instead of repent, men raise their fists towards God and curse Him to His face. While the Saints are in tribulation, Christian men are martyred at the hands of ungodly men that have the mark of the beast. On the other hand, during the day of vengeance; unbelievers die at the hand of God. While it is true some holy men may die during great tribulation, their ultimate destination will be heaven as opposed to unbelievers that will die as the vials are being poured out.

WHO SUFFERS DURING THE DAY OF VENGENCE

It is abundantly clear that unbelievers, not the Saints of God, die during the wrath of God with the ultimate destination of death, hell and the grave. In fact, hell is only a temporary holding place for unrepentant sinners.

> "15 And out of His mouth goeth a sharp sword, that with it
> He should smite the nations: and He shall rule them with
> a rod of iron: and He treadeth the winepress of the
> fierceness and wrath of Almighty God." --Rev 19:15

At this point, men are given a chance to repent before they are destroyed, with the ultimate judgment to experience the second death. It is true that during tribulation of those days or great tribulation, the same Gentiles or "one world order" that persecutes the Saints, are given a last opportunity to repent before the day of wrath. But when the great tribulation of the Saints ends, and later caught up to meet the Lord in the air, then the day of wrath shall begin at an unprecedented level. Revelation 19 reveals the destruction of ungodly human life after the second advent of Christ.

> "[17]And I saw an angel standing in the sun; and he cried with a loud voice, saying to all the fowls that fly in the midst of heaven, Come and gather yourselves together unto the supper of the great God;"   --Rev 19:17

The scene on earth is as the Lord's wrath unfolds with the eating of the flesh of kings, captains, mighty men, horses, riders and the flesh all bond, free, small and great. There is a stark difference between the tribulation of those days, where the Saints are tribulated by the Gentile beast or false prophet before the day of vengeance and wrath of our God.

When you seek God for revelation, interestingly enough, several things are at play simultaneously,

1. Tribulation of the Saints through persecution
2. The unmitigated suffering of the Saints
3. Pouring out of the wrath of God
4. Catching away of the Saints
5. The death of unrepentant men
6. The judgment of those whose names are not written in the Lamb's book of life

> "[1]And I heard a great voice out of the temple saying to the seven angels, Go your ways, and pour out the vials of the wrath of God upon the earth."   --Rev 16:1

While the beast persecutes the Saints, the angels are pouring out the vials that give men a chance to repent, and if they do not many are killed.

I will not reiterate this in its entirety because I mentioned this in another chapter entitled "The Saints during Tribulation" but you will notice that not all men die during tribulation of the

Saints. The Apostle John witnesses an innumerable multitude of blood washed believers coming out of great tribulation.

THE SEAL PROTECTS THE SAINTS IN TRIBULATION

> "¹⁴And I said unto him, Sir, thou knowest. And he said to me, These are they which came out of great tribulation, and have washed their robes, and made them white in the blood of the Lamb."   --Rev 7:14

Any idea how it is possible for any Saint to survive tribulation? We can get an idea when looking at the Jewish believers in Revelation 7.

> "³Saying, Hurt not the earth, neither the sea, nor the trees, till we have sealed the servants of our God in their foreheads."   --Rev 7:3

> "¹And I looked, and, lo, a Lamb stood on the mount Zion, and with him an hundred forty and four thousand, having His Father's name written in their foreheads."   --Rev 14:1

> "4And it was commanded them that they should not hurt the grass of the earth, neither any green thing, neither any tree; but only those men which have not the seal of God in their foreheads."   --Rev 9:4

Here we find the name of their father written in the foreheads and the seal of God in the foreheads. Why is this significant? First, having the name of their God in the foreheads implies that they are God's remnant and are not servants of Satan. By examination, they do not have 666 upon the palm of their hands. And second because the seal of God is stamped into the foreheads. The seal serves as protection before the wind blows during the tribulation of those days. In fact, not even the locusts

200

that come from the bottomless pit can harm the Saints of God during great tribulation.

Think of it as the blood over the doorpost of each Hebrew house in Egypt as the death angel passed over to kill the first born of every Egyptian. This great innumerable multitude that could not be counted of all nations, all ethnicities, kindred's, people, and tongues that stood before the throne, and before the Lamb, are able to survive tribulation because they are marked by God's angel. Like the 144,000, so do Christian Saints bear the Seal of promise on their foreheads when they are baptized and filled with the Holy Ghost.

> "In whom ye also trusted, after that ye heard the word of truth, the gospel of your salvation: in whom also after that ye believed, ye were **sealed** with that Holy Spirit of **promise.**"   --Eph 1:13

Those that do not die physically but endure persecution of unrepentant men during the tribulation of those days, are protected by both the name of their God and the seal in their foreheads.

> "Him that overcometh will I make a pillar in the temple of my God, and he shall go no more out: and I will write upon him the name of my God, and the name of the city of my God, which is new Jerusalem, which cometh down out of heaven from my God: and I will write upon him my new name.:"   –Rev 3:12

Notice that the former scripture quote suggests that you don't need to be of Jewish descent to qualify to have the name of God written on your forehead. You just need to be someone that has overcome the wicked one.

To finalize this chapter, when Christ returns we see the armies in heaven following Him, some of these are the Saints that were caught up to meet the Lord in the air. But then who are the "camp of the Saints" that are surrounded in Revelations 20:9?

> " [9]And they went up on the breadth of the earth, and compassed the camp of the saints about, and the beloved city: and fire came down from God out of heaven, and devoured them. "   --Rev 20:9

I believe that the "camp of the saints" consists of all nations of godly men that have been washed in the blood of Jesus. These have the seal of God in the foreheads that are standing with the lamb on mount Zion. Empowered by the Lamb, the Saints take back the kingdom with violence of praise and worship. Remember what James spoke in Acts 15, that God was restoring the tabernacle of David that had fallen and that all nations would serve in Jerusalem.

Contrary to public opinion, during the battle of Armageddon, the Saints don't just stand around in heaven like a group of "good for nothings" in retirement but take back the kingdom from Satan with violence. The tabernacle of David, apart from the temple of Herod, was constructed on mount Zion. However, in that day, when the metaphoric Davidic temple is restored, it shall be a temple of praise which shall be critical in winning the final battle.

As Saints, the wrath of God has no effect because we are sealed in our foreheads. Don't be carried about by fears and phobias regarding the wrath of God, it can't touch a Saint. For that reason, we need to put emphasis on preparation, not looking for an escape from wrath. Preparation for what? The Saints need to be equipped with warfare praise during the battle so that we can effectively win souls for Christ during one of the most critical times in the history of Christianity.

Chapter 12

THE SAINT'S
DURING TRIBULATION

"[11]And He gave some apostles; and some, prophets; and some, evangelists; and some, pastors and teachers; [12]For the perfecting of the Saints, for the work of the ministry, for the edifying of the body of Christ"   --Eph 4:11, 12

"To all that be in Rome, beloved of God, called to be Saints: Grace to you and peace from God our Father, and the Lord Jesus Christ."   --Rom 1:7

Unlike the interpretation of the Catholic Church, in the first century, Saints, both Jew and Gentile, were living human beings who were called by the name of the Lord. Paul, by faith, called those that were predestined to serve the Lord, Saints.

In the first century model, the word Saints was commonly used to refer to Christians in the primitive church. Interestingly enough, during Paul's generation, there was no real distinction between a Jewish Saint and a Gentile Saint. When Islam came on the scene in 632AD, both Jews and Gentiles parted ways creating a major rift between brethren. Later, certain schools of thought started to develop the substitution doctrine metaphorically substituting the Gentiles for the Jews.

As we shall shortly see, in the next few quotes, the word Saints was understood to be a convert to Christianity in the primitive church by the authors of the New Testament.

> " [33]For God is not the author of confusion, but of peace, as in all churches of the saints"   --1 Cor 14:33

> "[15]I beseech you, brethren, ye know the house of Stephanas, that it is the first fruits of Achaia, and that they have addicted themselves to the ministry of the saints,"   --1 Cor 16:15

> "[1]Paul, an apostle of Jesus Christ by the will of God, and Timotheus our brother, [2]To the saints and faithful brethren in Christ which are at Colosse: Grace be unto you, and peace, from God our Father and the Lord Jesus Christ. "   --Col 1:1, 2

In fact, any person that converts to Christianity and is washed in the blood has the right to become both a son of God and a Saint of God. We shall soon see why the word Saint is so important and relevant to the tribulation of those days.

THE ELECT OR ELECTION OF GOD

Who are the elect or election of God? Are both Jews and Gentiles considered the elect of God? Consider the following references and notice that the words election, elect, and chosen are interchangeable between verses:

1. Jews

"For Jacob my servant's sake, and Israel mine **elect**"
--Isa 45:4

"As concerning the gospel, they are enemies for your
sakes:" but as touching the **election**, they are beloved for
the father's sakes"   --Rom 11:28

"Israel hath not obtained that which he seeketh, but the
election hath obtained it, and the rest were blinded"
                                                    --Rom 11:7

2. Christians

"According as He has **chosen** us in Him before the
foundation of the world"   --Eph 1:4, 5

"Put on therefore, as the **elect** of God, holy and beloved,
bowels of mercies"   --Col 3:12

"The church that is at Babylon (Rome) **elected** together
with you"   --1 Pet 5:13

Albeit during the middle ages, both Jews and Gentiles were
divided due to anti-Semitic views, all worshipped together in the
first century at the inception of the primitive church.
The etymology of the word church G1577 is derived from the
Greek word ἐκκλησία or ekklēsia meaning: *"to call out implying a
gathering of people called forth, i.e. the town meeting at Ephesus,
or Israel called out of Egypt."*

During the twentieth century, the word "church" applied
exclusively to gentile Christians to the exclusion of Jews, but in
the twenty-first century that has been slowly changing. In fact, by
excluding the Jews from church, they without us shall not be
made perfect and Christ will not come.

"Thou art Peter and upon this rock I shall build my
church and the gates of hell shall not prevail against it
"   -- Mt 16:18.

Church buildings were not constructed until the 4ᵗʰ century. Here Jesus is referring to His house which is us, not a building:

> "But Christ as a son over His own house, whose house are we, if we hold fast the confidence and the rejoicing of the hope firm unto the end"   --Heb 3:6

Ostensibly, the book of Revelation mentions the word churches in Revelation 1:11 "What thou seest, write in a book and send it unto the seven churches which are in Asia..." After chapter 3 of the book of Revelations, John does not mention the word church again until chapter 22. I submit that this chapter will prove that Christian Saints will go through tribulation as well as great tribulation until the tribes of the earth witness the clouds open and mourn "behold Faithful and True sitting on a white horse"(Rev 19:11-14).

CHURCH AGE IN TRIBULATIONS

In fact while in Rome, Peter endures tribulation while writing his two Epistles I & II Peter, before suffering martyrdom under Nero in AD 65. Again, John writes in the book of Revelation 1:9 "who also am your brother, and companion in tribulation", attempting to comfort the generations to come with revelation that tribulation will only continue to exacerbate with each passing year. Let's be honest, most things are not sudden by nature, there is always a slow progression. Sudden events would be an angelic visitation or when John said he saw the clouds open and behold a white horse. Great tribulation will not be a sudden event but gradual just like everything else in our existential realm of experience.

Most scholars of Revelation (meaning the disclosure of that which was previously hidden or unknown) know that in the book of Revelation, John only references the word "church" in chapters 1-3 and 22. What's the relevance? I propose that the focus on church diminishes while the emphasis on the Saints continues to increase until the white horse appears.

For the last two centuries, theologians have purported that since the words "church" or "Christian" are not used after Rev 3, it must infer a mystical "secret coming" referenced by 1 Thessalonians 4:16, 17.

> "[16] For the Lord himself shall descend from heaven with a shout, with the voice of the archangel, and with the trump of God: and the dead in Christ shall rise first: [17] Then we which are alive and remain shall be caught up together with them in the clouds, to meet the Lord in the air: and so shall we ever be with the Lord."

Notice the following four essential elements of the return of Christ:

1. Dissension
2. Voice of the angel
3. Sound of trump
4. Gathering the Saints together

But no scholar with any accuracy has been able to correlate the above four essential elements to a timeline within chapters 4-18,20-22 of Revelation, and when any attempt is made, it is mere conjecture. However, these four essential elements are crystal clear in the book of Matthew 24 verses 29-31:

> "[29]Immediately after the tribulation of those days shall the sun be darkened, and the moon shall not give her light, and the stars shall fall from heaven, and the powers of the heavens shall be shaken: [30]And then shall appear the sign of the Son of Man in heaven: and then shall all the tribes of the earth mourn, and they shall see the Son of Man coming in the clouds of heaven with power and great glory. [31]And He shall send His angels with a great sound of a trumpet, and they shall gather together His

elect from the four winds, from one end of heaven to the other."

Note that immediately after the tribulation, we find the four identical elements of this coming:

1. Dissension
2. Voice of the angel
3. Sound of trump
4. Gathering the Saints together

There is a transition taking place from Church to a Saints movement (Age) between Revelation chapters 4 - 22. Technically we don't see the church in heaven but the temple of God is filled with Christian Saints.

UNITY OF BOTH GENTILES AND JEWS IN TRIBULATION

As most biblical scholars are aware, both Messianic Jews and Gentiles served together in the primitive church of the first century. Apostle Paul writes the following in his letter to the Ephesians:

> "[11]Wherefore remember, that ye being in time past Gentiles in the flesh, who are called uncircumcision by that which is called the Circumcision in the flesh made by hands; [12]That at that time ye were without Christ, being aliens from the commonwealth of Israel, and strangers from the covenants of promise, having no hope, and without God in the world: [13]But now in Christ Jesus ye who sometimes were far off are made nigh by the blood of Christ."   -- Eph 2:11-13

Prior to the New Testament, salvation was exclusively for the elect, Hebrew/Jew alike, while the Gentiles were aliens from the commonwealth of Israel. As a stranger, unless you converted under the Law of Moses or were converted to Judaism, the only option that remained was eternal separation from God.

When Jesus died on the cross, those that were foreigners, as wild branches, were grafted into the vine by the blood of Jesus Christ. Furthermore, Paul writes in Ephesians 2: 14:

"[14]For He is our peace, who hath made both one, and hath broken down the middle wall of partition between us; [15]Having abolished in His flesh the enmity, even the law of commandments contained in ordinances; for to make in Himself of twain one new man, so making peace; "

The inference is that now both Jews and Gentiles are made one new man. Effectively, Jesus had destroyed the enmity between both camps thereby reconciling the Gentiles unto God. What does this have to do with the price of beans in China? Reality is that it has far reaching implications that are ignored by biblical scholars.

However, the unity between Jews and Gentiles did not endure the Roman Empire. At one point, perhaps during the Counsel of Nicaea, Christians began to part company with the Jews. God obviously allowed it and soon animosity developed between the two groups. Further separation occurred after the founding of Islam in 632 AD. Moreover, anti-Semitism was widespread during the 3rd Reich Nazi Germany era when Hitler insanely concluded that it was his destiny to cleanse Germany of the Jewish population by genocide that killed some 6 million Jews.

However, today, there is a movement that is reconciling both Christians and Jews together. A Jew that converts to Christianity is called a messianic Jew. Albeit some of the customs differ in the church culture, but nevertheless, both Jew and Gentile are washed in the same blood of Jesus.

I submit that God is authoring the fulfillment of Ephesians Chapter 2 back to its original state. Case in point, one of the most well knows Jews are evangelists like Benny Hinn who has converted to Christianity. For the sake of this writing, I acknowledge that he does not necessarily call himself a messianic Jew but theoretically Hinn is a messianic Jew or better yet a Christian. I've heard reports that many Jews believe that Jesus is the Messiah and are converting to Christianity. According to Romans 11:25, Paul writes that Israel was blinded until the fullness of the Gentiles which correlates to Peter's vision of the sheet coming down from heaven by the four corners containing unclean animals (Acts 10:11). God made it clear that the Gentiles were clean according to this vision. God grafted the Gentiles into the vine while the Israelites were removed temporarily to provoke jealousy. But Israel cannot be perfected without the manifestation of the fullness of the Gentiles first.

Today certain circles have developed a substitution doctrine where God has removed the natural branches from the vine permanently. This notion is just not true, Israel is being reconnected to the vine and hence one with the Gentile nation. Paul the apostle in Romans 11:25 declared that Israel has been blinded for 2000 years until the fullness of the Gentiles has been completed:

> " [25]For I would not, brethren, that ye should be ignorant of this mystery, lest ye should be wise in your own conceits; that blindness in part is happened to Israel, until the fullness of the Gentiles be come in. "   –Rom 11:25

Now that the fullness of the Gentiles is presently being fulfilled, signs of unity between Jew and Gentile have been coming to fruition around the world. Albeit a large group of Jews living in Israel remain blind, but the process of grafting them into the vine has already started.

For the last 2,000 years, God has been taking out, and consecrating a people for His name.

> "[14]Simeon hath declared how God at the first did visit the Gentiles, to take out of them a people for His name. [15]And to this agree the words of the prophets; as it is

written, [16]After this I will return, and will build again the tabernacle of David, which is fallen down; and I will build again the ruins thereof, and I will set it up: [17]That the residue of men might seek after the Lord, and all the Gentiles, upon whom my name is called, saith the Lord, who doeth all these things."   –Acts 15:14-16

DAVID'S TEMPLE OF PRAISE IS UNDER CONSTRUCTION

Recently, there have been negotiations in Israel to begin rebuilding the temple in Jerusalem. Not only is there a remnant of Jews alive today, but there is also a remnant of Christians as well. I believe that Christians as well as Jews shall descend on Jerusalem and participate in the process of rebuilding the temple of David. Metaphorically, we understand the temple of David, which is a temple of praise, has been in the process of being rebuilt by the Gentiles who have learned how to access God by entering into the Holy of Holies with their praise and worship. Praise and worship, one of the "lost art forms" during the dark ages, was restored during the restoration of the Prophetic ministry. As prophets in the early 20th century like William Branham began to utter revelation, prophets sent by God revealed the need for restoration of praise and worship during church service. In today's church services, praise and worship are the centerpiece that initiates every Protestant and Catholic service. I said Protestant because most scholars understand that Christianity is divided between both Catholics and Protestants.

There is a movement within Israel today and around the world where Jews are converting to Christianity and collectively, slowly but surely, becoming twain in one body, hence, the Saints of God. And Saints of God, both Jews and Gentiles, this one body shall take back the kingdom from the little horn referenced in the book of Dan 7:18-21:

" **18**But the saints of the Most High shall **take** the kingdom, and **possess** the kingdom forever, even forever and ever. **19**Then I would know the truth of the fourth beast, which was diverse from all the others, exceeding dreadful, whose teeth were of iron, and his nails of brass; which devoured, brake in pieces, and stamped the residue with his feet; **20**And of the ten horns that were in his head, and of the other which came up, and before whom three fell; even of that horn that had eyes, and a mouth that spake very great things, whose look was more stout than his fellows. **21**I beheld, and the same horn made war with the saints, and prevailed against them."

TAKING THE KINGDOM BY FORCE

It is abundantly clear that God empowers His Saints to take back the kingdom by force from the beast and the horn in the books of Daniel and Revelation. For this reason, God completed the rebuilding of the prophetic and apostolic office because the Saints will need leadership in the middle of tribulation.

Daniel is a book of eschatology written in Aramaic, the language of Jesus. Many scholars hold that eschatological references of the word Saints during great tribulation must refer exclusively to Hebrew Jews because theoretically Jesus would have already raptured the dead in Christ. However, that would contradict the writings of Paul the apostle to the Ephesians in Chapter 2 where he wrote that "He might reconcile both unto God in one body by the cross." Why would God wait until after tribulation or great tribulation to "reconcile" both Jews and Gentiles? Assuming that heaven is the ultimate destiny, there is no reference to the church, Jews or Gentiles in heaven, but they are called Saints!

Look, the wedding supper of the Lamb is referenced in Revelation 19:7-9, in the same chapter where the heavens open, and a white horse appears. If you've come out of great tribulation, and you've washed your robe white in the blood of the lamb, at that point you belong to Christ. Does it really matter in which chapter of the book of Revelation that your robe is washed white in the blood of the lamb?

Look, in Revelation 14:1, John makes it clear when he says, "a Lamb stood on the mount Zion, and with him stood a hundred and forty four thousand, having his Father's name written in their foreheads." These can't be grafted in until the fullness or completion of the Gentiles occurs. I submit, Paul makes it clear in Ephesians 2 that the "law of commandments in ordinances was abolished making in himself of twain one new man."

When Jesus steps onto Mount Olivet, crosses over to the east gate of the temple, at that moment, all Jews and Gentiles that have made their garments white in the blood of the lamb will be considered sons, the elect, twain one new man. All will have one title, Saint.

Listen, both Jews and Gentiles are resurrected in the first resurrection, there are no secret resurrections for Christians or Jews. In fact, there is a great distinction between catching away and the rapture! When I studied at ORU, one of the theological questions asked in exams was "name the three theories of the tribulation regarding the second coming." There are three theories, pre-tribulation, mid-tribulation, and post-tribulation. The answer included not just one, but all three answers.

For the Saints of God to be one body through tribulation, then the valid doctrine would be post-tribulation, in other words, Christ's one and only coming in all of His glory (Rev 19:11). Since there is only one advent of Christ, then the thief in the night clause must be related to Revelation 19:11. If truth be told, Christ cannot come as a thief in the night for Saints who are watching and praying as sons of the light.

I mention here in this book that the first publication of the rapture occurred in 1811 to a man by the name of Emmanuel Lacunza, a Jesuit priest. He introduced the doctrine in his book entitled "The Venida de la Messiah en Gloria y Majestad."

THE SAINTS OF GOD

OUTSIDE OF DEMOCRACY CHRISTIANS SUFFER TRIBULATION

After reading his work, I concluded that the rapture is a man-made doctrine. Did you ever ask yourself why the dire need for the existence of the rapture doctrine? The rapture doctrine implies pre-tribulation, where the catching away infers no particular timetable, just speculation. Let's be clear, Emmanuel Lacunza's publication inferred a pre-tribulation event. My opinion is that we, the Saints of God, live in a fight or flight society, no one wants to survive the great tribulation. No one enjoys being denied the right to buy and sell. Who wants to be on the earth when the seven trumpets sound and the vials are poured out?

If truth be told, we are already in tribulation, open your eyes. Look, Christians that confess Christ in Pyongyang North Korea under Kim Jong-un are taken to political prisoner of war camps as spies and simply disappear. Furthermore, we can clearly see that Democracy in the United States mitigates the full impact of tribulation or even the initial signs of great tribulation. As I so eloquently detailed the meaning of tribulation in another chapter, it is now apparent that atheists, agnostics, and worldly god-haters don't experience tribulation, but the wrath of God.

Christians, God's precious Saints suffer during tribulation. Wrath or the terrible day of the Lord found in chapters 19 & 20 of Revelation is reserved for ungodly men who explicitly will not submit to God even while murrain disease comes from the heavens.

Look, the fact remains, if you want to have eternal life, you must be a part of the first resurrection, there are no options for the 144,000 that have been sealed by God. During tribulation, Jews will continue to receive Jesus as their savior and as such, they will be grafted back into the olive vine during tribulation. Jesus appears in Revelation chapter 19, and finally in chapter 20 the first resurrection occurs. The following key verse tells us that the

214

Jews are only temporarily separated from the vine which is Jesus in Romans 11:25:

"²⁵For I would not brethren that ye should be ignorant of
this mystery, lest ye should be wise in your own
conceits; that blindness in part is happened to Israel, until
the fullness of the Gentiles be come in. "

It's clear that the division between Gentiles and Jews is temporary until the fullness of the Gentiles occurs and we obtain mercy to believe in Jesus through their unbelief. Fact is, many Jews are receiving Jesus and becoming one with Christians right now, every second of each day.

Look, the Bible does not make any distinction between Jewish Saints and Gentile Saints. It's utterly ridiculous to carry this to a conclusion that there are Jews and Gentiles in heaven. In heaven they are all simply Saints, not Greeks nor Jews, male or female, bond or free, just Saints of God.

It's undeniable that the Jewish remnant will join Gentiles during the great tribulation period. Regarding the 144,000 Hebrew tribes that are sealed, in order to be saved, they too must wash their robes in the blood of the lamb and be called Saints. Christ is that lamb and anyone who is washed in His blood is a Christian. The 144,000 that are on mount Zion with the Lamb are part of the remnant that Paul references in Romans 11:5 that endure great tribulation. Christians are the other part of the remnant.

BLOOD WASHED JEWISH AND GENTILE SAINTS

I think that theologians have stayed up late at night trying to validate the rapture doctrine. We know that there is only one way, the truth and the life, and that there is none other name under heaven given for salvation by which we must be saved (Acts 4:12). Even though the Jews today are grafted into the natural vine does not mean they gain access to heaven by some other means. Every man must be born again by the blood of Jesus. The

215

divisions between Jews and Gentiles are changing by the day. There are more Messianic Jews today than ever before. I don't see two different events or two different resurrections, one for gentile Christians and the other for Messianic Jews. I believe it is an all-inclusive catching away that includes both Jews and Gentiles during great tribulation. Hence by definition we can conclude that there is neither Jew nor Gentile, male nor female, bond or free, for we are all one in Christ, for as many of us (Jew or Gentile) has been baptized into Christ, we have all put on Christ (Gal 3:28).

THE ARMIES OF HEAVEN THAT FOLLOW CHRIST

What's been left unspoken for generations is the fact that right now there are a group of Old Testament Saints in heaven. When did that happen? How did they get there? After Jesus died, the Bible proclaims that the veil of the temple was ripped down the center, the graves were opened as a sign and many Old Testament Saints that slept were resurrected. It should be also evident then when the Second Apocalyptic Advent of Christ occurs in the future, the armies that follow Him from heaven are composed of these Saints. We then must conclude that on the third day after these Old Testament Saints were resurrected and finished witnessing that Jesus was the son of God, they then joined Christ in heaven.

> "[52]And the graves were opened; and many bodies of the saints which slept arose, [53]And came out of the graves after His resurrection, and went into the holy city, and appeared unto many."   --Mt 27:52,53

Please reference (Deuteronomy 33:2, Judges 1:14) where the writer pens that the "Lord will come with ten thousand Saints." I want to show you how Matthew understood the word tribulation in Matthew Chapter 24. Notice in verse 21, Matthew uses the words "great tribulation" but later in the same context, he uses the word "tribulation" prior to seeing the Son of Man coming in the clouds of heaven. Great in the Greek simply means "mega", or "mega tribulation."

TRIBULATION VS GREAT TRIBULATION

The events taking place in great tribulation are the same as tribulation; it is the persecution of the Saints from Chapters 4-22. Not only are the Jews considered to be elect, but we as gentiles are the elect of God also.

> "21 For then shall be **great tribulation**, such as was not since the beginning of the world to this time, no, nor ever shall be. 22 And except those days should be shortened, there should no flesh be saved: but for the elect's sake those days shall be shortened. 23 Then if any man shall say unto you, Lo, here is Christ, or there; believe it not. 24 For there shall arise false christs, and false prophets, and shall show great signs and wonders; insomuch that, if it were possible, they shall deceive the very elect. 25 Behold, I have told you before. 26 Wherefore if they shall say unto you, Behold, he is in the desert; go not forth: behold, he is in the secret chambers; believe it not. 27 For as the lightning cometh out of the east, and shineth even unto the west; so shall also the coming of the Son of Man be. 28 For wheresoever the carcass is, there will the eagles be gathered together. 29 Immediately after the **tribulation** of those days shall the sun be darkened, and the moon shall not give her light, and the stars shall fall from heaven, and the powers of the heavens shall be shaken: 30 And then shall appear the sign of the Son of Man in heaven: and then shall all the tribes of the earth mourn, and they shall **see the Son of Man coming in the clouds of heaven** with power and great glory."

The authors of the New Testament make reference to the Saints of God approximately 46 times and 13 times in the book of Revelation depending on your translation.

THE SAINTS OF GOD TAKE CENTER STAGE

I happen to believe that the King James translation is the most authentic minus some of the italicized words by authors like C. I. Scofield. Paul the Apostle, perhaps the greatest contributor to the New Testament, explicitly declares that he will minister to the Christian Jewish Saints at Jerusalem (Rom 15:25). But be mindful that on the day of Pentecost, those men that were blessed to experience the outpouring of the Holy Ghost were both Jews and Gentiles from every nation.

> "[9]Parthians, and Medes, and Elamites, and the dwellers in Mesopotamia, and in Judaea, and Cappadocia, in Pontus, and Asia, [10]Phrygia, and Pamphylia, in Egypt, and in the parts of Libya about Cyrene, and strangers of Rome, Jews and proselytes, [11]Cretes and Arabians, we do hear them speak in our tongues the wonderful works of God. "

Can you imagine that in Acts 2 even Arabs who would later be deceived by Muhammad, a religious, political, and military leader, would also be converted and witness the promise of the Holy Spirit?

But let's reason together, do you really believe that Paul would allow a Saint to remain a Jew without converting him or her to Christianity? It's unconscionable. Moreover, the first century primitive church had no division between Gentile and Jewish Christians. Apart from some traditions, they all worshipped together. Paul makes his position emphatically clear with statements such as "to all that be in Rome, beloved of God, called to be saints: Grace to you and peace from God our Father, and the Lord Jesus Christ" (Romans 1:7). Even when Paul returns from his journey back to Jerusalem, he writes " [25] But now I go unto Jerusalem to minister unto the saints"(Romans 15:25). Hence, not only had the Gentiles from Rome become Saints, but those in Jerusalem whether Jews or Gentiles were also converted by Paul when he preached the gospel of Christ.

One of the first clues that the bride of Christ suffers in tribulation is the prayers of the Saints that come before God in Revelation 8:3. We know that the prayers are not from heaven because the Saints in heaven are not praying; they are worshipping God day and night. During tribulation however, the presence of church is evident when the angel offers incense in the golden censer with the prayers of the (living) Saints before the throne (Rev 8:3). It's a travesty that mainstream theology teaches that the Saints are only Messianic Jews and not Gentiles saved through tribulation. But this doctrine is inaccurate for at least the first 3 ½ years of tribulation.

Back a few chapters, in (Rev 5:8), notice again that the vials are full of incense which are the "prayers of the Saints", Jews and Christians, but in verse 9 and 10, some translations erroneously imply that the song that twenty four elders sing around the throne refers to them, when in reality their new song refers to the Saints. Erroneously, some translations use the antecedents "us" and "we" like King James, while other versions employ antecedents "them" and "they" referring to the Saints:

> "You purchased men unto God from every tribe and language and people and nation. And you have made them (Saints) a kingdom (royal race) and priests to our God, and they (Saints) shall reign [as kings] over the earth."   —AMP

The Darby translation is similar:

> "And they sing a new song, saying, Thou art worthy to take the book, and to open its seals; because thou hast been slain, and hast redeemed to God, by thy blood, out of every tribe, and tongue, and people, and nation, and made them (Saints) to our God "kings and priests"; and they (Saints) shall reign over the earth."

Furthermore, BIB 101 in seminary school illuminates the Bible student with the knowledge that Revelation 1:6 refers to Christian Saints:

> "And hath made us "kings and priests" unto God and His Father; to Him [be] glory and dominion for ever and ever. Amen." —Rev 1:6

So where does great tribulation begin anyhow? I believe that great tribulation begins in Revelation Chapter 12:14 where the author says the women will fly into a place where she is nourished for a time, and times, and half a time (Rev 12:14).

Albeit I don't believe the book of Revelation is in chronological order, please note that Revelation 12:1-17 is at the halfway point within the 22 chapters of the book of Revelation.

SAINTS PLAY A KEY ROLE IN THE BOOK OF REVELATION

Invariably throughout the Bible, God has always had an army to confront His enemies. From the Bible we know two things:

1. For though we walk in the flesh, we do not war after the flesh; Our weapons of warfare are not carnal but mighty through God to the pulling down of strong holds; casting down imaginations and every high thing that exalteth itself against the knowledge of God -- 2 Cor 10:4,5

2. Christ is preparing His bride without spot or wrinkle for the marriage supper of the lamb. --Eph 5:27, --Rev 19:9

Several things are happening today. Not only is God raising up an army of Saints, but He completed the rebuilding of the Fivefold offices, and continues to use Fivefold leaders, or generals, to impart, and equip Christian Saints for some eternal purpose. But for what purpose?

If Christ comes tomorrow, Rev 19:11, what purpose did discipleship training and evangelical training serve? A similar question would be, why do we as leaders oppress believers with huge financial burdens such as 10,000 sq ft temples if the advent of Jesus might occur tomorrow? There can only be one explanation, God is preparing an army of believers that will participate in the end-time revival campaigns. I can imagine that in part God knows that His people will need to be equipped, empowered and anointed for the tribulation period.

THE WOMAN IN REVELATION 12 IS THE CHURCH

As I previously mentioned, Apostle John says in Rev 1:9 "John your brother in tribulation." John who was in tribulation on the Island of Patmos, was consoling Christians for the centuries to come.

In Revelation 12:1-5, a great wonder appears in heaven, a woman clothed with the sun trailing to give birth to a man child, Jesus Christ. Understand that the women is fed for 1260 days or 3 ½ years then the dragon makes war with her. If the word "Woman" is metaphorically Mary, Israel or the Christian Church then the man child is metaphorically Christ. In the same context, Satan is cast down from heaven with great wrath against the Saints of God. Satan a.k.a Lucifer is both jealous and angry because he lost his former position as a light-bearer. Since then, his sole desire has been to kill the remnant of her seed and appropriate their inheritance.

Now, the Bible stipulates that whosoever is born of God overcomes the world, (1 Jn 5:4) implicitly inferring that they, Christian Saints, have "overcome him (Satan) by the blood of the Lamb, and by the word of their testimony, and they loved not their lives unto the death."

I guess God has not set the stage for a "tiptoe through the tulips", isn't that right Tiny Tim? Every Bible scholar knows that Christian Saints have overcome him by the blood of the lamb, and within that same context, remnant of her seed (Rev 12:17) the offspring of Jesus or better yet, the Saints of God.

Just a sidebar, every week in churches across the nation, Saints stand up to declare "we overcome him by the blood of the lamb" yet if truth be told, hello, we are in the middle of the tribulation period. How can Christian Saints appropriate these words out of context if they are pre-tribulation believers? To be politically correct, if the pre-tribulation crowd wants to encourage themselves, technically, they should only apply scriptures from Revelation Chapters 1–4. However, this is not the case. It is further proof that as believers we extract any scripture out of context that is convenient, it's similar to "Soup de Jour", bad grammar but good gospel. Just like the precious Saint Benny Hinn, a Jew, became a Christian by the blood, only by the blood of Jesus may man have eternal life (John 5:19) so shall others become Christians during tribulation.

Let me highlight one very important key point. We are living in the day when the dragon was "wroth with the woman and went to make war with her remnant" (Rev 12:17). We are entering a season where the persecution or tribulation against believers will reach an unprecedented level, and while Christ will defend His people, we need to be equipped to fight with our weapons of warfare that are not carnal.

Revelation suggests that the eyes of leaders will open to begin developing prophetic apostolic teams for the purpose of evangelism but they first must understand grace, mantels and anointing for this generation. "I won't be here during tribulation" you say. Really? Did you ever consider what will happen when tribulation transitions into great tribulation? I believe that many Saints will become disillusioned and discouraged ultimately leading to apostasy due to an inaccurate interpretation of the Bible? Due to the rapture doctrine, people were simply not prepared for great tribulation when it came.

While escaping before the vials are poured out and the seven trumpets sounds nice, a reality check reveals that we need to be equipped, prepared, anointed, and trained when the dragon empowers the beast to war with Christian Saints and to overcome them (Rev 13:7). Why fear? Remember, we win as denoted by the beast and false prophet being cast into the lake of fire.

Truly, this writing was not intended to be a book of revelation, but to empower Christian Saints through tribulation by informing them of their duty to prepare for maximum performance as the bride of Christ. This work was never intended to cause the readers to say "Wow" but to invoke a passion that says, "I want to demonstrate and walk in His glory.

THE SEAL OF GOD IN THEIR FORHEADS

Often in the Old Testament, a king would seal a decree by depressing his ring into the parchment making an official seal of authenticity. Beginning in Revelation Chapter 5, there are seven sealed books that only Christ can open. Bible students become aware of the fact that Christians have been established, anointed and sealed as Saints (2 Cor 1:21, 22). Moreover, Christian Saints are "sealed with that Holy Spirit of promise" (Eph 1:13). Paul admonishes the church at Ephesus to walk as believers and grieve not the Holy Spirit of God, whereby Christian Saints are sealed unto the day of redemption (Eph 4:30).

Not only does the seal represent ownership, but also provides protection during tribulation. John reveals that servants of God are sealed in their forehead against the wrath of God in tribulation (Rev 7:3,4) and the seal protects servants of God during great tribulation (Rev 9:4).

For those who are not sealed, apocalyptic events will be very lethal. John prophesizes that out of the bottomless pit will come locust like scorpions that are commanded to hurt those without the seal of God on their foreheads. Therefore, the seal in the forehead of the living Saints will serve as protection from every plague of God's wrath.

THE ENEMY IS PREPARING FOR A FIGHT

For years we have been duped by the religious institutions that since we are under grace somehow we don't have to fight anymore. That could not be any further from the truth, in fact Islam and other groups are ready to take the fight to our borders again. Many Saints sit around with the wool pulled over their eyes because they read somewhere that Jesus will snatch them from earth bald-headed before the trouble starts. And yet, look at the attacks America sustained on September 11, 2001, when two jets piloted by ten trained Islamic Al-Qaeda Terrorists slammed into the twin towers, symbolizing western prowess. Nevertheless, Christianity has been hood-winked by the rapture indoctrination since 1811, when Emmanuel Lacunza published his infamous book implying a "secret coming" of Jesus Christ. Prior to that date, the holy fathers were all apocalyptic mid/post-tribulation proponents. Heretofore, I have made a clear case that the Saints, believers in Jesus Christ, are in the midst of tribulation, and it will only be exacerbated as time goes on. Having said that, in Revelation 12:17 and 13:7, after the woman gives birth to a man child, the dragon becomes very angry with the woman. Since he obviously cannot damage her, he goes after the remnant of her seed. Of course, that "seed" is metaphorically Jesus Christ and the "remnant" represents the Saints of God.

> "[17]And the dragon was wroth with the woman, and went to make war with the remnant of her seed, which keep the commandments of God, and have the testimony of Jesus Christ."   --Rev 12:17

> "[7]And it was given unto him to make war with the saints, and to overcome them: and power was given him over all kindreds, and tongues, and nations"   --Rev 13:7

In Galatians 3:16, notice that the word "seed" is not plural but singular, symbolizing Christ, but the "remnant" of her seed, which

224

is her offspring, must refer to Christians or spiritual sons of Jesus Christ. Although Christ Jesus had no natural Jewish offspring, we are his brethren, heirs, and joint heirs by faith (Rom 8:17).

THE MARK OF THE BEAST IS 666

Moreover, Revelation 7:3 describes how Christian Saints shall be protected by the seal, survive the winds released to destroy the earth, sea and trees. In fact, the word "Saints" spans a wide gamut that includes Messianic Jews, Greeks, and Gentiles that converted to Christianity. When the gathering of Saints occurs, they come from all parts of the globe including Israel, Europe or even gentiles from America. Those however whose names are not written in the book of life, but have the number of his name 666 in their foreheads, will suffer the ultimate demise of death because they are not protected by the seal of God.

> " [16]And he causeth all, both small and great, rich and poor, free and bond, to receive a mark in their right hand, or in their foreheads"   --Rev 13:16

UNSUBSTANTIAL FEAR DURING TRIBULATION

Its unfortunate the amount of unsubstantiated fear that is propagated today regarding the "tribulation of those days" in seminary school. Albeit we see a multitude coming out of great tribulation (Rev 7:9) protected by the seal of God and washed by the blood of the Lamb, religion still persists in perpetuating fear that somehow no believer in Jesus can survive. This is just preposterous. If Christian Saints cannot survive during the tribulation of those days, who will preach to the nations? For this reason, God has sealed His people with the Holy Spirit of promise. The imprimatur or mark of His Spirit will protect every believer during tribulation.

Look, it's evident that the angel will have the everlasting gospel and will preach to them that dwell on the earth (Rev 14:6) but he is not the only one with a message. God commands John to "prophesy again before many peoples, nations, tongues and kings" (Rev 10:11). Moreover, the two witnesses also begin to prophesy for 3 ½ years during great tribulation. Furthermore, Daniel prophesied in Chapter 12:

> "³And they that be wise shall shine as the brightness of
> the firmament; and they that turn many to righteousness
> as the stars forever and ever."   --Dan 12:3

Guess who the wise are? The Saints of God will be very active with lots of celestial help to get the message across to the inhabitants of the earth during the tribulation of those days.

WITHOUT THE MARK YOU CAN'T BUY OR SELL

You're familiar with scripture that warns believers that if you don't have the number "666" the mark of the beast or some IC chip under your skin, that you cannot trade, buy or sell. However, did the children of Israel that walked through the wilderness during a 40-year period, barter, buy and sell? I submit that during the tribulation, Christian Saints with the seal of God in their foreheads do not have to worry about buying and selling for they are preserved and protected.

> "¹⁶ And he causeth all, both small and great, rich and
> poor, free and bond, to receive a mark in their right hand,
> or in their foreheads:¹⁷ And that no man might buy or
> sell, save he that had the mark, or the name of the beast,
> or the number of his name"   --Rev 13:16,17

Look, to be subject to deception, you must be living during the days of tribulation. Believers will not be hiding in a cloud somewhere, this is simply a fallacy.

Ever think for a moment how Israel survived in the wilderness with no food or water during forty years? Where did their food come from? Was it heaven? Did not their drink come from the rock that followed them through the wilderness which was Christ? But somehow, when trouble comes, we forget that we serve a super natural God. If truth be told, faith, the kind that is required to walk through the wilderness while trusting God has been forgotten. On one hand we boast that the children of Israel ate angel food, and on the other hand we are completely dependent on our bank account. I always believed that there was a heavenly storehouse, not of this earth, that could not be affected by the economy of our world.

> "[10]Bring ye all the tithes into the storehouse, that there may be meat in mine house, and prove me now herewith, saith the LORD of hosts, if I will not open you the windows of heaven, and pour you out a blessing, that there shall not be room enough to receive it."--Mal 3:10

Perhaps that is why pastors attempt to help you understand that giving is worship unto God. Whatsoever a man soweth he shall reap, or does that just apply outside of great tribulation? I guess we throw out all of the principles of established scripture during great tribulation? My Bible declares that "whatsoever a man soweth he shall reap" (Gal 6:7).

PROPHETS DURING TRIBULATION

Did you know that there shall be prophets of God prophesying during great tribulation? Scholars believe that John already prophesied to the nations when the book of Revelation was published fulfilling the prophetic word of the angel. However, I believe that the Apostle John will prophesy again at the end of the age.

> "[11]And he said unto me, Thou must prophesy again before many peoples, and nations, and tongues, and kings."   --Rev 10:11

Not only is the prophecy regarding the Apostle John unfulfilled but he is one of several prophets that will prophesy during tribulation. One of the most remarkable events from heaven is when God gives power to his two witnesses who shall prophesy for one thousand two hundred and threescore days (Rev 11:3).

LEADERSHIP DURING TRIBULATION

Like any military force, the army of God requires leadership logistics, reconnaissance, strategy, training, and deployment I submit that God will deploy some apostles, prophets, evangelists, pastors, and teachers for the edification and perfection of the Saints during tribulation. War denotes a fight, but to fight you need Generals, Captains, Sergeants, battle plans, and reconnaissance.

In fact, apostles, prophets, and evangelists were given to perfect the Saints (Eph 4:12) during tribulation, why else would he have completed the rebuilding these offices if the Saints did not need to enter strategic warfare?

During war, we will need leaders like apostles, prophets, evangelist, pastors and teachers, to equip, anoint, impart, direct, and prophesy to the troops as they fight a good warfare with the dragon and false prophets. Some battles will take place right in church during praise and worship where the Saints will learn to use their weapons of warfare that I have discussed in another chapter.

Since the Jewish nation will be perfected during tribulation, it will predominantly be the responsibility of Christian Saints to preach the gospel. In Revelation 7:9-14, there is a large multitude of all nations, and kindreds, and people, and tongues, standing before the throne, clothed with white robes that were washed in the blood of the lamb. Arguably, this multitude heard the gospel preached during tribulation.

SAINTS ARE EQUIPPED TO PREACH TO THE NATIONS

Revelation 7:14 validates this hypothesis by recording a great multitude of every nation that washed their robes making them white in the blood of the Lamb (Christ) thereby becoming Christians Saints. Let's be perfectly clear, whether pre-tribulation or post-tribulation, any man washed in the blood of Jesus is a bona fide Christian. But how can this great multitude (Gentiles) become Saints without hearing a preacher? During at least the first 3 ½ years of tribulation, Christians Saints had preached the word to them (Gentiles). Again, by virtue of the fact that their white robes were washed in the blood of the Lamb is evidence that they had been converted to Christianity (Rev 7:10).

While the gospel is being preached during the tribulation period, God dispenses plagues to coerce men to repent of their sins and be converted. It's a horrible scene as horse tails like serpents kill men with plagues, as God during his wrath attempts to persuade men who still will not repent from worshipping devils (Rev 9:18-21).

ONLY TWO GROUPS IN TRIBULATION

There are only two groups that exist during great tribulation, those who have washed their robes in the blood of Christ whose names are written in the lamb's book of life and those who wondered, served, and who were deceived by the beast and false prophet. So we can conclude that if you're washed in the blood of the Lamb, then you must be a Christian because there is no other access to enter heaven.

"⁸And all that dwell upon the earth shall worship him (the beast), whose names are not written in the book of life of the Lamb slain from the foundation of the world."
--Rev 13:8

THE SAINTS OF GOD

Look, there will be living breathing Christian Saints during tribulation whose names are written in the book of life of the Lamb. When we see the word Saint in the book of Revelation, we must understand that it is referring to both Jew and Gentile who are all one in Christ.

Look, some 3,000 people including Jews, and Gentiles that had become Christian Saints were added to the church in Jerusalem. As I have state with ad nauseam, I believe that the word Saints refers to both Jewish, Greek and Gentiles grouped together. In fact, the apostles were Jewish Christian Saints. Paul was a Gentile Christian Saint. I see church as the Saints and Saints as the church, and there should be no separation between church and the Saint.

By chapter 21 of the book of Revelation, the wrath and judgment of God has ended. In Revelation 20:9, all nations, including Gog and Magog, are led by their leader Satan to launch a final assault against the beloved city Jerusalem. Greatly outnumbered, a small minority is left to defend the beloved city filled with Jews y gentiles (Arab, Palestinians, Orientals, Anglo-Saxons). These Christian Saints that are encompassed by Satan and the nations must be blood washed, and have their names written in the Lamb's book of life. In fact, these are the same ones that formerly came out of Great Tribulation. Why? Because Christ has already returned with his army.

Many will say that the armies that followed Christ upon white horses will consist of men that were part of the catching away of the church. True, but don't forget that many Saints arose from the dead in Mt 27:52 which were Old Testament Hebrews. Finally, during the millennium, the Saints will rein with Christ. The real question is where will this take place? Since we will witness Christ coming to the earth in Rev 19:11, the Saints will probably reign with him in Jerusalem during the millennium. Furthermore, after the millennium, the Saints, his army of Saints, and those Saints that were resurrected will be with Christ in the Holy City when they are surrounded by the nations from the four corners of the earth (Rev 20:9).

THE SAINTS OF GOD

Chapter 13

THE MYTHS OF
THE RAPTURE

The word Rapture is not a biblical word, but a Latin word that was popularized in 1827 by men like John Darby. However the origin of its implication began with a Jesuit Spanish priest by the name of Emmanuel Lacunza .who published a book in 1811 entitled, "La venida del Messiah en Gloria y Majestad" which was later published in English in 1833 by Darby himself. Prior to 1811, the word "rapture" was never associated with the "catching away" (1 Thes 4:16) or what theologians infer to as the "secret coming." Lacunza initiated the idea that Christ would come two more times in the future. The rapture implied a "secret coming" or rapture, then after tribulation, third return upon his white horse referenced by Revelations 19:11.

The etymology of the word "catching away" comes from the Greek, *harpazo* meaning to seize, carry off by force, and claim for one's self eagerly, to snatch out, away. It is derived from the word *haireo* meaning to take for oneself, prefer, and choose by vote elect to office.

Rapture doctrine became popular over the last 170 years, promoted by C. I. Scoffield D.D. 1843 and Darby, both scholars of the scriptures. However, no scripture supports a *harpazo* or catching away before tribulation, it's just an accepted doctrine over the last century. Again, it's more of "an escape from trouble mentality" than good sound doctrine.

If I were to define the difference between the catching away, and the rapture, I would definite it like this: where the rapture implies pre-tribulation or when the coming of Christ will occur, the "catching away" from the scriptures simply reveals that it will happen but makes no prediction as to when. Notably, prior to 1843, the catching away was taught mid-tribulation referenced by Revelations 19:11, and Matthew 24:30.

PROPAGATION OF THE RAPTURE

Later, others including John Darby in 1827, and Edward Irving, continued to expand the Rapture doctrine into its present day prototype. Moreover, others like Scofield also perpetuated the "rapture doctrine" in the footnotes of the King James Version of the Bible.

First of all, I submit that I Thessalonians 4:16 is connected with his coming in Revelations 19:11, but the idea of a "secret coming" before tribulation is an absurd notion among the Saints of God. While it appeared authentic, for the last 170 years or so, men have been falsely "comforting yourselves together" by misconstruing the scriptures with slogans like "fly in the sky, in the sweet by and by". When in reality, it is none other than a "fight or flight" behavioral response taught in psychiatry.

Let's face it, in light of etymology, every Saint has fear of the seals being opened and trumpets sounding. Moreover, why would a Saint be any more uncertain regarding their wellbeing during great tribulation than the children that walked through the wilderness for 40 years? Pastors have told me that their greatest fear relevant to mark of the beast 666 is sanctions that will prohibit Saints from buying or selling commodities. If God provided all the needs of the Saints in the old testament, and we know that God has not changed according to Heb 13:8 and if he performed the impossible 3,000 years ago, he can do the same during tribulation or better yet great tribulation.

A quick cursorily review of events during the last one hundred years clearly indicate that we are in tribulation and the seals are being opened by the Lamb. Unfortunately, if something does not fulfill our expectation, then it just can't be true. Today many believe for physical tangible healing and money but when it deals with resurrections, translations, the Shekinah glory cloud, walking on water, and dividing loaves many deem it all "spiritual." Can you imagine your response if I prayed for your metaphoric healing and symbolic money? No, we embrace our own schools of thought that stipulate that certain things must be tangible like health, wealth, and prosperity.

THE SIGNS DENOTE THE CHURCH IN TRIBULATION

We need to wake up and smell the proverbial coffee. We need to stop; denying the signs recorded by history in the twentieth century and the terrorism occurring in our country today. I truly believe that the FBI and CIA realize that they can no longer protect the US from terrorism due to the fact that the enemy has breached both the Pacific and Atlantic Oceans. With current technology, the two afore mentioned great bodies of water no longer protect the United States. Unlike Europe, no country could simply form an army and gallop into the United States borders to overrun our country like the Mongol Hordes did in 13 century that spread terror and panic from Asia to Europe. Horseback is no longer the conventional way to transport armies. Now terrorists use sleeper cells, walk through open borders, come over on student exchange programs, or carry in nuclear devices to create terror and havoc.

Christian, I hate to inform you but we are there now. Today, we see evidence of moral decadence and decline not recorded before in American history. It appears that immorality will continually exacerbate until we mirror the culture of the Roman

Empire that collapse in part due to disease, homosexuality and moral declension.

COMING AS A THIEF IN THE NIGHT

For years, Christians Saints have been hoodwinked regarding a "secret coming" of Christ which is scripturally inaccurate. In fact, I have proof that if you are a Saint of God, there should not be any secrets at all!

Let stop a moment and take a walk down memory lane by opening up to Revelation 3:3. It reads like this:

> "If therefore thou shalt not watch, I will come on thee as a thief, and thou shalt not know what hour I will come upon thee"   --Rev 3:3

Now Saints, if we take the scriptures at first glance, it would appear that the coming of Christ is a secret, but what is not said is that John is referring to those walking in complacency. Let's say for a moment that you are a Saint of God, you fast, watch, pray, graduate from discipleship training, and have a personal relationship with God 24 hours a day. Now, let's negate the scripture for a moment. Relax, I am not committing heresy, it's just for the purpose of illustration.

> "If therefore thou shalt ~~not~~ watch, I will *not* come on thee as a thief, and thou ~~not~~ shalt know what hour I will come upon thee".   --Rev 3:3

Notice, I simply negated the sentence to imply the opposite meaning, namely that we are "watching." Let's be honest, generally speaking, our society rarely knows how to recognize, positive virtues in the life of a Christian or for anyone for that matter. Society is geared towards emphasizing the negatives with the intent of developing perfection.

Saints, we realize that the angel of the Lord is reprimanding the church of Sardis for their lackadaisical posture. In other words, you have a good name, but there remain some issues within the rank and file, some are sleeping on the job. Watching implies alertness, preparedness, being center stage, obedience, patience, dressed for the wedding feast, praying, and fasting to mention a few.

HIS COMING IS NO SURPRISE AT ALL

Let's take another walk down memory lane so that you can be center stage before this assertion. This time follow me to (Matthew 25:1-13) where we can explore the setting of the ten virgins.

> "Then shall the kingdom of heaven be likened unto ten virgins, which took their lamps, and went forth to meet the bridegroom. And five of them were wise, and five were foolish. They that were foolish took their lamps, and took no oil with them. But the wise took oil in their vessels with their lamps. While the bridegroom tarried, they all slumbered and slept. And at midnight there was a cry made, Behold, the bridegroom cometh; go ye out to meet him. Then all those virgins arose, and trimmed their lamps "
> --Mt 25:1-7

In short, we see that there are ten virgins, five wise and five foolish. Oil, a type of the presence of God, was not purchased by the five foolish virgins so they implored the other five to give them some oil. Now in verse 5;

> "While the bridegroom tarried, they all slumbered and slept. "

Notice that all are sleeping during the night, and that the lamps extinguish for the five that did not purchase oil. Even the five wise virgins are sleeping. But wait, although all are sleeping, (hmm, maybe not all) fortunately, someone was awake at midnight. Read verse six:

"And at midnight there was a cry made, Behold, the bridegroom cometh; go ye out to meet him."--Mt 25:5

SOME PEOPLE ARE FAITHFULLY WATCHING

I submit that some will be awake, cry, and see the bridegroom coming, although they did not know the hour of his coming. The assertion that the Messiah's secret coming will be a surprise to all Christians that are living is but a myth. Now let's take a look at a bigger than life scripture, I Thessalonians 5: 2.

"For yourselves know perfectly that the day of the Lord so cometh as a thief in the night. [3] For when they shall say, Peace and safety; then sudden destruction cometh upon them, as travail upon a woman with child; and they shall not escape."   --1 Thes 5:.2,3

"[10]But the day of the Lord will come as a thief in the night; in which the heavens shall pass away with a great noise, and the elements shall melt with fervent heat, the earth also and the works that are therein shall be burned up. "   --2 Pet 3:10

Notice Paul makes the inference to those who "cry peace and safety, then sudden destruction." Conversely, in verse 4:

"[4] But ye, brethren, are not in darkness, that that day should overtake you as a thief. "

Since we are children of the light and the children of the day, we are not of the night or darkness, meaning we watch and pray. Watch the semantics; do you really believe he was referring to shutting of the eyes in the following verse?

"Therefore let us not sleep, as do others; but let us watch
and be sober"   --I Thes 5:6).

I'd be a train wreck if I never closed my eyes, so if he does
not refer to closing the eyes what then? Metaphorically speaking,
he quite clearly is stating that we should not become lax and
complacent in our intimacy with the Lord. Being drunken infers
being catatonic, dull of hearing, mediocre, not ignited, distracted,
delusional, calloused, blind, stubborn, rebellious, without
revelation, uncommitted, traditional, without expectation,
faithless, lethargic, apostate, and not intimate with God. I'm sure
that you could add to this list. I assert that for Christians who do
not sleep, there is no secret coming of Christ but one coming.
How then could he come as a thief in the "night" if we are
children of the light? Now if His coming is not symbolic or
metaphoric, then it's tangible, if it's physical, then it is no secret.
According to the scriptures it is a stunning event that all will view.

"behold, He cometh with **clouds**; and every eye shall see
Him, and they also which pierced Him: and all kindred's
of the earth shall wail because of Him."   --Rev 1:7

GET READY BEFORE THE DOOR CLOSES

Saints, often we hear in church you need to be ready or the
door will close, yet we never ask the question, how about those
Christians that left the earth saved? Why is the door that the
groom closes only a threat to those who are physically alive but
not a threat to those who have left to be with the Lord? I always
thought that God was fair and balanced.

Each generation, for the last 492 years since Martin Luther
nailed the proclamation against the doors of St. Peter's Basilica,
have been admonished with the same words by church leaders.
Yet are they not with the Lord right now, or is there something
else that is left unsaid?

Please note that the doctrine of the "catching away" and resurrection that is referenced by 1 Thessalonians 4:16 cannot be correlated to the book of Revelation outside of Revelation 19:11 which states:

> "[11]And I saw heaven opened, and behold a white horse; and he that sat upon him was called Faithful and True, and in righteousness he doth judge and make war. "
>
> --Rev 19:11

The above scriptural reference from the book of Revelation is the only verse that references an explicit coming.

GOD ALWAYS BROUGHT MEN THROUGH

Moses through the Red Sea, Joshua through Jordan, Lazarus and Jesus through death, Shadrach, Meshach, Abednego through the fire, David through the valley of the shadow of death, Noah through the great deluge, and Jehoshaphat's valley of Tekoa. All of these illustrate a variety of examples where God developed character in His people by leading them through insurmountable odds. From my recollection, God never pulled Israel out of tribulation or trouble, but always led them through. If that was the prototype that God established from the beginning, why should He deal with us any differently today?

> "[4]Yea, though I walk through the valley of the shadow of death, I will fear no evil: for thou art with me; thy rod and thy staff they comfort me. "   --Psal 23:4

Another myth that I would like to address is the phrase "he could come any day." Most Bible scholars would agree that before Jesus could come any day, there are certain prerequisites according to scripture that must happen first.

MANY SHALL FALL APOSTATE BEFORE HIS COMING

" [1]Now we beseech you, brethren, by the coming of our Lord Jesus Christ, and by our gathering together unto Him, [2]That ye be not soon shaken in mind, or be troubled, neither by spirit, nor by word, nor by letter as from us, as that the day of Christ is at hand. [3]Let no man deceive you by any means: for that day shall not come, except there come a falling away first, and that man of sin be revealed, the son of perdition;"

Sometimes I stand back amazed at the things the Saints listen to each week without question. In the previous scripture, it is abundantly clear that the day of Christ will only happen after a "falling away first" takes place. I think sometimes we just can't help ourselves speak talking points every service during the week without thinking whether what we are saying agrees to scripture. Not only is there a required "falling away first", but the son of perdition and man of sin must be revealed.

Again, just to make it clear, the appearing of the white horse, and the catching away, are all relevant to the "day of the Lord" or the "day of Christ". I don't know about you but I am tired of semantics each Sunday morning. And to exacerbate matters, since the revelation of the Jesuit Priest Manual Lacunza, leaders have attempted to "comfort yourselves with these words" even though there is no proof that the catching away refers to a pre-tribulation second coming.

The catching away is an event of epic proportion that carries certain characteristics of which I would like to discuss at length. There are many allusions to a catching away in the scriptures. Some include events with the clouds, "Then we which are alive and remain shall be caught up together with them in the clouds" (1 Thes 4:17). Or the catching up of the dead we find in Matthew 24:31 where the writer uses the words "and they shall gather together His elect from the four winds, from one end of heaven to the other."

In reality, when 1 Thessalonians 4:16 talks about trumpets, there are seven trumpets that sound in the book of Revelation and the last trumpet occurs in Revelation 11:15:

> "¹⁵And the seventh angel sounded; and there were great voices in heaven, saying, the kingdoms of this world are become the kingdoms of our Lord, and of Hs Christ; and He shall reign forever and ever."

The previous snapshot of scripture reveals the fact that the last trumpet that sounds in the book of Revelation occurs in Chapter 15 which just so happens to be in the middle of great tribulation. Could it be that the trumpet's sound is so secret that only certain living and dead can hear it? That's ridiculous, right?

At this point I pray

Father I pray, open the eyes of the reader to begin to see the truth regarding the correlation between the following references to scriptures.

Please note that I have itemized many of the strikingly same features as evidenced by the two tables below. Both books have the same elements; the only difference is that Matthew informs his reader that these events occur after great tribulation.

BOTH MATTHEW 24:29-31 AND 1 THESSALONIANS 4:16-17 CORRELATE PERFECTLY

Matthew 24:29-31	1 Thessalonians 4:16-17
1. Presence of the Lord	1. Presence of the Lord
2. Clouds	2. Clouds
3. Angles	3. Angels
4. Sound of trumpet	4. Sound of trumpet

242

5. Gathering the people   5. Caught up together

The following table represents a side by side correlation of the scriptures in their original King James translation of the bible for your own self edification.

Matthew 24:29-31	1 Thessalonians 4:16-17
Immediately after the **tribulation of those days** shall the sun be darkened, and the moon shall not give her light, and the stars shall fall from heaven, and the powers of the heavens shall be shaken:	
1. And then shall appear the sign of the Son of Man in heaven: and then shall all the tribes of the earth mourn, and they shall see the Son of Man coming in	1. For the Lord Himself shall descend from heaven with a shout,
2. the clouds of heaven with power and great glory.	3. with the voice of the archangel, and with
3. And He shall send His angels with	4. the trump of God: and the dead in Christ shall rise first:
4. A great sound of a trumpet,	5. Then we which are alive and remain shall be caught up together with them
5. and they shall gather together his elect from the four winds, from one end of heaven to the other.	2. in the clouds, to meet the Lord in the air: and so shall we ever be with the Lord.

THE SAINTS OF GOD

Please note that Paul does not tell the Thessalonians that "and so shall we ever be with the Lord" in the clouds. No sir. The Lord does not remain in the clouds, but He descends to fight with the nations:

> [15]And out of His mouth goeth a sharp sword, that with it He should smite the nations: and He shall rule them with a rod of iron: and He treadeth the winepress of the fierceness and wrath of Almighty God." --Rev 19:15

I always tell the Saints that Jesus did not project a passive posture but conversely a focused, intense, and determined redeemer. He might have been meek, but He wasn't weak. He's dressed to fight flanked with an innumerable company of Saints on horseback. Oh yes, the angels don't fight this one, that is why I stress training for reigning, and schooling for ruling. God prepares His Saints to fight with the dragon during tribulation in Revelation 12:17.

Why do we have seminars about weapons of warfare as well as warfare praise but when it comes to a battle with Satanic power, we become a generation of metaphoric wimps looking for Jesus and the angels to fight all our battles, when, in fact, He has been empowering, imparting, equipping, anointing, teaching, and training you to fight the good fight of faith.

Listen you may have had your tail whipped, you may be down for the count, you may have been a carpet to walk on all these years, the odds may be stacked up against you, but honey, your day is coming to fight. It's your hour to bounce back, jack!

> " [5]Let the saints be joyful in glory: let them sing aloud upon their beds. [6]Let the high praises of God be in their mouth, and a two-edged sword in their hand; [7]To execute vengeance upon the heathen, and punishments upon the people; [8]To bind their kings with chains, and their nobles with fetters of iron; [9]To execute upon them the judgment

244

written: this honour have all His saints. Praise ye the
Lord"   --Psal 149:3

No matter what your view is, Jesus does not remain sitting on
a horse in the cloud forever that is just silly. Remember, as the
Saints of God we rule and reign with Him while Satan is bound by
a chain for 1,000 years.

MY TRIP TO THE CLOUDS

I remember one day I was in church on a Sunday morning
and I had been praying about taking trips by translation to preach.
While standing in service one Sunday morning, I suddenly saw a
vision of the army of God on the earth. Small billows of smoke
were rising from the hoofs of the horse's feet. The soldiers
brandished point spears similar to javelins. Suddenly, I felt the
earth tip and I almost fell over because something was lifting me
into the air like an elevator. The next moment, I found myself in
the clouds with the army of soldiers, chariots and horses. It was so
real I could almost touch the clouds with my hands. One thing is
for sure, it was so wonderful that I did not want to return but in
the next moment, I found myself back in church, standing next to
my wife.

No doubt, some of you are saying "awesome", "you're
confirming some things that I have believed for a long time but
just did not have the firepower to prove".

CONCLUSION OF THE MATTER

To conclude my dissertation, well almost, the rapture is
man's doctrine contrived by a Jesuit Priest name Manuel Lacunza.
Before this manuscript, the holy fathers never wrote about two
more returns of Christ, just one, Rev 19:11. Where Lacunza
attached pre-tribulation to his manuscript, the catching away has
always been post-tribulation from the time of the apostle's
writings. The fly in the sky mentality fits into an ever-growing

unwillingness to face tribulation. Today, democracy has duped many Christians to believe that they are not in tribulation at the moment, but it's some future event. However, those Saints that have lived under communism or Islam understand the true meaning of biblical tribulation. I know, I have spent time in Pakistan, but unfortunately, Americans have slowly but surely become apostate, putting more faith in myths, cults, and new age religion. As Christian Saints, we should be setting the tone for our community, men that have hazarded their lives for the name of our Lord, but unfortunately, we are parochial, hiding in church buildings each week. I've got some good news, after some of you have read this book, I believe you're going to be the devil's worst nightmare.

Did you ever ask yourself, where is Uncle Joe? Whatever happened to Aunt Louise? Is sister Suzy with God? The answer is simple, if they were children of God, then, they are with God. If you contemplate the "rapture" doctrine, all those who died physically in Christ would have to remain in their graves until the beginning of tribulation. What other explanation can there be? If that were the case, why is it when a beloved Saint transitions from this world, the leader conducting the home-going service will say, "Brother Freddie went to be with the Lord." Arguably, according to the popular theory, the secret resurrection and catching away will occur prior to great tribulation. Do you really think that the leader was sincere or did he intend to say that Brother Freddie is waiting in a graveyard for a shout from heaven with the voice of the archangel? Or are theologians saying that Freddie is absent from his body but present with the Lord? If our proponent's theory is true, then when Chantelle returns with the Lord, will she perform a swan dive from heaven directly into her grave and then participate in the first resurrection?

For the record, I am not talking about unbelievers. Let's be honest, over the ages, better yet, over the last 2000 years, devout men have parted from the living believing in the first resurrection. It's obvious that they are not among the human race, so there are only two possibilities that explain their present state, either they are in their graves or with the Lord. I suppose the last generation, those who remain alive, will experience the "catching away". I believe those who have parted, if they were saved and baptized in the Holy Ghost, then before they died, they were resurrected in baptism. When they depart, they return to the Lord and remain there. The ultimate destination for all the Saints of God is the earth. That is why John wrote that the city, New Jerusalem, is coming down from God, to the planet earth or in other words, some day it will be heaven on earth. I'll talk a little more about this in the next chapter.

THE SAINTS OF GOD

Chapter 14

FIRST
RESURRECTION

In 1997, I was fortunate to have had the opportunity to be baptized in the river Jordan by Pastor Prophet David Paul. Watching that dark green water, I began to contemplate the significance of water baptism. You must understand that the holy sites in Israel are all precious to God. First of all, I was stunned that I was being baptized relatively close to the place where Jesus was baptized. As I came up out of the water, my hair was the same, I weighed about the same, apparently in the natural everything was the same. In short, I began to realize that my experience at the River Jordan was bigger than wet pockets and a nose full of water. I had actually experienced a resurrection from the dead according to Col 2:12 "being buried with Him in baptism, I was resurrected with Him through the faith of the operation of God." Undeniably, after I depart from planet earth, there will be a celestial body that is waiting for me at that day now that I have been quickened by the last Adam, even Jesus Christ (1 Cor 15:44). Some schools of thought embrace the concept that Christians sleep in graveyards after death until they hear a shout. On the other hand, I remember that scripture makes it emphatically clear that He is not the God of the dead but the living (Luke 20:38). I therefore submit that if you are a born again Saint washed clean in the blood, baptized in the name of the Father, Son, and Holy Ghost, you have been resurrected from the dead.

Did you know that the doctrine "resurrection" is a principle of Jesus Christ? Many call it a tenet of our Christian faith.

> "[1]Therefore leaving the principles of the doctrine of Christ, let us go on unto perfection; not laying again the foundation of repentance from dead works, and of faith toward God, [2] Of the doctrine of baptisms, and of laying on of hands, and of resurrection of the dead, and of eternal judgment." --Heb 6:1, 2

If you carefully scrutinize the previous scripture, you'll realize that resurrection is the fifth principle of the doctrine of Christ. In my experience, you'll find two prototypes of Christian Saints today, one which sleeps during the coming of Christ and the other which is ready, watching, on the cutting edge, and ready to fight with fasting and prayer. I often characterize those who sleep as passive complacent Saints (2 Thes 2) and those who are preparing to fight as those who know that they have been resurrected from the dead. Moreover, I believe I have already been raised from the dead by virtue of my baptism.

DEATH IN BAPTISM

> "[11]In whom also ye are circumcised with the circumcision made without hands, in putting off the body of the sins of the flesh by the circumcision of Christ: [12]Buried with Him in baptism, wherein also ye are risen with Him through the faith of the operation of God, who hath raised Him from the dead." --Col 2:11, 12

This is suggesting that when I was submerged in the river Jordan, while under the water, I died and was buried together with Christ, metaphorically of course. Once dead under the water, I was then raised to the surface by the faith of the operation of God. Paul writes in the book of Romans 6:1-6 that believers die in baptism and then are resurrected in the newness of life.

YOU HAVE BEEN RESURRECTED

Look, if you have not been raised from the dead in baptism, then you have not come full circle in the fifth principle of Christ. The cycle must be completed and in fact, everyone shall come full circle someday. When I came up out of the water, I still appeared to be my old fanatical, radical self, but something changed on the inside. I was resurrected from the dead.

While many are in the state of moral depravity, lost and undone, each sinner will experience a moment when they hear the shout of the Son of God. In a real sense we are dead in the uncircumcision of our flesh until He raises us up.

HEARING THE SHOUT OF THE MESSIAH

When the unsaved hear the voice of the Son of God they metaphorically come out of their graves (John 5:25). Some are condemned by the word of God, for others, it's a resurrection experience.

Ok, time to take on the big boy, the mother of scriptures, the one you've been waiting for, 1 Thessalonians 4:16. It states the following:

> " [16]For the Lord Himself shall descend from heaven with a shout, with the voice of the archangel, and with the trump of God: and the dead in Christ shall rise first: [17]Then we which are alive and remain shall be caught up together with them in the clouds, to meet the Lord in the air: and so shall we ever be with the Lord."
> --1 Thes 4:16, 17

Let me pose a question, those that are "alive and remain", when are they resurrected? If they will meet the Lord in the air, how do they participate in the first resurrection? Arguably, they are living human beings who are awake, not sleeping, and perhaps that last generation. I don't see them stopping by the cemetery, do you?

SOME WILL WITNESS HIS COMING

Could it be possible that there is a group who are watching and praying until the Lord comes in all of His glory? Could it be possible that these also have been resurrected in baptism? When these that are alive and remain meet the Lord in the air, then at that point, do they receive their new bodies? Look, not everyone will sleep, but they shall all be changed in the twinkling of an eye.

> "If therefore thou shalt not watch, I will come on thee as a thief, and thou shalt not know what hour I will come upon thee."   --Rev 3:3

Let's play with the words for a moment, let's negate the sentence, shall we? The affirmative must be negated to false, and the negative made positive. The following represents the negation:

> "If therefore thou shalt watch, I will (not) come on thee as a thief, and thou shalt know what hour I will come upon thee."

Even though I have negated the sentence, it is still true. I am merely inferring that a small remnant of Saints that are watching, will disallow Him from coming as a thief, hence, they will see Him when He comes. Sweet, right? Let's be clear, I am not implying that suddenly we shall know the times and seasons, I'm simply stating that we shall see Him coming. Plainly speaking, for some it will be no secret. I can't be any blunter than that. Conversely, those who do not pray, but are sleepy, lazy, lax, distracted, inattentive, uninterested, unmotivated, gossipers and unbelievers, shall not see Him coming but invariably be shocked when He does as a thief in the night.

This is all based on the hypothesis that we believe that we have been resurrected in baptism. For that reason, those which are alive and remain must already have been resurrected in baptism to then get caught up together in the clouds to meet the Lord in the air. Then we should suppose that those who "do not" believe that they have been resurrected in baptism, must get resurrected at that moment. Look, if you've received the truth that you've been resurrected in baptism, and depart from this earth, you shall be with the Lord, period.

DEBUNKING THE RAPTURE MYTH

Prior to the nineteenth century, the "catching away" of I Thessalonians 3:17 always referred to the accepted post-tribulation, mainstream doctrine. However, due in part to a variety of sources as I mentioned in a previous chapter, including the manuscript published by Emmanuel Lacunza in 1811 entitled "La Avenida de la Mesias En La Gloria", Margaret McDonald's prophecy, John Nelson Darby and C.I. Scofield DD's Bible, the pre-tribulation was popularized. Just at the turn of the nineteenth century, suddenly, the doctrinal church pendulum began to swing to the other extreme, namely the "fly-away-before-trouble-begins" doctrine. It is a travesty that so few people have knowledge of church history and could even care less for that matter. Through church history, the squeakiest wheels that get the most grease today are family, health, and prosperity.

For many years, we embraced the understanding that the tribulation days referenced by the book of Revelation, whether small or great, inferred judgment against the ungodly. However, a cursory review of the Book of Revelation reveals that in at least 90% of the New Testament where the word "tribulation" or "thlipsis" is found, no matter how great the destruction, it generally refers to the persecution of the righteous. In other words, ungodly men are not impacted by tribulation, but it's the Saints of God that endure great hardships. Conversely, it is abundantly clear that the "wrath of God" was reserved for the hordes of ungodly men that were deceived by Satan, the dragon. Ultimately, the fire coming down from heaven is a sign of the wrath of God intended on consuming wicked men that surround the camp of the Saints (Rev 20:9). Notice in particular that the fire of God consumes the armies of the beast but preserves the camp of the Saints.

FALSE DOCTRINE CAUSES APOSTASY

"[1]Now the Spirit speaketh expressly, that in the latter times some shall depart from the faith, giving heed to seducing spirits, and doctrines of devils; [2]Speaking lies in hypocrisy; having their conscience seared with a hot iron;"   --1 Tim 4:1, 2

I submit that in the days to come, many will be shell-shocked as Christendom continues to enter tribulation. Meanwhile, theology by and large continues to condition Bible scholars to buy into the "fly in the sky in the sweet by and by" mentality. As such, multitudes of good Christians are becoming discouraged day by day because they were not educated properly. Since the 1811 publication of Emmanuel Lacunza, Christendom has strived to inspire the church with "don't worry, He's coming tomorrow." Since I've discussed all of this in a previous chapter, I don't want to belabor my point.

THE NUMBER 666, MICRO CHIPS, AND THE INABILITY TO PURCHASE, ALL HAVE CREATED FEAR AMONGST CHRISTIANS

Apostle John writing in Revelation 1:9 said, "I am also your brother, and companion in tribulation." He was referring to the entire book of Revelation. For this reason, despair during tribulation will be the critical factor that will cause many to "fall away". More and more people are quitting God for other religions day by day. Quite frankly, I'd rather be honest with God's people so instead of quitting they can be equipped to fight during tribulation. I find it amusing that those who have already departed don't need to have anxiety about the "rapture" in as much as they are now with God. For generations, different leaders have perpetuated these fear tactics so that helpless souls would come flocking to the altars and make a public confession for Christ. Fear has been the main proponent of the rapture which is subject to the hypothesis that "Jesus could come tomorrow and some of you will be left behind."

Any Bible student will tell you that the former statement is false in that all the prerequisites for Christ's coming have not occurred yet. Let's be honest, who wants to suffer in tribulation when you can escape?

Unfortunately, many have committed a disservice to the Saints with this false doctrine. I submit that God is preparing his Fivefold leaders to carry the Saints through tribulation. In fact, if we had continued with the post-tribulation doctrine taught for the first 1,900 years, people would have no valid reason to be disappointed and become apostate as tribulation intensifies.

SECOND DEATH OF THE WICKED

After one thousand years of ruling and reigning with Christ, Satan will be loosed from prison. He shall then go and deceive all nations upon the face of the earth. Moreover, they will gather to battle at Gog, and Magog. Remember, at this point there is only a small remnant in the camp of the Saints in Israel. Suddenly, fire comes down from God out of heaven and kills all those who have encamped against the Saints. In a real sense, all the dead must be resurrected to stand before the throne of God to be judged. At this point every knee will bow, and every tongue shall confess that He is Lord.

" [12]And I saw the dead, small and great, stand before God; and the books were opened: and another book was opened, which is the book of life: and the dead were judged out of those things which were written in the books, according to their works. [13]And the sea gave up the dead which were in it; and death and hell delivered up the dead which were in them: and they were judged every man according to their works. [14]And death and hell were cast into the lake of fire. This is the second death. [15]And whosoever was not found written in the book of life was cast into the lake of fire."   --Rev 20:12-15

HELL WAS NEVER DESIGNED FOR ETERNAL JUDGEMENT

The sea, death, and Hell give up the dead so that the ungodly can be judged. It must be a horrible torment to experience a temporary resurrection from the dead only to die a second death. But contrary to legend, hell was never designed for eternal judgment, just a temporary staging area while God annihilates His enemies that hate Him. Ultimately, if your name is not written in the Lamb's book of Life, your destiny will be the lake of fire. There, Satan and the Beast will burn consciously in torment for an eternity

.

Chapter 15

LIVING IN
THE GLORY

For many, this chapter may seem surreal however, I am convinced that the glory began in the Garden of Eden, it departed during the dark or Middle Ages, and it is now returning again during the great and terrible day of the Lord.

As the children of Israel beheld His glory, so shall we, the last generation, behold the glory of God during the days of judgment. Unlike the rapture folk whom over the last 170 years have attempted to substantiate their doctrine based on the traditional "fly in the sky in the sweet by and by"; I believe God is preparing us to stay and fight. Unlike this generation, the first century was a generation of true Christians who put their lives at risk for His glory (Acts 15:26).

Even though Israel beheld the 10 plagues of Egypt, watched Moses divide the Red Sea, witnessed the Lord's shekhinah glory cover the mount, after years of warning the children of Israel, they witnessed the glory parting from their camp.

I Sam 4:20-22 because of the sins of Eli's sons Hophni and Phinehas, the glory departed from the camp at the time that Phinehas' wife died giving birth to a child named Icabod, meaning "the glory has departed".

Ironically, Israel [(H3479) meaning he will rule as God, (H8280) prevail have power, (H410) God great and powerful], was embarrassed by defeat because the glory had departed. When the arc was taken captive by the Philistines, it was symbolic of the presence of God departing from Israel.

The Philistines feared Israel continually calling them "mighty gods". When Israel shouted for war, it sounded like thunder and intimidated the Arabs in the region. How could the Philistines ever hope to defeat an enemy whose name was "God, great and powerful"?

VISIONS OF TANGIBLE GLORY CLOUDS ARE COMING

But God is providing a way for us to behold His glory by the restitution of all things which God had spoken by the mouth of His holy prophets (Acts 3:21). Fortunately, during Israel's captivity, the prophets continued to seek His glory. In fact, Ezekiel was a prophet who not only foretold the distant future, but also experienced the glory of the Lord. Note that the lack of a particular mantel or office does not mean you can't experience God's glory like His holy prophets. Each star has its own glory, the glory of the moon and the sun. The spirit of God lifted Ezekiel between the heaven and earth in visions to show him the wickedness of church elders Ezek 8:3. These men were offering incense to familiar idols in dark chambers. Finally, after years of warning, God's glory, His presence, lifts from the temple. But really what was God angry about? Could it have been:

- Complacency
- Disobedience
- Traditions
- Mind Sets
- Casual intimacy
- Passivity

258

- Weakness
- Impotence

We are much like those people in that "religion" conforms to the things of a particular century. We are a church culture filled with metaphors, compromise and substitutions for real glory.

SUBSTITUTIONS FOR THE GLORY OF GOD

- Humanism in exchange for fanaticism
- Passivity instead of violence
- "Jesus loves you" in place of demonstrating the character of God
- Catchy songs with lyrics using words like "glory"
- Eloquent preaching in exchange for demonstration of power
- Rigid edicts, commandments of men, substitute for agape love
- Discipleship training in place of real power
- Human abilities in place of the grace of God
- Bible tracts in place of prophetic unction
- Clapping hands in place of shouting and high praise
- Talented administrators in place of Apostles and Prophets
- Standard healing services substitute for the unexpected and unusual
- Airliners in place of real translations in the spirit
- Name tags replace the need of hearing names from heaven
- Missionaries in place of apostles, prophets, and evangelists
- Titles have replaced mantles, graces and anointing
- Spiritual earthquakes have substituted for the earth shaking after anointed prayer
- Spiritual quickening in place of physical resurrections from the dead

THE SAINTS OF GOD

ONCE UPON A TIME, BACK IN THE HEYDAY

This generation has become the most metaphoric, hermeneutic, homiletic, and apologetic than any other. There was a day when Jesus raised the physical dead, now Christian evangelists talk about "being quickened from the dead." We don't raise the physical dead anymore because it's taboo, uncouth, unethical, uncultured, stigmatic, and passé.

In the first century they opened the eyes of the blind, even born blind, now they say "let your spiritual eyes be open."

At one time after the apostles were threatened, they prayed to the God of heaven causing the place to be shaken by an earthquake. Now they say, "God is sending an earthquake into your life", a complete reversal from the first century mantel of anointing.

Can you imagine, some are just satisfied with building projects, big choirs, television, radio broadcasts, eloquent preaching, and altar calls?

At one time, men were caught up by the Spirit, transported to re-appear in Azotus, to preach on the other side of town. Today the elect say " I'll fly Southwest and earn extra sky-mile points."

At one time men filled with the Holy Ghost confronted sorcerers and witches, casting out spirits of divination, even prophesying blindness to one named Elymas, that he should be blind for a season (Acts 13). Today they admonish you in discipleship training to "pray for them."

Some psychics and diviners need strong correction to let them know that we, men and women of God, have the signature

260

of God resting on our lives, that when we speak according to God's divine timing, things happen. And like the first century primitive church, the only way to convince some of these spiritualists and those observing is through demonstration of God's power.

Granted, apostles and prophets when directed by the Holy Ghost will speak to sorcerers, witches, and psychics in an unapologetic fashion. I understand that in some cases those in laity may not be equipped to discern the kind of spirit that is opposing them. Instead of rebuking a witch or sorcerer, in the final analysis, many ever pray for a false prophet to be delivered. But in my humble opinion, there is no excuse today for not promoting these kinds of mantels and anointing in the church that can properly deal with a counterfeit anointing. In fact, I believe that the world needs to witness the dunamis power resting on the lives of believers.

Curious enough is the argument that we are supposed to minister exclusively by love to others in the New Testament, that I understand. But remember the apostolic doctrine began in the New Testament. So, what changed?

In the first century, angels unlocked prison doors, ministered to people after fasting, and brought messages to devout men. But today, our angels are both in retirement and out of commission.

In the heyday of the Apostles, men by the gift would discern names like "thou art **Simon,** the son of **Jonas,** the son of **Cephas**", but today men will ask before they minister, "what is your name?"

In one occasion when Jesus saw a complete stranger approaching by the name of Nathanael He said "before Philip called thee I saw thee standing under the fig tree". Now they say "sister loose-lips told me that she saw you under the fig tree two hours ago".

IT'S TIME TO SEE A VISION OF THE CLOUD AGAIN

Men saw Moses and Elias, the tangible glory cloud coming down, overshadowing them, they heard heaven speaking, but today men say "oohh I feel Holy Ghost chill bumps running up and down my spine."

One day a man stepped out of his ship and walked on water to go to Jesus, but today they say "you need to walk on the waters of your faith."

Granted, not everything is tangible, but we need to strike a balance between the metaphoric and the physical. Otherwise what separates Christian Saints from the other cults of the world?

So what are the requirements for living and experiencing the glory of God? We need to live in the glory, walk in the glory, remain in the glory and seek His tangible presence. For all those that may say "yeah right", I believe that all the Saints should have a supernatural manifestation of glory. Something unusual that will cause uproar in every church once in a while. Jesus did!! Jesus consistently sought for the glory of Him that sent Him by rising early, and being sent on assignments. Jesus never returned home without a glorious testimony of how God showed up during a divine encounter.

GLORY ON THE MOUNT OF TRANSFIGUARATION

One of the most compelling stories of the Bible occurred on the mount of transfiguration, Matthew 17:1-9. Jesus explained to His disciples that the Son of Man shall come in the glory of His father with His angels and reward every man for his works according Matthew 16:27, 28. Jesus exclaimed that there were "some standing there that shall not taste of death, until they see

262

the Son of Man coming in His glory." With the benefit of hindsight, we now know that Jesus was talking about a vision of the glory.

In these days, there are increasing testimonies of phenomenal manifestations of glory occurring in services around the country. It was common place for tangible shekhinah glory to appear in the Old Testament. After Solomon finished the house and brought in all things that David had made, including gold and silver, then everything was placed in a particular order in the house of God. The priests took their places, the arc was put in place, the singers had unity in praise and worship, and sang "for He is good and His mercy endureth forever" and suddenly the house was filled with a cloud. Likewise, when Solomon dedicated the temple for prayer and worship, and made burnt offerings unto the Lord, then the glory of the Lord filled the house and fire came down from heaven to consume the sacrifice (2 Chr 7:1,2). As every star has its own glory, one glory of the moon, one glory of the sun, and one glory of the stars, so was there a unique manifestation of glory on the day of Pentecost.

There is a pattern throughout the Bible that precedes the manifest glory of God. Fifty days after the resurrection, about 120 disciples were united in Holy Communion, waiting for the promise of the father. In unity, in one mind, one purpose, no big or small in authority but one spirit, continued in one accord in prayer and supplication. I believe this should be the model for invoking the shekinah glory of God in the days to come. Suddenly, while in one accord, in one place, there came a sound from heaven as a rushing mighty wind and it filled the house.

Filling the house was the pattern that God established from Old to New Testaments when He wanted to confirm and put His seal of approval on a particular hour according to His choosing. Again, fire is associated with His presence as tongues of fire descend from heaven to cleanse and purge the disciples in preparation for the chapters to come.

THE FIRE OF GOD IS REAL

Today during many religious events, fire is still coming from heaven as a seal of God's approval that will usher in His glory in the twenty first century. I'll never forget about our gathering in the Walmart parking lot while we were asking God to send angels and pour out His spirit upon us to work the works of God. Suddenly, a fire began to burn in our midst. This smell, distinct from any other, was a sign from God to confirm His approval that we were in the right place at the right time doing the right thing.

As I mentioned in previous chapters, when the scripture in Acts 2:17 declares that "I will pour out in those days of my Spirit and they shall prophesy", God is referring to this generation. This century shall enjoy a taste of His glory as a witness to the whole world. For our benefit, God speaks through Haggai 2:9, that "the glory of this latter house shall be greater than of the former."

REQUIREMENTS FOR THE GLORY TO RETURN

Let's refer back to our theme scripture Matthew 17:1 for the following narrative. Here in Matthew 17, we see all the elements associated with the glory of God. Shock and awe left them speechless as the heavens began to speak over the life of Christ, "this is my beloved son, hear ye Him." What do you think is lacking for the glory of God to manifest again in the twenty first century?

I want to give you 11 important rules that will transform the pseudo-glory of God of this century into a tangible glory of biblical proportions again.

1. A separate, consecrated life before God
Jesus consecrates His inner circle James, John, and Peter from others and takes them into the mountain apart to pray (Mt17:1).

Church is derived from the word Ecclesia which means to come out from among them and be separate (Rev 18:4). Even the antichrists "went out from us, but they were not of us, for had they been of us, they would no doubt have continued with us" (1 Jn 2:18, 19). Moses wrote in the law Num 8:14 "Thus shalt thou separate the Levites from among the children of Israel: and the Levites shall be mine." He foreknew the divine integral role that these would play in the future and that great grace would fall upon them. As for the rest, they would experience a lesser glory in the following years. You must know them that labor among you when you choose your inner circle of intercessors. In this hour, God is raising up a contingency of bold men and women who will not be deterred from believing for the unusual.

2. Worship and high praises

Jesus strategically led his powerful trio into a high place for praise and worship. It was metaphorically a heavenly place, where they had an opportunity to give high praise in unity (Psalm 149:6). Until we are not embarrassed for being cocky, arrogant, and violent in praise, we shall see only diminished manifestations of glory. Until high praises of God are in your mouth, you will not be equipped with a sharp two-edged sword in your hand to execute vengeance upon the heathen and punishments upon the people. Many churches have rather casual praise unto God; it's not violent and loud as the first century standard. We need warfare praise to be restored in the midst of the camp if we want God to intervene in the affairs of man. Back in the first century, bona fide, ground shaking earthquakes manifested after men congregated to pray.

WARFARE PRAISE CAUSED THE GROUND TO SHAKE

In fact, God used earthquakes or caused the earth to shake as a seal of His approval over Paul and Silas when they were beaten and shackled in the dungeon at Philippi. Unlike the typical response, these men responded by praying and then praising God so loudly that the other prisoners would witness the relationship between praise and the earthquake that caused the jail cells to open.

3. Sacrifice and self-denial

Prior to the prophetic statement that His disciples would see the Son of Man come in His glory, Jesus declares that His apostolic team members must deny themselves if they want to follow Him (Mt 16:25).

If they were not prepared to forsake all that they have (Luke 14:33) they cannot be His disciples. We lose our lives when we deny ourselves to take up the cross and follow Him. Jesus was the epitome of self-denial and sacrifice. No wonder God was pleased to transfigure Him before these men of destiny. Paul in writing to the Galatians alluded to the fact that he was "crucified together with Christ, yet nevertheless "I live, yet not I but Christ that liveth in me"(Gal 2:20). No wonder Christ manifests God's glory, because He laid down His life for humanity.

There is some glory behind the story of your life; your suffering is not in vain. Humanity by nature does not want to yield to suffering, but without dying to the appetites of our flesh, the light of Christ cannot shine through a dark vessel. Controlling His mouth when beaten and persecuted was one of the outstanding virtues of His life.

One of the overarching truths of the Bible is denial, death to attitudes and emotions of the flesh. Else, how will the glory of God manifest? Sacrifice is a quintessential aspect in the life of a believer who wants to experience first-hand, the tangible manifestations of the glory of God. Let's be honest, today's Saints use metaphoric substitutes for God's literal glory. We sing about it, dance in it, boast about it, shout about it, get emotional about it,

266

but if truth be told, how many have raised the dead lately? How many have taken a trip to heaven? How many have opened the blind eyes of a person from birth? How many have had an encounter with an angel? Scholars would say those things are spiritual, but that's exactly the point. The amazing bona fide works of yesterday arguably have been reduced to metaphors or symbolism in today's Christendom.

Folks, in essence, those are the things we should be boasting about, not just philosophical semantics, or just emotional thrills. Isaiah pens "⁷He was oppressed, and he was afflicted, yet he opened not his mouth: he is brought as a lamb to the slaughter, and as a sheep before her shearers is dumb, so he openeth not his mouth (Isaiah 53).

Jesus was a lamb slain before the foundations of the world, when they beat Him, He opened not His mouth, and He was a lamb dumb before His shearers. In fact, if more of our thoughts were transformed into prayer, God would have the opportunity to tweak our ungodly thoughts. No wonder we are embarrassed so often when we speak presumptuously, when the Holy Ghost could have tempered the thought process before we opened our mouth.

4. Without a vision my people parish
Most adherents of the scripture do not realize that the disciples had seen a vision of an event to come in the future, but it was as tangible as a cool breeze and full of glory. When the disciples began to inquire what had just happen, Jesus replied "Tell the vision to no man, until the Son of Man be raised again from the dead." Amazingly, that suggests that a vision is just as real and palpable as any physical experience that confirms the laws of time and space. When Jesus was transfigured, He stepped out of time into eternal glory. Don't leave home without a vision; every man needs to see something about his future. Paul in Ephesians 1:18 wrote a letter of empowerment to the Saints asserting that he

"ceases not to give thanks, making mention of them in his prayers "and that they would have wisdom and revelation of Jesus Christ. He goes on to say that "the eyes of your understanding be enlightened, that ye many know what is the hope of your calling." This generation needs a revelation from the Holy Ghost with respect to "Living in the Glory".

5. Revelation of the truth

How many have heard theologians decry signs and wonders for today? Today, even if God wanted to move He couldn't because we are too steeped in tradition. Part of my studies at ORU included researching the life of Oral Roberts, the founder and chancellor of that evangelical university. Oral Roberts, a forerunner of the "power gifts" had a mantel of healing and miracles resting on his life which clearly was not the norm in the twentieth century. In fact, most religious institutions are proponents of cessationism meaning that many believed that the sign-gift ministry ceased after the death of the apostles.

Without a doubt, the eyes of the apostles were wide open as Jesus is transformed or transfigured before their eyes. Jesus called it a vision, or revelation of things that were previously hidden, but now unfolding before their eyes, in fact they witnessed Jesus entering the kingdom.

Ask God to open your eyes with revelation to see the coming glory upon the face of the earth.

One of my favorite scriptures is Acts 3:21 "whom the heaven must receive until the times of restitution of all things, which God hath spoken by the mouth of all His holy prophets." Restitution speaks to:

- Raising the dead
- Being transported to preach in another place

- Visions of the glory cloud
- Shaking of the earth
- Fire coming down from heaven
- Apostolic ministers
- Prophetic ministers
- Evangelists in position
- Signs of the moon changing to blood
- Wonders in heaven
- Acceleration of time and reversal of time

Training and equipping of Christian Saints should be part of the revealed truth that you seek in the word. Contrarily, adding an addition to your church building should be secondary next to training and equipping so that the Saints may fight a good warfare against the principalities of this world (I Tim 1:18).

6. Strategically assembled in unity

When the Saints assemble in one place, know their position for that season and are in one mind, then the door of opportunity will open to manifest God's glory. As you know, each moment with Jesus was strategically planned to maximize the outcome of glory. We see evidence of this when Jesus takes his disciples to the mountain. At that moment, four men with a common purpose assembled on the mount to witness the glory of God.

Jesus in His omniscience knew that it was high time to prepare his disciples for the theatre of battle. Therefore at the appropriate hour, charged his apostles to "tarry in the city of Jerusalem, until ye be endued with power from on high" (Luke 24:49).

The hour has come for this generation to assemble together and tarry in the place specified by heaven, so that we may receive the promise of endowment under open heavens. Tarry, a word foreign to the vocabulary of many, means to labor, fast, pray, wait, yield, and be unanimous in a particular place until something happens.

Some of the most captivating moments in scriptures were marked by unusual sudden events such as the time when the angel suddenly appeared in Herod's prison and smote Peter upside the head to wake him up. Maybe we need a good slap to wake us up out of passivity and stop messing with God.

While there is disunity or division, which means two visions, we will continue to operate like children, carnal, able to exploit natural material things of this world for the good, but unable to experience a measurable tangible glory of God like the apostles. While in the upper room, waiting to be endued with power, 120 men, in unity, of one mind, in one accord, were expecting for something to happen.

Folks we need to change our thinking and start expecting the unusual. These men were desperate for His presence, such that they continued in fasting and prayer for ten days without ceasing. Can you imagine walking through the pages of the first chapter of Acts again in the twenty-first century? In that day, the assembling of the Saints of God moves heaven. If one can put one thousand to flight, then ten can put ten thousand to flight, but we must understand membership ministry. If the foot shall say because I am not of the hand, I am not of the body? We need each other, for together we shall conquer the strongholds of our enemies.

7. Obedience and Submission to leadership
Can you imagine the eternal state of man if Jesus had not decided not to submit to God? But Jesus taught them the cost of discipleship by example. Interestingly enough, denial of oneself and following Him was precisely the lesson.

Listen, you might be one of the greatest prophets that God ever called upon the face of the earth since Moses but you must be able to yield to authority and be obedient. Had they not been obedient to Jesus in Luke 24:49 "tarry ye in the city of Jerusalem, until you be endued with power", the events of Pentecost may have been totally different. Because so many want safe religion, convenience, and don't want to stand in jeopardy, we see only mediocrity amongst the rank and file Christian Saints. Obedience to a leader, master, Angel or God is imperative for a move of glory to manifest in your church provided that the angel is not preaching "another gospel."

8. Repentance, Fasting, and Prayer

Categorically each time there was deliverance from an enemy, restoration from destruction or imminent danger, there was a repeating theme before the glory manifested. Today, most people don't want to fast, pray, and least of all repent of their faults and those of previous generations. Moses was a high priest-prophet that had deep convictions regarding the heart of God. As a contemporary apostle, Moses spent a large amount of time on his face interceding for the "children" of God because that was exactly how they acted, childish. Right before Jesus is transfigured; He demands that that adulterous and sinful generation repent from being ashamed of Him and of His words.

Continual fasting and prayer was analogous to the lifestyle of Jesus Christ. This lifestyle of complete denial was synonymous with His holiness that manifested itself as a shimmering entity exceedingly white as snow, whiter than any fuller on earth. At that moment, the apostles witnessed Jesus coming in glory.

In the narrative Exodus 33, we see Moses summoned to the mountain, apart with God. During a long fast of 40 days, Moses seclusion allows him to give God his undivided attention for what he was about to receive. While in the glory of God's presence, the face of Moses begins to glisten as white as the sun. Moses received a taste of the transformation while still in his earthly body. Christ was the epitome of self-denial and God said that He was well pleased. No wonder Jesus experienced the glory on that day.

9. Expecting, Seeking his Glory

As creatures of habit, sometimes we just can't help ourselves from behaving like the previous generation. For that reason, having your eyes opened by the word is important for change. Change takes people out of a comfort zone which is not very comfortable. Nevertheless, change is here and change is now.

What level of expectation did the apostles have compared with us since we are some 50 generations removed from the first century? Expectation is the key that unlocks the door of change. The trendy expression heard today in the halls of most churches is "how many are desperate for his presence?" By and large, Christianity as a whole is at best both passive and lethargic.

Why? Because all of life's commodities is at our fingertips, one does not have to be desperate for his or her needs to be met today. Without desperation, we can hardly expect to see His glory. Jesus was a fanatical radical, a very intense individual who was determined to do God's will.

His existence revolved around seeking the glory of Him that sent Him in a nutshell. We need to return to our first love, experience the embers burning, desire for the fire to fall again, covet a passion for His presence and be desperate for his glory in the twenty first century.

10. Idolatry, Iniquity, Witchcraft

Often when we become angry, the imagery of our mind can quickly convert to idolatry without intervention. Usually, a lack of forgivingness towards a particular person in the past can result in obsessive compulsive thoughts which will impair our fellowship with God. Jesus was consistently one with God. When we are one with God, the stronghold of stubbornness and rebellion must

272

come down. Sometimes only the anointing can help us break the yoke of bondage. For this reason Christians must learn to use their weapons of warfare to cast down strongholds. If left alone, arguments of the mind can arguably evolve into evil thoughts including the desire to settle a score or vengeance towards another person. These relentless arguments about other people in your mind will be contrary to the glory of God.

11. Uniqueness in Glory

When referring to the glory, the apostle John purports in John 1:14 that "we beheld His glory", inferring that there were different expressions of glory, in as much as the only begotten Son was one of the expressions of God's glory. During our time of suffering with Him (Rom 8:18), a glory shall be revealed in us, "Christ in us, the hope of glory" (Col 1:27).

When glory manifests amongst the Saints of God, it will be unique by nature. Like norm, I believe bona fide ground shaking quakes shall occur again wherever the Saints gather to pray..During the glory days of tribulation, we shall witness men standing on water again similar to the New Testament where two men walked on water. Case in point, when the angel descended upon the tomb of Christ and when Paul and Silas began to pray and praise God at Philippi. Unusual events that are not recorded in scripture have occurred and will occur again in the days to come including resurrections from the dead, steel plates changing to bone, bald heads growing hair, teleportation in the Spirit, gold dust accumulating on the surface and standing on water. When God's glory manifests during gatherings, an unlimited number of events could occur at any one time. But we need the knowledge of His glory as the waters cover the sea.

Did Jesus and Peter truly walk on water in the book of Matthew chapter 14:25, 29? I believe that the Bible is God-inspired, and God-breathed. It is not only a document filled with authentic evidence of events that have taken place some 2000 years ago, but of events yet to come. As we approach a one world system, the glory of God will increase commensurate with world events (signs of the times). The Bible records a gravity defying event in Daniel 12:7 where a man in linen is standing on the water. Since Daniel is a book of eschatological events, it only stands to reason that this event shall occur in the future occur during tribulation.

MAN SHALL WALK ON WATER AGAIN

"⁷And I heard the man clothed in linen, which was upon the waters of the river, when he held up his right hand and his left hand unto heaven, and swear by him that liveth forever that it shall be for a time, times, and an half; and when he shall have accomplished to scatter the power of the holy people, all these things shall be finished. "   --Daniel 12:7

I believe that gravity-defying feats, moving forward, backward, and stopping time were all norms throughout scripture. They were just as common as the jet that carries you across the country in several hours. So what happened? Did we stop believing, or did we simply become ignorant related to the glory of God.

"The heavens declare His righteousness, and all the people see His glory."   --Psal 97:6

In closing, I ask you to pray for me that I might publish this book across America in preparation for a great awakening.

TENETS OF CHRISTIANITY

1. Jesus Christ is the Only Way to Eternal Salvation with God the Father
2. We Are Saved by Grace Through Faith – Not by Works
3. Jesus Christ is the Son of God
4. The Incarnation of Jesus Christ
5. The Bodily Resurrection of Jesus Christ From the Grave
6. The Ascension of Jesus Christ
7. The Doctrine of the Trinity
8. The Holy Bible is the Inspired and Infallible Word of God
9. We Are Baptized with the Holy Spirit at the Moment of Salvation
10. The Doctrine of Hell
11. The 2nd coming of Jesus Christ Back to our Earth
12. Regeneration by the Holy Spirit

Additional Reading
http://www.Bible-knowledge.com/basic-tenets-of-christian-faith/#ixzz2XAatYI7j

BIBLIOGRAPHY

The encyclopedia of Christianity, Volume 5 By Erwin Fahlbusch
http://books.google.com/books?id=lZUBZlth2qgC&pg=PA437&l pg=PA437&dq=holiness+movement++1700's&source=bl&ots=R cFhMW-pMP&sig=q1yee9cnW2DF5KGhtncaszfz-Ug&hl=en&ei=A85RTfSxEYragAf1jdHHCA&sa=X&oi=book_r esult&ct=result&resnum=3&ved=0CCIQ6AEwAg#v=onepage&q =holiness%20movement&f=false

Puritan Movement
http://www.grossmont.edu/karl.sherlock/English231/Assignments /PuritanismEraTimeline.pdf

Protestant Reform
http://en.wikipedia.org/wiki/Protestant_Reformation#Puritan_mo vement

Christian Crusades
http://en.wikipedia.org/wiki/First_Crusade

Muslim Conquests
http://en.wikipedia.org/wiki/Muslim_conquests

Jim Jones
http://en.wikipedia.org/wiki/Jim_jones

Jim Jones Jamestown Nightmare in Paradise
http://www.youtube.com/watch?v=xfht6DveCRc

Gordon Lindsay - William Branham
http://www.williambranhamhomepage.org/mansent1.htm

Quran
http://quran.com/search?q=jews+christians+pagans
Does Army Consider Christians a Terrorist Threat?

BIBLIOGRAPHY

http://www.foxnews.com/opinion/2013/10/23/does-army-consider-christians-tea-party-terror-threat/

MICHAEL BIAGIONI MINISTRIES

Dear reader,

We trust that you've been enlightened by this timeless work entitled The Saints of God. Michael Biagioni Ministries was founded by Michael and his wife Neida Biagioni in 2005 who are currently residing in Kissimmee, Fl. Here in Florida, God has empowered us to transcend the language barrier in order to deliver an urgent message to our Spanish speaking friends.

Michael Biagioni who has a prophet-evangelist calling has had the opportunity to travel and preach around the world. Venues include Africa, Malaysia, India, Peru, and Pakistan. Currently God has been opening doors for this ministry in the United States including New York, Connecticut, and Florida.

God has given Michael the burden to provoke an awakening amongst Christian Saints in preparation for end time tribulation. An awakening implies returning to the norms of the first century standard when Jesus walked the earth. In part, the team approach concept originates from Jesus and his apostolic team of disciples who walked with great power as a witness of his resurrection.

Michael Biagioni Ministries is empowered by partners as yourself that selflessly donate to the work to which we have been charged. Thank you for all that you have done and may God bless you.

Michael Biagioni Ministries, Inc.
P.O. Box 450852
Kissimmee, FL 34745

www.michaelbiagioni.com - mabiagioni@gmail.com

Made in United States
North Haven, CT
23 March 2023

34453899R00167